ADVERTISING AND CONSUMER CULTURE IN CHINA

ADVERTISING AND CONSUMER CULTURE IN CHINA

Hongmei Li

polity

The right of Hongmei Li to be identified as Author of this Work has been asserted in accordance with the UK Copyright, Designs and Patents Act 1988.

First published in 2016 by Polity Press

Polity Press
65 Bridge Street
Cambridge CB2 1UR, UK

Polity Press
350 Main Street
Malden, MA 02148, USA

ISBN-13: 978-0-7456-7116-1
ISBN-13: 978-0-7456-7117-8(pb)

A catalogue record for this book is available from the British Library.

Library of Congress Cataloging-in-Publication Data

Names: Li, Hongmei,1974- author.
Title: Advertising and consumer culture in China / Hongmei Li.
Description: Malden, MA : Polity Press, 2016. | Includes bibliographical references and index.
Identifiers: LCCN 2015046121 | ISBN 9780745671161(hardback) | ISBN 9780745671178 (pbk.) | ISBN 9781509511136 (mobi) | ISBN 9781509511143 (epub)
Subjects: LCSH: Advertising–Social aspects–China.
Classification: LCC HF5813.C5 L484 2016 | DDC 659.10951–dc23 LC record available at http://lccn.loc.gov/2015046121

Typeset in 11.5 on 15 pt Adobe Jenson Pro
by Toppan Best-set Premedia Limited
Printed and bound in Great Britain by Clays Ltd, St Ives PLC

The publisher has used its best endeavours to ensure that the URLs for external websites referred to in this book are correct and active at the time of going to press. However, the publisher has no responsibility for the websites and can make no guarantee that a site will remain live or that the content is or will remain appropriate.

Every effort has been made to trace all copyright holders, but if any have been inadvertently overlooked the publisher will be pleased to include any necessary credits in any subsequent reprint or edition.

For further information on Polity, visit our website: politybooks.com

Contents

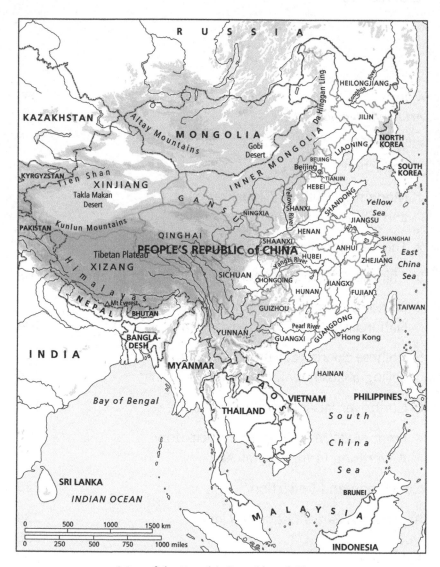

Map of the People's Republic of China

Acknowledgments

This book is the outcome of my ten-year observation of the advertising industry in China. I became interested in Chinese advertising and consumer culture when I was a graduate student at the University of Southern California (USC), where I completed my dissertation on the subject. My advisor Marita Sturken, and dissertation committee members Larry Gross, Stanley Rosen, and the late Richard Baum (at UCLA) provided tremendous support and encouragement. Larry and Marita have been providing continuous guidance after I graduated from USC.

I continued the research while I was a George Gerbner postdoctoral fellow at the Annenberg School for Communication, University of Pennsylvania in 2008–2010. I am very grateful to Dean Michael X. Delli Carpini for providing a stimulating and nurturing research environment while I was there. This project received Georgia State University's (GSU) research initiation grant in summer 2012. I also want to thank Richard Campbell, chair of Department of Media, Journalism and Film at my current home institute Miami University, Oxford, Ohio, for providing funds for indexing the book.

Jade Miller read through my dissertation manuscript at USC. Many of my graduate students at GSU read part of the book manuscript and provided useful feedback. In particular, I want to extend my appreciation to Carmen Goman for her meticulous editorial support. Mina Ivanova, Chris Michael Toula, and Laci Lee Adams also provided useful assistance.

I would especially like to thank the advertising and media professionals and scholars who agreed to be interviewed. To preserve their
anonymity, I cannot list all of them. Among them, however, I want to
mention Huang Shengmin, Chen Gang, Raymond So, Josh Li, Thomas
Mok, and Liu Guoji. I also thank Liu Changming, Ruby Wu, Xu
Zheng, Zhang Xiangying, and Li Mei for arranging my internships in
Beijing in a Japanese firm, a Chinese firm, and a Western media-buying
agency.

My family provided tremendous support. My two kids Sam and
Joseph made the writing much more enjoyable. My husband Xu Cao
provided a lot of encouragement. My brother-in-law and sister-in-law
in Beijing provided support while I was conducting research there. My
parents Li Linhui and Liu Zizhen always have a steadfast belief in me.
This book is dedicated to them.

Chronology

1839–42	First Opium War
1861–95	Self-Strengthening Movement
1894–95	First Sino-Japanese War
1911	Fall of the Qing dynasty
1912	Republic of China established under Sun Yat-sen
1915–20s	New Cultural Movement
1919	May Fourth Movement; Founding of the Chinese Communist Party
1937–45	Second Sino-Japanese War
1945–49	Civil war between KMT and CCP resumes
Oct. 1949	KMT retreats to Taiwan; Mao founds People's Republic of China (PRC)
1966–76	Great Proletarian Cultural Revolution; Mao reasserts power
Dec. 1978	Third Plenary Session of the 11th Central Committee; Deng Xiaoping assumes power, launches Four Modernizations and economic reforms
1978	One-child family planning policy introduced
1979	U.S. and China establish formal diplomatic ties; Deng Xiaoping visits Washington
1982	Census reports PRC population at more than one billion
1982	China issues Provisional Regulations for Advertising Management

1987	China issues Regulations for Advertising Management
1989	Tiananmen Square protests culminate in June 4 military crack-down
1992	Deng Xiaoping's Southern Inspection Tour re-energizes economic reforms; China further commercializes media
1993–2002	Jiang Zemin is president of PRC, continues economic growth agenda
Oct. 27, 1994	Advertising Law is passed, which comes into effect on February 1, 1995
Dec. 11, 2001	China joins WTO; further liberalizes media and advertising
2002–2012	Hu Jintao, General-Secretary CCP (and President of PRC from 2003)
2003	Chinese ad revenue exceeds 100 billion yuan for the first time
Jan. 1, 2004	Investors from Hong Kong, Taiwan and Macau are allowed to fully own ad agencies
Dec. 10, 2005	Foreign investors are allowed to fully own ad agencies
2008	Number of Chinese Internet users surpasses the United States
Aug. 2008	Summer Olympic Games in Beijing
2010	Shanghai World Exposition
2011	Internet surpasses print media and becomes the second largest advertising medium
2012	Xi Jinping is appointed General-Secretary of the CCP (and President of PRC from 2013)
2014	Internet surpasses TV and becomes the largest advertising medium
Apr. 24, 2015	China passes revised Advertising Law, effective September 1, 2015

Introduction

Since China opened its doors to domestic and international capital in 1978, the "low salary, low consumption" system prevalent during the first three decades of Communist rule (since 1949) has gradually been replaced by a political economy that promotes higher salaries and higher-level consumption. Before 1978, almost all daily necessities were rationed, with prices determined by the central authorities. Producing and saving were two core values of China's economy. Ideal socialist Chinese cities were "Spartan and productive places with full employment, secure jobs with a range of fringe benefits, minimal income and lifestyle differences, an end to conspicuous consumption and lavish spending, and with decent consumption standards for all" (Whyte & Parish, 1984, p. 16).

Despite a thriving advertising industry in Shanghai in the 1920s and 1930s (Jian Wang, 2000; Jing Wang, 2008), China gradually eliminated commercial advertising after the founding of the People's Republic of China in 1949. During the Cultural Revolution (1966–1976), there were almost no commercial ads except for limited information about foreign exports (Chen, 2010). People were predominantly dressed in blue, gray, brown, or military green, prompting French journalist Robert Guillain (1957) to call the Chinese "the blue ants...under the red flag." The streets were devoid of outdoor advertising, except for political slogans or publicity columns filled with printed or handwritten political announcements and propaganda.

Since 1978, China has undergone tremendous changes. Consumerism, attacked as decadent capitalism during the Mao era, has now become a key driving force to economic development. In the last two decades, the Chinese government has actively promoted domestic consumption as a way to restructure the economy. Current Chinese cities resemble the urban centers in any capitalist society, and attract pleasure-seeking consumers, with towering buildings, ubiquitous outdoor TV commercials, alluring neon-lit billboards, bulletins, posters, outdoor TV screens, mural ads, massage bars, beauty salons, department stores, and many brands of automobile. Chinese consumers have access to a wide range of local and foreign products, wear clothes in any color or style that one can imagine, and are exposed to domestic and foreign advertisements that sell customized luxury products as well as mass-produced daily necessities.

The "three big items"—the staple consumer goods (a bike, a watch, and a radio set) that symbolized a well-to-do family in urban China in the Mao era—have been replaced by the new three big items: an apartment in a good location, an automobile of a good brand, and the opportunity for foreign education. With increasing disposable income, a rapidly growing middle class, and an increasing number of millionaires and billionaires, China is now flooded with luxury foreign products, making the country the third largest luxury market in the world. A McKinsey report estimates that China will account for 20 percent (180 billion yuan or approximately $27 billion USD) of global luxury sales in 2015 (Atsmon, Dixit, & Wu, 2011). China has become the world's largest market for automobiles, personal computers, smart phones, and a long list of other consumer products and production materials.

Advertising, arguably the most important institution driving consumer desires, has developed rapidly in China. From a previously negligible sector, advertising has grown into a gigantic industry at double-digit and sometimes triple-digit rates, with an average annual rate of growth of 35 percent in the last three decades (Cheng & Chan, 2009). Advertising revenue continues to grow, often at a rate much higher than the general economy growth.

The development of advertising goes hand in hand with China's economic globalization, political liberalization, cultural transformations, and technological development, especially since 1992. As will be discussed in chapter one, four major factors—policy, market, technology, and culture—have shaped Chinese advertising. The dynamics of these interdependent forces are embodied in three key relations: state-media, producer–consumer, and China–West relations. These sets of relationships constitute and determine crucial features of advertising culture in China.

China joined the World Trade Organization (WTO) in 2001, further liberalizing the media and advertising markets. In the post-WTO era, the authorities have tightened control over media's ideological functions while simultaneously liberalizing their economic potentials. New advertising and marketing trends and practices have emerged in conjunction with new communication technologies and social media.

In this interdisciplinary project, I analyze advertising in China since 1978 as an industry, a profession, and a discourse in the broader context of China's search for modernity and economic integration with global capitalism. This book emphasizes the ways in which advertising practitioners negotiate between the local and the global, the state and the market, China and the West, and tradition and modernity. Thus it can be read as a cultural history of advertising as well as an analysis of China's broader societal and cultural transformations.

My investigation centers on Chinese ad agencies and brands, with limited discussion of foreign advertising, for three reasons. First, in the Chinese market, the majority of advertising agencies and marketers are local. Second, scholars such as Jing Wang (2008) and Jian Wang (2000) have discussed foreign advertising in China.

Gerth (2003) analyzes advertising in the early twentieth century in great detail. However, research on Chinese ad agencies and brands published in English is limited. And third, the tactics and strategies used by Chinese ad agencies and brands reflect challenges and opportunities facing less-developed countries entering the global market.

This project is the outcome of my cumulative fieldwork and observation over the last ten years. I draw upon materials from advertising campaigns, trade journals, news reports, documentaries, and interviews. In summer 2005, I conducted participant observations in a Chinese advertising agency, a Japanese firm, and a Western media firm. Additionally, I conducted thirty-four interviews with advertising professionals, including ten working in Japanese firms, ten in Western firms, twelve in Chinese firms, and two in Taiwanese firms. I also interviewed several leading scholars. Further, between 2008 and 2012 I conducted repeat interviews as well as new interviews with ad professionals.

This book is among the first scholarly works in English that systematically analyzes Chinese advertising from the perspective of Chinese ad professionals, ad agencies, and advertisers. It contributes to an emerging body of literature that examines the tension between nationalism and cosmopolitanism in China's engagement with globalization. This book provides insight into China's evolving media industries as they are affected by communication technologies. It also allows readers to understand the changing relationship between the media and the ad agency, the advertiser and the consumer, and the regulators and regulated in post-WTO China.

Chapter one introduces the conceptual and analytic framework for understanding Chinese advertising. It discusses key theories and historical contexts that allow readers to look at Chinese advertising as an industry, a profession, and a discourse. I focus on China's search for modernity and cultural globalization, as well as the dialectical relationship between nationalism and cosmopolitanism, and Orientalism and Occidentalism. The chapter stresses how key advertising influencers, including factors such as policy, market, technology, and culture, mutually shape the key sets of relations: state–media, producer–consumer, and China–West.

Chapter two discusses advertising and consumer culture since 1978 in the broader context of China's modernization, economic liberalization, and media commercialization. It provides an overview of advertising development and analyzes three phases in conjunction with China's political and economic liberalization. The government's support for domestic consumption as well as the rise of the middle class play roles here. My analysis centers on the interplay between the market and the state, the local and the global, and technology and ideology.

Chapters three through five analyze the tension between nationalism and cosmopolitanism and the convergence of the two. Specifically, chapter three focuses on how neoliberal policies and the imagined West-China relations shaped advertising ideas and practices prior to China's entry into the WTO and during the subsequent grace period until 2005. Such an analysis is also complemented by an understanding of important competition tactics and advertising strategies proposed by leading Chinese ad professionals in post-WTO China. The chapter investigates the transformation of Chinese advertising agencies (state-owned and private) and the discourse of Chineseness, focusing on how advertising has become a site for negotiating Chinese identity as a business and cultural strategy.

Chapter four studies how Chinese advertisers sell nationalism and cosmopolitanism by conducting an in-depth analysis of selected TV commercials and print ads. Given that Chinese advertisers and ad agencies often claim to represent more authentic Chinese feelings and values, an analysis of these ads helps us understand how Chinese advertisers reflect and produce Chinese identity, which further reflects a conflicting understanding of China as a nation, a state, and a people in an increasingly globalized market. This chapter is a modified version of a journal article published in the *International Journal of Communication* in 2008.

In chapter five, I extend the discussion from chapter four and investigate China's most prominent sportswear brand, Li Ning, in relation to global brands and other Chinese brands. The chapter analyzes Li Ning's marketing and advertising strategies, centering on the Beijing Olympics and beyond. The analysis specifically explores how and why the brand balances nationalism and cosmopolitanism to produce a cosmopatriotic image.

Chapter six looks at China's controversial advertising in the context of the country's changing regulations and its sociopolitical, economic, cultural, and technological transformations. Topics explored include the nature of advertising controversies; the differences between local and foreign ads; the impact of technologies; and historical, political, and cultural contexts that contribute to controversial advertising practices.

Chapter seven continues the discussion of the impact of digital technologies and analyzes how trend-setting advertising practices have changed the relationship between the media, the advertiser, the consumer, and the ad agency. I discuss three major advertising practices that have exerted lasting influences, including CCTV's annual auction, Unilever's branded entertainments, and Chinese smartphone Xiaomi's participatory social media marketing. The three different advertising practices illustrate China's shift from mass marketing to more responsive strategies catering to consumer needs and sentiments.

I should note three things: first, in the book I convert Chinese currency into US dollars using the exchange rates at the time of each occurrence; second, advertising revenue figures are not deflated because they are mainly used to illustrate general trends; last, the name of a Chinese person is spelled out mostly following the Chinese convention—that is, one's given name follows the family name. However, if a scholar is based in the West or has an English first name, the first name precedes the family name.

An incomplete list of links of ads discussed is included as an appendix.

1 Modernity, Cultural Globalization, and Chinese Advertising

Modernity is the transient, the fleeting, the contingent; it is one half of art, the other being the eternal and the immovable.

Charles Baudelaire, 1863

Advertising represents a key site of cultural negotiation in China, a society that otherwise limits political expression. Advertising shapes and is shaped by China's sociopolitical, economic, cultural, and technological transformations. Through advertising, we can understand not only the challenges and opportunities facing China's corporate world but also the ways in which corporations respond to local, regional, and global forces in China's rapidly globalizing market.

This chapter sets up an analytical and theoretical framework for understanding advertising conditions in China. It situates advertising development in the broader context of China's search for modernity and cultural globalization. By emphasizing the productive dialectics between tradition and modernity, nationalism and cosmopolitanism, Orientalism and Occidentalism, and cultural globalization and localization, this chapter maps out cultural theories that help make sense of Chinese advertising as an industry, a discourse, and a profession. It concludes with a conceptual model that incorporates major factors shaping advertising in China.

CHINA'S SEARCH FOR MODERNITY

As a grand narrative, Chinese modernity is inherently associated with global influences, ranging from China's semicolonial history to its current participation in the global economy. Modern China is characterized by a constant struggle between emulating Western modernity and creating an alternative model of development. Consequently, China has demonstrated an ambivalent attitude toward the West: a strong desire to imitate the West and a powerful resentment toward the West, largely due to the nation's historical suffering from Western domination and imperialism.

Modernity is often understood as the Western mode of sociopolitical and economic arrangements—characterized by industrialization, mass production, the division of labor, and urbanization—which lead to and are further shaped by a new ethos that supports rationality, efficiency, democracy, material progress, freedom, newness, and individualism. Mike Featherstone (1991) summarizes modernity as follows:

> From the point of view of late nineteenth- and early twentieth-century German sociological theory,…modernity is contrasted to the traditional order and implies the progressive economic and administrative rationalization and differentiation of the social order (Weber, Tonnies, Simmel): processes which brought into being the modern capitalist-industrial state and which were often viewed from a distinctly antimodern perspective (p. 3).

The "anti-modern perspective" quoted above refers to how modernity is experienced as a way of life that produces "a sense of the discontinuity of time, the break with tradition, the feeling of novelty and sensitivity to the ephemeral, fleeting and contingent nature of the present" (Featherstone, 1991, p. 4). A modern person constantly experiences newness and "the shocks and jolts of modernity" (p. 5). Discontinuity, fear, uncertainty, anxiety, a sense of loss of traditions, and nostalgia for the past have also been referred to as postmodern, post-traditional, or post-industrial conditions (see Berman, 1982; Frisby, 1985; Giddens, 1991; and Lyotard, 1984).

Similarly, Giddens argues that modernity needs to be understood as "an increasing interconnection between the two 'extremes' of extensionality and intentionality: globalising influence on the one hand and personal disposition on the other" (1991, p. 1). Giddens believes that modernity can be understood as a global structural arrangement as well as one's subjective experience.

China's modernity has been largely shaped by its relationship with the West. Semicolonialism and modernity came to China simultaneously. To become modern is a "grand narrative" (Lyotard, 1984) that has obsessed China in the last two centuries since the first Opium War (1839–1842) when the country, under the Qing Dynasty (1644–1911), was defeated by the British army. After the Opium War, China suffered many more military defeats and was forced to open up its trading ports, cede territories, pay indemnities, and grant extraterritorial legal rights to Westerners. These military defeats gradually transformed China into a semicolonial society, and forced Chinese intellectuals and reform-minded officials to implement measures to save the nation. For example, statesman Zhang Zhidong launched the Yangwu Yundong (Self-Strengthening Movement, 1861–1895) to promote Western science and technology in order to defeat foreigners. The Movement's pivotal principle was encapsulated in the slogan "Chinese thought as the foundation, and Western learning as the practical application." Unlike Japan, however, which was successfully transformed into a modern nation during the Meiji Restoration in the nineteenth century, Chinese elites still clung to the autocratic monarchy. The movement's failure was symbolized by China's tragic defeat by Japan in the first Sino-Japanese War (1894–1895). The failure produced "a new national mode of unparalleled apprehension, frustration, and anger" (Pusey, 1983, p. 5), resulting in Chinese people's painful conclusion that China was inferior not only in armaments but also in political institutions, culture, and civilizational achievement. James Pusey (1983) argues, "this was a loss of 'faith in our fathers' probably more traumatic for the Chinese than the post-Darwinian loss of 'faith of our fathers' was for so many nineteenth-century Westerners" (p. 201).

Since then, a central question persisting in Chinese society is how to strengthen China. Generations of Chinese intellectuals severely criticized Chinese culture and some even advocated a complete elimination of Chinese traditions. Nationalism and racism, in conjunction with social Darwinism, also took root among many Chinese elites and in popular imagination. While a few scholars attempted in vain to rejuvenate China with Confucianism,[1] many others turned to radicalism and advocated complete Westernization of China's institutions and culture. Since then, inferiority and superiority complexes have simultaneously formed opposing Chinese sentiments regarding the West: while Chinese traditions are selectively eulogized and criticized, Western modernity is also admired as well as despised. These positions are not fixed; they shift and overlap with contextual changes.

MODERNITY IN THE EARLY TWENTIETH CENTURY

The early twentieth century (1910s–1920s) is commonly considered the starting point of China's serious engagement with modernity, symbolized by the New Culture Movement and the subsequent May Fourth Movement. Launched by radical and bourgeois intellectuals, these enlightenment movements resisted feudalism and Confucianism and promoted science and democracy as two main principles. They also aimed to produce vernacular literature to replace Confucian classics and establish a new system of morality based on Western democracy, science, and individualism. Prominent intellectuals including Lu Xun, Hu Shi, Wen Yiduo, Chen Duxiu, and Qian Xuantong embraced Westernization as the model to save China (Shih, 2001; see also Lu, 2002). Shu-Mei Shih (2001) argues that Chinese modernists (a broad term including different groups and ideologists from 1917 to 1937) associated Western modernity with progress, scientific advancement, efficiency, newness, rationality, democracy, individual freedom, cosmopolitanism, and power, in contrast with a traditional China that was considered backward, parochial, spiritual, and weak.

While these movements enabled Chinese society to be critical and self-reflexive concerning its traditions and culture, they also produced a lasting rift among Chinese scholars and people. The few scholars such as Gu Hongming and Wang Guowei who promoted traditional Chinese culture were marginalized. Radical intellectuals who favored the elimination of Chinese systems and culture became dominant in the twentieth century, and the ideas formed during this period still resonate with China today.

MODERNITY IN THE MAO ERA

The People's Republic of China, founded in 1949, implemented a new socialist political system and a centralized planned economy, which is commonly considered an alternative model to Western modernity. Chinese citizens were expected to consume little and sacrifice individual pleasure for the collective good of building a rich, powerful, egalitarian, socialist future. Capitalism and Western imperialism as well as Chinese traditions were severely criticized in favor of a new socialist ethos. Toward this goal, marketplaces, recreation centers, religions, and ritualistic cultural gatherings as well as commercial activities were suppressed.

While Mao's model seemed to be different from Western modernity on the surface, it still endorsed a linear understanding of history and naturalized the binary between China and the West (Chen, 1995). The model was also conditioned by the regime of knowledge and the socialist history constructed by the West about itself and China. Not surprisingly, Mao's China also emphasized efficiency, rationality, and technological determinism. What distinguished China and the West was merely different "cultural claims on the modern" (Dirlik, 2002, p. 17). Indeed, Gillette (2000) argues that to the Communist regime as well as the Nationalist government "modernization was measured primarily through material terms, with technology serving as the main index; 'civilization' was its ideological and ethical counterpart" (p. 14).

CHINA'S MODERNIZATION SINCE 1978

After China implemented its open-door policies in 1978, statesman Deng Xiaoping promoted four modernizations: industry, agriculture, science and technology, and national defense. In 2013, Chinese President Xi Jinping added modernization of state governance to the list. Establishing an economically efficient society was the top priority. Economic reform has since become a grand narrative that gradually delegitimizes socialist egalitarianism and instead validates income inequality as necessary for economic development. This pragmatic discourse is encapsulated in Deng's "cat theory," which states, "It doesn't matter whether a cat is white or black, as long as it catches mice," and in his policy that "lets some people become rich first." A realistic pursuit of power and wealth, an assertion of collective identity, and China's ambivalent attitude toward the West constitute a large part of China's modernity (Lin & Galikowski, 1999).

The idea of complete Westernization in the 1980s was very influential, despite opposing official slogans such as "building socialism with Chinese characteristics" and "modernization with unique Chinese features." Scholars demonstrated an insatiable yearning for outside knowledge. Qin Xiao (2009) argues that the 1980s could be viewed as the second enlightenment movement, even though it was an unfinished project. Further, many influential Chinese scholars equated modernization with Westernization, even though some advocated an alternative path (Chong, 2002). For example, Josh Li, former managing director of Grey Advertising in Beijing, recalled that many college students then felt that "China will be better off if the American President Ronald Reagan would be the Chinese president" (personal interview, July 6, 2005). In another telling example, Liu Xiaobo, a professor and literary critic who won the Nobel Peace Prize in 2010, stated that China could only be saved by "three hundred years of foreign *colonialization*" (Chong, 2002, p. 223). While Liu's statement resonated with Chinese society in the 1980s, many now criticize his submissive attitude toward the West.

A third example concerns an influential TV show titled *River Elegy* (*He Shang*), broadcast in 1988 and subsequently banned. The show sharply criticized and reinterpreted Chinese culture, civilization, and communist symbols: the Great Wall, the Yellow River, the Dragon, and the Red Flag, among other icons. It contrasted China's "yellow land culture," symbolized by decadence, incompetence, superstition, and icons of the distant past, with the "azure blue ocean culture" of the West, representing "youthfulness, adventure, energy, power, technology, and modernity" (Chen, 1995, p. 31). The show also ascribed new meanings to many Chinese cultural symbols. For example, the Yellow River was depicted as a source of poverty and disasters instead of China's mother river. The Great Wall was portrayed as a defense mechanism isolating China rather than a symbol of diligence and national pride. The Chinese dragon was described as an evil monster instead of an icon for good fortune and happiness. Su Xiaokang, the program's primary producer and writer, was on China's most wanted list after the government cracked down on the 1989 student democracy movement (a.k.a. the June Fourth Movement). Despite the program's short lifespan and simplistic portrayal of China, the key themes still resonate in China today.

All these examples imply a pervasive influence of Western modernity in Chinese society. In the aftermath of the student democracy movement, pragmatism intensified, resulting not only in the government's embrace of economic development in order to legitimize its rule but also in individuals' single-minded pursuit of monetary gain. In conjunction with economic development and globalization, some elites also show support for an alternative modernity.

CHINA'S SEARCH FOR AN ALTERNATIVE MODERNITY

Alternative modernities evidence differences, conflicts, contradictions, and contingencies of modernity in different societies. Rather than focusing on *the* modernity, researchers of such alternative models explore *many* modernities produced as a result of "the articulations, productions, and struggles between capitalist forces and local communities in different parts of the world" (Nonini & Ong, 1997, p. 15; also see Gilroy, 1993; Ong, 1997, 1999). Ong (1997) treats modernity as "an evolving process of imagination and practice" in specific historical context (p. 171). Concepts of alternative modernities challenge the hegemonic conceptualization of modernity as a Western construction. Chinese modernity, as Ong argues, represents "knowledge-power processes that arise out of tensions between local and regional forces, and not merely in reaction to the West" (p. 172). In this sense, situating advertising in China's search for an alternative modernity requires us to consider how local and regional forces shape China's advertising practices.

In the last two decades, the government has attempted to de-Westernize China through selectively restoring pre-communist traditions as well as the communist legacy. For example, Confucianism was revived as an instrument to increase China's soft power.[2] Further, "main melody" films and shows (*zhu xuanlv*), productions sanctioned by the party-state, appeared with increasing regularity. Sun (2010, April 1) argues that these programs "are propagandist in nature, usually re-affirming the official narrative of modern Chinese history and sug-arcoating communist revolutionary heroes" (para. 2). Some recent state-sponsored big-budget productions increasingly employ tech-niques of commercially successful blockbusters to target younger audi-ences, with a few becoming very profitable.

A discourse of "Chinese traitors" has emerged in popular literature, and those who cannot stand up against foreign powers are accused of "losing their backbone" (Lin & Galikowski, 1999, p. 161). Scholars and writers such as Zhang Chengzhi, Liang Xiaosheng, and Han Shaogong, who advocated complete Westernization in the 1980s, have gradually shifted their positions and have begun promoting Chinese culture and traditions. The success of Asian economies has also stimulated scholars to argue that there is an Asian model of development based on shared values of Confucianism.

In the academic field, "new left" intellectuals—many endorsed by the government—advocate a "critical rethinking of the assumptions of developmentalism, modernization, linear progress, absolute market, and autonomous individuality" (Zhang, 2001, p. 40). However, these scholars are strongly influenced by Western postmodern theories, ranging from postcolonial studies (e.g. third-world literature), cultural studies (e.g. Said, Spivak, Appadurai), and postmodernism (e.g. Fredric Jameson) to post-structuralism (e.g, Foucault, Derrida). Thus China's postmodernism is "often synonymous with a discourse on nationalism, which reinforces the China/West paradigm" (H. Wang, 2003, p. 170). Chinese postmodernism has also been characterized by a valorization of popular culture and consumerism, making it difficult to generate serious critique of capitalist activities and China's political reforms. Indeed, consumerism has become a dominant value among urban Chinese (Zhang, 2000). According to Xia Xueluan (2001), Chinese society has shifted from traditional values to modern values (prioritiz-ing career mobility, pursuit of diverse lifestyles, competitiveness, and consumption), from other-orientation to self-orientation, from obligation-orientation to profit-orientation, from collectivism to individualism, and from idealism to pragmatism (pp. 77–89). Furthermore, China's single-child policy has produced little emperors or empresses showered with gifts from their parents, grandparents, and relatives, resulting in a pleasure-seeking consumerist ethos.

Wang Hui (2003) argues that neoliberalism, in the forms of deregulation, privatization, and free trade, has become the predominant ideology in China. The combination of neoliberalism as an economic ideology and authoritarianism as a political system (Harvey, 2005) has produced a unique mode of economic production, referred to as "state capitalism" and "crony capitalism" (Bremmer, 2011), which favors those with political connections.

China's economic and political model was recently labeled the "Beijing consensus" (Ramo, 2004), an alternative model to the "Washington consensus" that promotes a free market and democracy. While scholars differ on what constitutes the Beijing consensus, whether there is a Beijing consensus, and whether the Chinese model is desirable, the concept of the Beijing consensus has attracted some attention, especially in nondemocratic countries. Even so, voices advocating an alternative modernity still occupy a marginal position. In the advertising arena, alternative modernity in China is often packaged as a competitive profit-making strategy, a practice that evidences Western influence. Diverse voices, then, still ultimately serve the interests of capitalism (Dirlik, 2002).

Knowledge of both modernity and ideas of alternative modernity provides essential background for understanding advertising in China as a profession, an industry, and a discourse. Advertising symbolizes China's desire to emulate the Western development model while simultaneously incorporating Chinese culture, balancing tensions between nationalism and cosmopolitanism, the local and the global, and tradition and modernity.

CULTURAL GLOBALIZATION IN CHINA

Globalization today is only partly westernization. Globalization is becoming increasingly decentered—not under the control of any group or nation, still less of the large corporations.

—Anthony Giddens, *Observer*, April 11, 1999

Cultural globalization is characterized by increasing interconnections and a dramatic "compression of space and time" (Harvey, 1989). Since Marshall McLuhan coined the term "global village" in the 1960s, heated discussions about globalization (economic, financial, cultural, media, and technological) have appeared in academic writing and popular literature. Arif Dirlik (2002) argues that the idea of globalization that "perpetrates the goals of modernization is prepared now to invite into modernity traditions that had been condemned to irrelevance" (p. 20). Here I will review Orientalism and Occidentalism, and discuss nationalism and cosmopolitanism, cultural imperialism and hybridity, to provide context for understanding Chinese advertising.

ORIENTALISM AND OCCIDENTALISM

"Orientalism" is the cultural and ideological expression and representation of the Eurocentric construction of the Orient, with "supporting institutions, vocabulary, scholarship, imagery, doctrines, even colonial bureaucracies and colonial styles" (Said, 1978, p. 2). It is a general style of thought that gives the West the power required for "dominating, restructuring, and having authority over the Orient" (p. 3). The Orient is *othered* as "an integral part of European material civilization and culture" and simultaneously contrasted to embody different images, ideas, personalities, and experiences, thus creating and naturalizing binary constructions (p. 2). In the process, "the Oriental becomes more Oriental, the Westerner more Western" (Said, 1978, p. 46). Another facet of Orientalism concerns how non-Westerners self-impose and internalize the logic of Orientalist discourse, consequently losing agency and reinforcing Eurocentric modernity.

Orientalism and self-Orientalism are important concepts for understanding popular culture in China because the Western Other has often been used either to push for reforms or suppress dissident voices. The West functions as an entity for China to either emulate or overcome. Specific to Chinese advertising, Orientalism provides a lens through which we can understand China's yearning for Western practices in contrast with local experiences.

Given China's active and voluntary participation in the global economy and media culture, Orientalism has to be reconsidered "not simply…as a system of mystification and manipulation imposed from the outside, but also as an on-going process of self-realization and self-fashioning" (Chow, 2007, p. 292). Indeed, Xiaomei Chen (1995) points out that social movements in China are not mindless Western replications; rather, they are new modifications situated in specific social and historical contexts. Chen coined the term "Occidentalism," as a supplement to Said's Orientalism, to describe how discourses about the West enable the Chinese to generate new discourses and practices for domestic purposes. While Chinese officials criticize the West for decadence and corruption to justify social control and monitor dissidents, Chinese intellectuals invoke the West to resist domestic political suppression and support economic and social reforms (Tang, 2000). This suggests the complexity of invocations of the local and the global in popular and advertising discourses.

Although support for alternative modernities and indigenous culture often privileges local resistance, an insistence on local purity may serve as an excuse for a reactionary revival of older forms of oppression (Dirlik, 1996). Indeed, Asian values and "Chineseness" are often used to legitimize China's authoritarian control. The local is thus valuable as a site for resistance to the global only insofar as it also serves as the locus of negotiation to abolish inequality and oppression inherited from the past. As will be discussed in chapter three, the discourse of Chineseness and an alternative modernity are used in advertising partially as a way to legitimize local exploitation and labor control. Furthermore, Chineseness is inherently related to the issues of nationalism and cosmopolitanism, predominant schema through which Chinese advertising professionals and citizens/consumers understand the world.

NATIONALISM AND COSMOPOLITANISM

The discourses of nationalism and cosmopolitanism are different responses to globalization. Though nationalism may be viewed as different from patriotism, in this book I will treat the two as one and the same, because the line between them is often blurred. Many scholars agree that nationalism is socially constructed (e.g., Anderson, 1991; Gellner, 1983; Duara, 1993) and not some primordial identity waiting for people to discover it. For example, Anderson (1991) argues that the emergence of print media resulted in the construction of nations as "imagined communities." The formation of national identity involves the processes of selection, reorganization, and re-creation of historical materials. Further, Duara (1993) contends that nationalism is best viewed as a relational identity, a site of dynamically competing and shifting representations and discourses. For example, he states, "What we call nationalism is more appropriately a relationship between a constantly changing Self and Other, rather than a pristine subject gathering self-awareness in a manner similar to the evolution of a species" (p. 9).

In China, the erosion of communism and collectivism has left ample room for the revival of traditional culture and nationalism, which are also reactions to the challenges of globalization. Official nationalism in China embodies two converging narratives: China as a victim of foreign imperialism and China as a victor under the leadership of the Chinese Communist Party (Gries, 2004). Since the 1990s, Chinese media increasingly emphasize the victimization narrative, especially when China experiences conflict with the US and Japan. Most recently, especially after the Beijing Olympics that corresponded with the beginning of the Western financial recession, the narrative of China as a victor has been intensified.

Even though scholars (such as He & Guo, 2000; Zhao, 2000; Hughes, 2006; Shirk, 2007) often focus on state or official nationalism, popular nationalism has become increasingly prominent. Popular nationalism in China often develops along with official nationalism, but can also form independently. A typical example of Chinese nationalism is the widely cited bestseller *China Can Say No* (Song, Zhang, Qiao & Gu, 1996), which was published by book merchants and distributed through nonofficial channels, with the main purpose of making money. The authors criticize Chinese leaders' worship of America, American hypocrisy, hegemony, individualism, containment policy toward China, and the US support for Taiwan, in which the authors believe some Chinese elites are complicit. A few months later, the authors issued the sequel *China Still Can Say No*, attacking Japan as "even more wicked than America" (Gries, 2004). The two books symbolize China's popular nationalism and its strong resentment toward the US and Japan, as well as a deep-rooted fear that the West does not welcome a rising China.

An important part of popular nationalism is "economic nationalism" and a hope to establish an economically strong China (Zhang, 2001). Zhang (2001) argues that nationalism in China results from the market reform that has encountered a global context "mediated, filtered, and sometimes blocked by the nation-state" (p. 42). Zhang continues:

Apart from an enhanced sense of geopolitical and economic interest and a more assertive cultural self-identity vis-à-vis the West, this popular nationalist sentiment is little more than a reflection of a renewed national confidence based on the continued growth of the Chinese economy. (2001, p. 42)

Consumer nationalism in China has also become an important part of popular and cultural nationalism (Li, 2008, 2009; Jian Wang, 2005, 2006). Chinese nationalism since the 1990s has become a middle-class consumerist phenomenon, and a widely shared sentiment associated with global capitalism. Jian Wang (2005) defines consumer nationalism as "the invocation of individuals' collective national identities in the process of consumption to favor or reject products from other countries" (p. 225). A nationalistic consumer base is reflected through consumer ethnocentrism that stresses the virtues of buying domestic products and the rejection of foreign products in general (Shimp & Sharma, 1987; Wang, 2005) or through animosity expressed toward brands of specific countries (Klien, Ettenson, & Morris, 1998). Given that China has benefited enormously from its open-door policies, these nationalisms do not necessarily contradict globalization; rather, they represent different responses triggered by China's perceived unequal footing in the global community.

Cosmopolitanism, in contrast with nationalism, is another response to globalization. Diogenes the Cynic (404–323 BC) is credited as the first to think about cosmo-political identity as a focus on the "inner life of virtue and thought" (Nussbaum, 1997, p. 57). Emmanuel Kant (1795) developed the idea into a moral philosophy that concerns universal humanity and community. In his treatise *Toward Perpetual Peace* (1795) Kant argued that our sense of right and wrong should encompass not just what happens to ourselves or to those within our own communities but also to the universal community. Nussbaum (1997) argues that cosmopolitanism is an identity whereby people can "see themselves not simply as citizens of some local region or group but also, and above all, as human beings bound to all other human beings by ties of recognition and concern" (p. 10). Cosmopolitans make a conscious and self-critical move to encompass all people in their moral concern, even those who live beyond the boundaries of their national identity (and other domains of identity) (Goman, 2015). Cosmopolitans reject "exclusive attachment to parochial culture" and promote cultural diversity, multiculturalism, and the rejection of nationalism (Kleingeld & Brown, 2011).

Cosmopolitanism can also be understood as produced by a post-modern condition characterized by interactions among various local and global forces. Cosmopolitanism results from particular media systems that produce cosmopolitan values (Norris & Inglehart, 2009). While this may seem to equate cosmopolitanism with globalization, there is an important distinction. Globalization does not necessarily lead to cosmopolitanism. An increasing body of literature documents how globalization triggers parochial identities such as fundamentalism and nationalism as reactions. For example, Manuel Castells (1996b) discusses how identity politics ("legitimizing identity," "resistance identity," and "project identity") is reconfigured through opposing globalization processes and "systemic disjunction between the local and the global" (p. 11). Globalization can result in nationalism and/or cosmopolitanism.

Taken together, cosmopolitanism and nationalism are different constructions of communities and shared meanings in response to globalization. While cosmopolitanism is produced by openly embracing border-crossing activities, which can be physical, symbolic, or imaginary (Clifford, 1992; Kelsky, 1996), nationalism represents an inward retreat defined by existing boundaries. While cosmopolitanism often has favorable connotations, a common critique of cosmopolitanism is that it is not sustainable because it privileges rich travelers. Another critique is that the concept is imperialistic and hegemonic, given its Western origin.

Nationalism and cosmopolitanism do not necessarily oppose each other; rather, they may occupy "poles in a dialectical relationship" (Van der Veer, 2002, p. 10). De Kloet and Jurriens (2007), in the edited collection *Cosmopatriots*, propose the concept of cosmopatriotism as one's quest for "the double articulation that is placed and displaced, territorialized and deterritorialized" (p. 12). Cosmopatriotism simultaneously captures the openness and rootedness of one's geographic and cultural identity. Indeed, there are popular cultural examples that conflate Chineseness and cosmopolitanism (de Kloet, 2007). Cosmopatriotism is not necessarily shaped by the nation, however. It may also be "an affect rooted in memories and shared experiences of the familiar and the everyday" (Leung, 2007, p. 22).

Since the 1990s the import of foreign media, products, values, and ideas in China has occurred in conjunction with a revival of traditional culture, leading to the use of cosmopolitanism and nationalism as a business strategy. Specifically, in the corporate context, Chinese advertisers and advertising agencies attempt to sell both nationalism and cosmopolitanism in a way that resonates with dominant Chinese values. While selling nationalism often relies on the appropriation of Chinese symbols, images, rituals, historical heroes, and China's anti-imperialist history, promoting cosmopolitanism celebrates the country's imagined integration with the West, which will be discussed in greater detail in chapters three to five.

Just like nationalism, cosmopolitanism has become central to middle-class consumer culture (Rofel, 2007). Chinese cosmopolitanism encompasses two aspects: "a self-conscious transcendence of locality posited as a universal transcendence, accomplished through the formation of a consumer identity; and a domestication of cosmopolitanism by way of renegotiating China's place in the world" (Rofel, 2007, p. 11). Rofel calls this "cosmopolitanism with Chinese characteristics" that both opens and closes the conceptual horizon. Further, it is in line with a transnational imaginary that is produced by a wide range of media images, domesticated in specific locality, and interpreted by historically and spatially situated consumers (Wilson & Dissanayake, 1996).

Cultural globalization is often embodied in postmodern pastiche and bricolage. Yet a central concern is whether cultural globalization produces and is produced by unequal power relations. This concern requires us to closely examine globalization as products and processes. The following sections will discuss cultural homogeneity, heterogeneity, and hybridity, which will further lay the groundwork for understanding how Chinese advertisers and advertising agencies deal with local, regional, and global forces.

CULTURAL HOMOGENEITY, HETEROGENEITY, AND HYBRIDITY

Cultural globalization produces debates of homogenization and heterogenization. Both views are based on the premises of increasing economic interconnections within and among regions; the speedup of communication; the erosion of old hierarchies and communities; the possibility of forming new identities; and social, economic, and cultural changes (for a detailed review of globalization, see Held & McGrew, 2000).

Those who view globalization as cultural homogenization criticize the imperialistic nature of global cultural flows and equate globalization with Americanization (or Westernization). They are concerned that Western corporations such as McDonald's, Coca-Cola, and Disney promote Western values and culture at the expense of more authentic local cultures (Dorfman & Mattelart, 1984; Schiller, 1996). For example, cultural critics Ariel Dorfman and Armand Mattelart (1984), in *How to Read Donald Duck*, contend that Donald Duck and other Disney cartoon characters promote American imperialism and paternal authority in South America.

Despite its usefulness as a model, cultural imperialism has been criticized for its simplicity, conceptual vagueness, and epistemological ambiguity (Fejes, 1981; Straubhaar, 1991). It has also been criticized for not considering audiences as active agents (Andrew, Carrington, Jackson, & Mazur, 1996; Notoji, 2000; Sturken & Cartwright, 2001). The simple portrayal of Western dominance fails to recognize that any culture is in essence a mixture of different cultures. Culture always involves a give-and-take relationship and cultural products do not travel in one direction from the Western center to third-world peripheral countries, but in a non-unitary process, as is demonstrated in Martin-Barbero's "mediation" (1993), Canclini's "cultural reconversion" (1992), Arjun Appadurai's five "scapes" (1996), and Manuel Castells' "space of flows" (Castells, 1996a).

Appadurai (1996), for example, conceptualizes global cultural processes in terms of five "scapes": ethnoscapes, mediascapes, technoscapes, financescapes, and ideoscapes. Each scape stresses a different flow along which populations, media, technologies, finances, and ideologies travel across national boundaries. According to Appadurai, modern mass media and migrations are two interconnected forces that affect the imagination of a modern individual and further define ideas of nation, nationhood, and identity. Mass media provide resources for imagination, which defines fields of possibilities and blurs the distinction between the local and the global.

Appadurai (1996) argues that cultural globalization is not homogenization, but rather a cultural diversification process that absorbs global cultural elements into local politics, culture, and economy. He states, "globalization is itself a deeply historical, uneven, and even localizing process" (p. 17). Robins, Cornford, and Aksoy (1997) also argue that globalization promotes ethnic, cultural, religious, and linguistic diversity within nation states. Global programs adapt to local cultures, and global producers have to collaborate with local producers (Croteau & Hoynes, 1997). In addition, countries often impose export quotas, investment limitations, and ownership restrictions; they provide subsidies to assist local production, suggesting that global producers only have limited control over local cultures (Humphreys, 1996; Raboy, 1997).

Another critique is that cultural imperialism does not consider local interpretation of global media products. When culture travels, new meanings are produced. Cultural globalization is believed to open up new space for imagination, identity formation, and cross-cultural communication, through which different citizens/consumers continuously negotiate with complex power relations (Appadurai, 1996; Castells, 1996a, 1996b; Kraidy, 2002; Morley & Robins, 1995). Homi Bhabha (1994) also argues that global flows create "the third space of enunciation" (p. 37), leading to the enacting of agency and the enrichment of local cultures.

Theory of hybridity celebrates cultural export as fusion between local and global forces and asserts that global audiences reproduce media products in the process of consumption, which leads to the empowerment of local audiences and enrichment of local cultures (Appadurai, 1996; Bhabha, 1994; Canclini, 2006). For example, the popularity of the Korean video "Gangnam Style" not only suggests the power of cultural fusion but also the global influence of non-Western media products (Jung & Li, 2014).

In the business world, multinational corporations actively incorporate local talent, content, and cultural values, merging the global and the local to produce glocalization. Proposed by Robertson (1992), the concept of glocalization is formed from the widely used phrase "think globally, act locally," which neutralizes tensions between local and global forces. Those who advocate hybridity and glocalization argue that local culture can be maintained and even strengthened in the midst of globalization. In business practices, glocalization means that locally tailored products or services or their advertising messages—ranging from minor modifications for a given market to complete redesign—are more likely to succeed. Glocal advertising, as pointed out by Wind, Sthanunathan, and Malcom (2013), follows three general principles: (1) a global concept based on a universal human motivation; (2) a unified brand vision that allows for local modifications; (3) and an infrastructure, including culture, technology, and other resources, that facilitates the collaborations between global and local players.

The idea of hybridity, however, has also been criticized for neutralizing power relations and endorsing a multiculturalism co-opted by corporate powers. Responding to these criticisms, Kraidy (2002) proposes a critical theory of hybridity that captures the dynamic power relations and the "dialectic articulation" between structure and agency. Instead of describing the production of cultural hybridity, his theory stresses that "hegemonic structures operate in a variety of contexts to construct different hybridities" (p. 334). Kraidy's conceptualization recognizes hybridization as a useful form of cultural production without losing sight of the hegemonic possibilities. Chinese advertising is a key site for situating and understanding cultural homogeneity, heterogeneity, and hybridity.

UNDERSTANDING CHINESE ADVERTISING

The information discussed above about China's search for modernity, the pursuit of an alternative modernity, and cultural globalization provide important context for understanding Chinese advertising. As a significant site for negotiating cultural identity and power relations, advertising addresses issues concerning dynamic global and local interactions, evolving advertiser and consumer relations, and shifting state and media relations. In the last decade, China has been increasingly treated as part of the global market. Advertising professionals working in both multinational and Chinese advertising agencies share the idea that a multinational corporation's success in China is essential for its overall global success. Since the 2007–2008 global financial recession,

Western modernity has been increasingly questioned. Chinese people are becoming more assertive, consequently changing the dynamics among local, regional, and global forces.

In this section, I propose a conceptual map illustrating major factors that shape Chinese advertising (see Figure 1.1). Advertising in China is generally shaped by four interdependent factors: market, policy, culture, and technology. While these four factors do not necessarily have equal weight in any given situation, they represent common influencers in advertising practices. These factors shape and are shaped by three sets of key relations: state-media relations, local-regional-global relations, and advertiser-consumer relations.

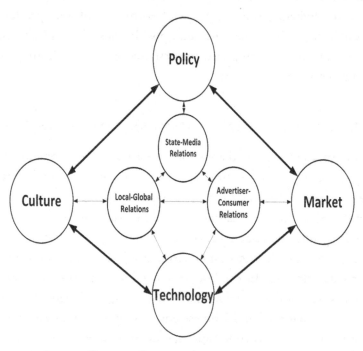

Figure 1.1 Factors Shaping Chinese Advertising

"Market" refers to various economic factors, including competition, market demand, business models, and perceived best practices. Prior to China's implementation of economic reforms in 1978, there was no market because the government managed a centralized planning system. Following market reforms, various competitive measures— foreign and domestic—were introduced. Market pressures and the profit motive, as well as politics, generally shape advertising and media practices. Marketers, often supported by the government, use a wide range of advertising and marketing practices to cater to and engineer consumer demands, consequently shaping the power relations between advertisers/consumers and the state/businesses.

Marketization in China is inherently complicated by global neoliberal policies and discourses. Indeed, neoliberalism, with pivotal principles of deregulation, privatization, and marketization, has defined policy, economy, politics, and ideology in the past few decades in China (Harvey, 2005; H. Wang, 2003; Xie, 2014; Zhao, 2008). Wang Hui (2003) argues, "the so-called marketization is not simply an affirmation of the market, but represents an effort to subsume all the rules of social activity to the functions of the market" (p. 148). As stated before, in contrast with neoliberalism in the West, China incorporates neoliberal elements while simultaneously maintaining the authoritarian centralized control (Harvey, 2005, p. 120). Liberalization and privatization have been gradually accepted as progressive and facilitating economic efficiency. Therefore, global capitalists, party officials, and local entrepreneurs work together to exploit the Chinese market to maximize their profits.

"Policy" includes issues of regulation, ownership, censorship, and media subsidization that define state-media relations and advertising practices. As advertising develops in parallel with China's economic and political liberalizations, policies are constantly introduced to regulate or deregulate the market. Thus, advertisers, ad agencies, and advertising professionals constantly deal with inherent contradictions in

Chinese media, acting as both party-state mouthpieces and profit generators.

"Culture" refers to values, attitudes, and norms that influence advertising practitioners' and consumers' choices and behaviors. Competing values such as traditional Chinese culture, Confucianism, socialism, and capitalism are reflected in advertising discourses and practices. In this book, I especially focus on the tension between nationalism and cosmopolitanism, as well as the strain between tradition and modernity. These are defined by changing local, regional, and global forces. I take the position that Orientalism and Occidentalism, nationalism and cosmopolitanism, and Chineseness and Western values, do not oppose each other, but rather are different business and advertising strategies exploited by different players at different times. The local and the global must not be understood as opposing forces but as constituting each other; their interactions also involve regional forces.

Technology, especially digital technologies and social media, opens new channels for cheaper and easier content production and distribution; intensifies the exchange of ideas; and further challenges advertising practices that are generally within national, cultural, and linguistic boundaries. New marketing platforms have changed advertiser-consumer relations in unprecedented ways; advertisers also face new opportunities and challenges when addressing unintended audiences. Mass marketing, together with emerging practices that employ consumer-centric strategies and consumer participation, has further complicated advertising practices.

In short, these interlinking factors influence Chinese advertising, which works interdependently with how state and media, local and global, and advertiser and consumer relations are imagined and managed. The West-China relationship, in particular, plays a crucial role in influencing how Chinese advertising is understood and understands itself.

CONCLUSION

This book analyzes advertising as an industry, a profession, and a discourse in the broader context of China's transformation in the last three decades. When we situate advertising in China's search for modernity and cultural globalization, we can see how local, regional, and global forces shape advertising practices and discourses. Chinese ad professionals and advertisers have to constantly negotiate their relations with Chinese tradition and an imagined West in launching specific advertising campaigns. This book uses multiple theories, methodologies, and perspectives to explore advertising in the rapidly globalizing Chinese market.

Unlike the situation in the West, where consumer culture is sanctioned by political democracy, China's consumer society grows under an authoritarian political system. In this context, advertising functions simultaneously as an apolitical activity and a political project that diverts citizen-consumers' attention from politics.

Sentiments and values employed in Chinese advertisements are fluid. Whether advertisements use nationalism or cosmopolitanism, they have to deal with dynamic power relations and the changing role of Chinese media: media that function both as the government's mouthpieces and as profit-generating entities. Given that the emergence of consumer culture in the past three decades has been accompanied by rapid social and cultural transformations that produce deep anxiety, advertising promises to reassure and comfort by providing identity, certainty, and direction.

The Development of Advertising in China

Chinese advertising has developed rapidly since 1978. It is inherently related to media commercialization: advertising embodies and realizes the commercial value of media in Chinese society. Following the analysis of media commercialization is the investigation of three stages in the development of advertising, corresponding with China's economic reforms, political liberalizations, and cultural transformations. We will arrive at the professionalization of the advertising industry in the context of a rising middle class, in conjunction with the government's ambivalence toward advertising and consumption. Following the diagram discussed in chapter one, this chapter also focuses on major influencers, including market, policy, culture, and communication technology, and explores the dynamic relations among the state and media, advertisers and consumers, and local, regional, and global forces.

CHINA'S MEDIA COMMERCIALIZATION

In the past three and half decades advertising in China has grown at double-digit and sometimes triple-digit rates into an extremely large industry, arising from a negligible sector worth only 10 million yuan (approximately $6 million USD) in 1979, which employed around 4,000 people. In 1981, China had approximately 1,000 advertising operating units licensed to advertise, which included advertising agencies as well as media organizations such as newspapers, magazines, radio, and television stations. In 2011, this increased by nearly 300 times to almost 300,000. According to the State Administration of Industry and Commerce's director Zhao Mao, China has become the world's second largest advertising market, with advertising revenue worth 500 billion yuan (approximately $81 billion USD) ("China has world's second largest advertising market," 2014, May 10).[3] The industry now employs more than two million workers. While advertising spending constituted only 0.024 percent of China's gross domestic product (GDP) in 1981 (Fan, 2009), it reached 0.66 percent in 2011 (*Modern Advertising*, 2012). Chinese advertising revenue continues to grow, often at a rate much higher than the general economic growth.

Chinese advertising has grown in conjunction with media commercialization. In 1983 China had only 305 newspapers, 633 magazines, 57 TV stations, and 115 radio stations that were allowed to carry advertising (Fan, 2009). Chinese media licensed to advertise have grown at an exponential rate since the 1990s, with 3,959 magazines, 2,917 TV stations, 2,496 websites, 1,833 newspapers, and 784 radio stations that currently advertise in 2011 (China Advertising Yearbook of 2011, 2012, p. 69). Not only has China founded an increasing number of new media outlets, but existing media have also drastically expanded advertising space and time, with newspapers adding more pages, TV stations adding more channels, and emerging players offering cable, satellite, and other new services. Newspapers, in particular, have created special editions (*zhuan kan*) and supplemental editions (*fu kan*) to accommodate advertising needs. For many newspapers, advertising staff (rather than news departments) often oversee special editions' contents, suggesting that special editions are predominantly instruments for advertising (personal interview with media expert Yao Lin of *Hui Cong*, July 21, 2005).

In the past, Chinese media were funded exclusively by the state and functioned as the party-state's mouthpieces. Now, they are simultaneously instruments of social control and profit-driven businesses. Chinese media thus serve three overlapping but different constituents:

the party-state, the market, and the public (Zhu, 2012). Because the state has considerably reduced fiscal support and subsidies in the last two decades, most media currently rely on advertising as a major or sole source of income; their content thus must satisfy market needs (Cheng & Chan, 2009; Zhao, 2008; Zhu, 2012). All these changes are accompanied by China's neoliberal policies and deregulations (Harvey, 2005; Xie, 2014; Zhao, 2008), creating and reinforcing interdependence between media and advertisers.

Growing rapidly in number, Chinese media have also become a scattered economic space. Since the mid-1990s, China has consolidated the media to improve their competitiveness vis-a-vis foreign media. Often resulting from top-down administrative orders, media groups were established to achieve an economy of scale and facilitate the government's control (Zhao, 1998). Starting with the Guangzhou Daily Newspaper group in 1996, China had established sixty-nine media groups by 2003, including thirty-eight newspaper groups, thirteen broadcasting groups, nine book-publishing groups, five distribution groups, three film groups, and one magazine group ("Zhongguo chuanmeijituan fazhan baogao," 2004, May). While only same-medium communication groups are officially allowed, cross-media groups based in the same geography have also been formed.[4] Consolidation further strengthens the bargaining power of Chinese media, making strong media stronger and weak media weaker. Although local media may have an oversupply of advertising space or time, strong provincial and national media spaces are in high demand. Chinese media have reportedly broken existing contracts and increased advertising prices after forming media groups (Huang, Zhou, Qi & Wang, 2003, August).

The establishment of media groups is also accompanied by ad agencies' strategies to expand their businesses into content production. Because of China's official policy of separating television transmission from production (since the 1990s), some leading Chinese ad agencies have taken advantage of this opportunity and produced a number of

TV dramas. For example, Guo-An Advertising Company and Hai Run International Advertising Firm are well-known investors in TV productions. According to Hai Run's general manager Liu Yanming,

> [Investing in TV dramas] intends to create two legs to walk on...[and] drive our advertising business. We gain a lot of advertising time through selling dramas, which allows us to offer airtime to our clients at very good prices....Another key point is that...we always earn profits through TV productions. When [the] advertising market is not so good, earning from TV productions provides very good support. [5]

Content production provides at least two advantages for ad agencies: first, it allows their advertising clients to integrate commercial information with media programming and content; second, the strategy counterbalances ad agencies' relatively weak position and makes them more competitive through exclusive rights to powerful TV stations' airtime. Accordingly, ad agencies normally sell their programs to TV stations not for direct payment but for exclusive rights to advertising time. The deep involvement of advertisers in programming has contributed to a growing trend in product placements and branded entertainment (which will be discussed in chapter seven).

Further, different media have experienced varying growth patterns in China. Figure 2.1 illustrates the development of Chinese advertising during 1983–2011, with Internet advertising being excluded. Television since the 1990s has consistently been a dominant advertising medium, taking up approximately one-third of the market share. Newspapers are an important advertising medium, but the growth rate of newspaper ads has slowed. Radio advertising is stagnant, except for traffic programs, largely because of rapidly growing numbers of private automobiles in urban China. The market share of magazine advertising is small, but most fashion magazines depend exclusively on advertising for survival. Multinational corporations especially like to advertise on

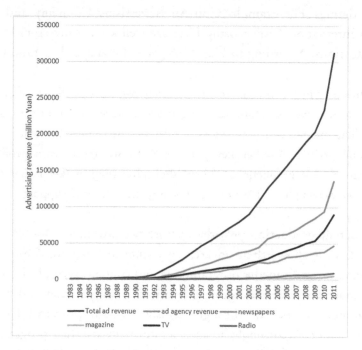

Figure 2.1 Advertising Development in China in 1983–2011

international fashion magazines that target the middle class and new rich (Frith & Yang, 2009; Song & Lee, 2010). Noticeably, the years 1992 and 2001 also marked the turning points for advertising— corresponding with China's economic liberalizations, which will be further discussed in later sections.

Of all the modern media, the Internet experiences the fastest growth in China. China has the largest number of Internet users of any country, totaling 649 million by December 2014, with a penetration rate of 48 percent (CNNIC, 2015, Jan.). The majority of Internet users are well-educated young consumers. Among users, 471 million are urban residents and 557 million use mobile phones to access the Internet. Internet surpassed print media and became the second largest advertising medium in 2011. For example, in 2011, China's TV advertising spending, totaling 72.44 billion yuan (approximately $11.63 billion USD), took up 39 percent of the market share; Internet advertising, totaling 51.19 billion yuan (approximately $8.22 billion USD), constituted 27 percent of the market share; newspaper advertising spending, totaling 45.36 billion yuan (approximately $7.28 billion USD), took up 24 percent of the market share (Sohu IT, 2012, Jan. 1). Internet advertising in 2014 increased by 40 percent over 2013 and reached 154 billion yuan (approximately 25 billion USD) (iResearch, 2015; 2015, March 2). Online advertising has surpassed television and become the largest advertising sector. Baidu, Taobao, and Tencent are leading online advertising publishers, followed by Google China, Sohu, Qihoo 360, Sina, and Youku Tudou. Among Internet advertising, search engine advertising constitutes approximately one-third of the market share, followed by e-commerce, brand graphic, and in-video advertising (iResearch, 2015; 2015, March 2). While search engine, e-commerce, and in-video advertising are expected to continue to grow, brand graphic advertising is expected to decline in the future. In 2014, Baidu had 82 percent of the search engine advertising market, followed by Google (about 10 percent) and Sogou (about 4 percent). In contrast to scattered traditional media, the top fifteen Internet players constitute 80 percent of the total market share (iResearch, 2012, Jan. 13).

The use of mobile phones and social media has developed quickly. A report put China's mobile phone use at 1.22 billion lines (XinhuaNet, 2013, Nov. 12). By 2014, the country had 532 million social media users and 437 million bloggers.[6] Sina Weibo and Tencent WeChat are leading social media platforms. Sina Weibo claimed to have more than 500 million registered users by December 2012, with 46 million active daily users (XinhuaNet, 2013, Feb. 21). Now Tencent WeChat has more than 500 million users. Social media have become important platforms for political participation, cultural production, e-commerce, entertainment, online video, and gaming services (Guobin Yang, 2009).

While China has traditionally kept separate the three networks—telecommunication, broadcasting, and the Internet—it has recently launched initiatives to integrate them into one platform. Trial services to converge traditional and new media platforms have been launched in multiple cities, with more expansions under way.

Generally speaking, there is a positive correlation between advertising growth and economic development. More developed coastal areas experience greater advertising development, followed by inland regions, with far-flung areas such as Xinjiang and Tibet having the least development. As a result, Chinese advertising is characterized by the dominance of first-tier cities, including Beijing, Shanghai, and the Guanzhou-Shenzhen Areas.[7] These three areas often constitute around 50 percent of national ad revenues, as is shown in Table 2.1. In the last decade advertising clusters have been formed, including the Pearl River Delta centered on Guangzhou and Shenzhen, the Yangtze River Delta centered on Shanghai and surrounding cities, and the Northern China Economic Circle centered on Beijing. More recently, advertising in cities such as Chongqing and Xi-An has experienced rapid growth, thanks to China's policies to develop the western regions.

Advertising in China is also concentrated in a few industries, such as pharmaceuticals, electrical appliances, food and drinks, and cosmetics/personal care. From 1995 to 1998, pharmaceuticals, food, cosmetics, medical equipment, medical service, and household electric appliances took up almost half of all advertising money. Since 2000, real estate, telecommunications, and automobiles, as well as service industries, tourism, insurance, and retail businesses emerged as large advertising spenders. For example, in 2011, in newspaper advertising totaling 48.73 billion yuan (approximately $6 billion USD), 55 percent was concentrated in three sectors: real estate, retail business, and automobiles, with a 23.6 percent increase in real estate advertising since 2010 but a general decline in automobile

Table 2.1 Advertising Concentration in Beijing, Shanghai, and Guangdong in 1983–2007 (million yuan)

City Year	Beijing		Shanghai		Guangdong		Subtotal		Total ad rev.
	Rev.	%	Rev.	%	Rev.	%	Rev	%	M. Yuan
1983	40	17	32	14	24	10	95	41	234
1986	145	17	86	10	82	10	314	37	845
1988	276	19	66	4	200	13	543	36	1,493
1990	491	20	228	9	389	16	1,099	44	2,501
1992	1,608	24	790	12	1,066	16	3,464	51	6,787
1993	2,911	22	2,108	16	2,147	16	7,166	53	13,409
1994	3,852	19	2,963	15	3,203	16	10,018	50	20,026
1996	9,247	25	6,421	18	4,045	11	19,713	54	36,664
1998	12,070	22	9,499	18	5,751	11	27,320	51	53,783
2002	16,754	19	14,556	16	14,318	16	45,628	51	90,315
2004	21,554	17	22,503	18	21,159	17	65,215	52	126,460
2007	31,252	18	29,895	17	25,671	15	86,818	50	174,096

Sources: International Advertising, 1999 (no.8); Modern Advertising, 2005 (no.6); China Advertising Yearbook (1988–2003), Beijing: Xinhua Chubanshe and Fan (2009). Note: Beijing's ad revenues exclude those generated by ad firms registered with SAIC as national companies, which means that the actual numbers should be higher. For example, in 2007 Beijing's ad revenues were 34.56 billion yuan, which was 3 billion higher than the data shown here. The data for Guangdong include Guangzhou, Shenzhen, and other cities in the province.

advertising (Miao, Yue & Lu, 2012). These statistics show that consumer goods lead China's advertising spending.

THREE ADVERTISING STAGES: FROM 1978 TO THE POST-WTO ERA

The following sections map out the historical development of advertising in relation to China's liberalization and reforms. Advertising is divided into three phases according to the diagram established in chapter one, with a focus on the interactions between the state and the market, economy and politics, and local and global forces.

Advertising as a Political and Liberalizing Instrument in 1978–1991

From 1978 to 1991, advertising was a controversial and contested site between conservative forces and reform-minded officials. As a symbol of modernity and Western capitalism, advertising highlighted the central government's willingness to open up the country, as well as the challenge the administration faced in managing citizen's perceptions toward the economic transition. Early advertising and media workers collaborated with reform-minded officials to spearhead China's political and economic reforms. Some advertising pioneers played a critical role in developing the industry by skillfully navigating China's political landscape. Since many newspapers were disbanded during the Cultural Revolution (1966–1976), media workers collaborated with ad professionals to fund newspapers in the restoration period.

In 1978, China started to establish or restore ad agencies. Shanghai Advertising Corporation (SAC), founded in 1962 mainly to paint Mao's portraits and propaganda slogans during the Cultural Revolution, established commercial advertising in 1978. Other state-owned agencies, including Beijing Advertising Corporation (BAC) and Guangdong Advertising Corporation (GAC), were subsequently founded in 1979. China had already established ten ad firms by 1979.

At that time, ad firms were either state-owned or collectively owned. State-owned firms generally received licenses to provide services to import and export businesses, while collectively owned firms received licenses to handle domestic businesses.[8] The businesses these two types of firms served had little overlap because China strictly limited a company's officially designated business scope. SAC, BAC, and GAC were the three most important ad firms tasked with handling import and export businesses. Indeed, foreign advertising businesses were mainly divided among BAC (in charge of Beijing and Northern China), SAC (in charge of Shanghai and Eastern China), and GAC (in charge of Guangdong and Southern China).

On January 4th, 1979, *Tianjin Daily* published China's first print ad in the reform era. The newspaper's editor-in-chief took the initiative to look for an advertiser and eventually persuaded a toothpaste manufacturer to advertise its products. In order to publish the ad, however, he had to fight with the Tianjin Municipal Party Committee, still controlled by the Gang of Four (the leftist political faction that launched and maintained the Cultural Revolution) (Hui, Wu & Wang, 1999). Although the 1.6-square-inch black-and-white ad, featuring the product functions of four toothpastes, seems unremarkable now, it was a big sensation then because of its symbolic political significance.

Other liberal-minded reformers followed suit. About ten days later, Ding Yunpeng, an SAC employee, who acquired knowledge about foreign advertising through his previous experience in import and export businesses, published a revolutionary article in *Wenhui Daily*, a newspaper owned by the Shanghai Municipal Commission. Aiming to "rectify advertising's reputation," Ding emphasized the dialectical nature of capitalism and advertising's potential positive role in China's socialist economy. Specifically, his new and heterodox claim was that advertising could tighten up the relationship between the mass, the producer, and the distributor. He had the courage to publicize his view largely because he had already published a similar piece in an internal publication and gained official support from the Shanghai Municipal Government. The Minister of China's Propaganda Department Hu Yaobang, who later became the Party Secretary and President of China, also endorsed his idea.

On January 28, 1979, the Shanghai Television Station (STV) aired China's first TV commercial, featuring a high-end oral tonic product. The spot showed Chinese citizen-consumers purchasing the product as a gift for their elders. The timing was strategic: it was aired during the Chinese New Year as well as during Deng Xiaoping's first trip to the United States as an indicator of China's march toward a market-oriented economy. Again, STV encountered tremendous political pressure. The commercial was made possible only through the courageous efforts of a few media and ad professionals, who received support from higher-ranking officials, including China's future president Hu Yaobang and Premier Zhao Ziyang. Subsequently, media organizations such as the *Liberation Daily* (a military-owned newspaper), the *Worker's Daily*, the *Wenhui Daily*, and the Shanghai Radio Station started to advertise domestic and even foreign products.

At that time, very few Chinese had ever seen an ad. Newly founded ad firms experienced difficulties in hiring qualified employees. As a result, ad professionals studied and emulated ads created in pre-1949 Shanghai. Xu Baiyi, a Shanghai-based copywriter and an entrepreneur who had received training through correspondence courses from the London-based Dixon School of Advertising in the 1940s, played a crucial role in educating first-generation Chinese ad professionals during the reform era. His 1979 book, *The Advertising Handbook for Practical Use*, was critical for the newly developing ad industry. Further, he was the first recipient of the Lifetime Advertising Award from the state-affiliated Chinese Advertising Association (CAA) (Jian Wang, 2000).

While advertising became more normalized in the 1980s, political movements still often condemned advertising and consumerism. Leading ad professionals were often summoned to write self-criticism reports, a common practice in the Mao era. Obtaining higher-level official endorsements beforehand thus became a strategy to secure protection and prevent harassment. Reform-minded officials were also willing to support advertising in order to deepen economic reforms. For example, in 1987, Beijing hosted the Third World Advertising Congress, sponsored by China's leading ad agencies and associations. Premier Zhao Ziyang sent a congratulatory letter to the conference and China's President Li Xiannian and many government ministers attended. Approximately 1,500 delegates from corporations, ad agencies, media, and research organizations in third-world countries were treated with special honors. The conference was hosted in the Great Hall of the People, a place designated mainly for official meetings of national significance.

Advertising Strategies in the 1980s

Reflecting unfamiliarity with modern advertising practices, most early ads used hard-sell strategies, highlighting production processes and product functions and quality. While ads using soft-sell tactics were rare, they were more successful than hard-sell ads. For example, a 1983 Yanwu Radio commercial on CCTV features a teenage boy playing guitar while dancing and singing, "Yanwu, Yanwu, singing together, bonding together." This ad turned the unknown product into a nationally renowned brand, which maintained the number-one position in sales revenue for eight consecutive years. In 1984 a Weili washing machine commercial, aired on CCTV-1, also became a sensation. The commercial portrays a daughter working in a city far away from home. She remarks, "Mama, I dreamed of playing in the spring creek again. I dreamed of my grandmother and you. Mama, I am now sending you something good." Her voiceover is accompanied by images of automobiles driving in the countryside, excited consumers, and a smiling mother. The commercial ends with the slogan, "Weili washing machine, love for mother." Weili subsequently used this slogan for more than a decade.

Another well-known commercial, aired in 1988, for the oral tonic compound Apollo—a pharmaceutical product produced by a township factory in Guangzhou—features a group of shirtless Chinese men working with vitality and great strength under the rising morning sun. Following a close-up of the brand's logo, the commercial ends with powerful music and lyrics linking the product with the rising sun and eternal love. The ad, together with advertorials, testimonies, paid news, and other promotional activities claiming that the product could calm nerves and invigorate the brain, boosted product sales from less than 100 million yuan in 1988 to 1.2 billion in 1994, a hundredfold increase in six years (He & Lu, 2004). This commercial is often considered a classic application of corporate identity system theory (CIS), a communication concept first introduced in China via Japan in 1984. CIS claims to integrate three dimensions of identity: concept, behavior, and visual perception. The theory aims to produce a coherent and consistent corporate image in consumers and employees through the use of logos, advertising strategies, and corporate communication. Following the success of Apollo, many companies applied the same theory (He & Lu, 2004). Despite the frequent use of hard-sell advertising that was developed in the local context, Chinese advertisers also learned from foreigners and implemented various ad theories to inform their soft-sell tactics, which often produced "magic" sales results.

Foreign Advertising in the Early Years

My discussion so far mainly concerns local advertising in China. Foreign advertising, however, has influenced Chinese advertising and been an integral part of advertising in China from the very beginning. Foreign advertising entered China immediately after the country resumed advertising. STV aired China's first foreign commercial on March 15, 1979, during the reform era. The one-minute commercial for the Swiss Rado wristwatch, which was not available in the Chinese market until 1983, was aired in English only twice, but produced a large impact.[9] In comparison with ad professionals dealing with Chinese advertising, those dealing with foreign advertising faced even more political pressure from conservative forces. Although these ad professionals received support from liberal and reform-minded officials, they also faced political risk and uncertainties, since foreign contacts were still viewed with suspicion.

In the late 1970s and 1980s, Japan dominated the foreign advertising market in China. Dentsu, the largest Japanese ad agency, was the first foreign ad agency to conduct advertising business in China. It began contemplating business with China in 1973 by establishing a China department immediately after the two countries normalized diplomatic relations. In 1979, Dentsu sent delegations and established business relations with state-owned Chinese agencies. A year later, Dentsu invited the first Chinese delegation to attend Japan's Dentsu Advertising Award, an annual event, which has since attracted China's regular attendance (interview with BAC's former general manager Cheng Chun, July 19, 2005). Supported by Japanese ad agencies, Japanese brands also had a dominant presence in China. For example, National, Panasonic, Sony, Toshiba, Toyota, Sanyo, and Rico became household names in urban China in the 1980s. Many brands erected large billboards at Beijing landmarks, attracting a lot of attention.

American advertisers and ad agencies also showed a keen interest in China early on. Young & Rubicam was the first American ad agency to conduct business in China. Its 1979 self-promotional ad in Chinese positioned itself as *the* agency skilled at introducing fine Chinese products to the world. In 1979, it signed a contract for collaboration with BAC. Using their branches in Singapore and Hong Kong, Western advertisers and ad agencies reached out to state-owned Chinese agencies, enabling ethnic Chinese in these areas as well as in Malaysia and Taiwan to play important roles in promoting foreign ad practices in China.

In 1986, DYR—Dentsu and Young & Rubicam—established a joint venture with two Chinese partners, supported by China's Foreign Economy and Trade Ministry (now the Ministry of Commerce). Of the $600,000 USD registered capital, DYR invested 70 percent, New York China Trade Center contributed 20 percent, and the Chinese International Advertising Firm invested 10 percent. The joint venture aimed to support foreign advertisers, import technology and equipment, and train Chinese professionals. With almost no competitors,

DYR grew quickly in the 1980s, but it lost many foreign clients in the 1990s when other foreign agencies founded joint ventures in China.

The state-owned Chinese ad agencies were officially charged to handle foreign advertising and thus had access to foreign expertise. They directed advertising development and enjoyed enormous cultural and financial advantages in China for almost two decades. For example, BAC conducted the first nationwide marketing research project in China and its marketing research department was modeled after the Japanese Dentsu Corporation. While early Chinese ad agencies were often design boutiques, BAC transformed into a full-service agency in 1984 because of its knowledge about Dentsu operations.[10] BAC became a model for the Chinese advertising industry in the mid-1980s. Furthermore, foreign advertising was a major source of income for these Chinese ad agencies, since foreign advertisers were required by the government to pay Chinese agencies with 15 percent commissions.

Chinese ad agencies were eager to learn foreign practices. For example, BAC, SAC, and GAC modeled their corporate structure after Japanese agencies. In 1981, BAC's general manager Cheng Chun studied at Dentsu for six months. According to Cheng, this experience "was a very important breakthrough": he learned what an ad was like, but he also discovered much about the artistic and scientific aspects of advertising (personal interview with Cheng Chun, July 19, 2005). In addition to learning foreign practices, Chinese workers were willing to collaborate with foreigners. For example, SAC collaborated with Ogilvy & Mather (O&M) and founded a joint venture in 1991.[11] Chinese ad agencies in Guangzhou also learned advertising practices from agencies in Hong Kong because of the program spillover. They were more creative and innovative in comparison with agencies in other places. A few agencies in Guangzhou—such as the White Horse Advertising Agency, the Black Horse Advertising Firm, and the Southern China Advertising Agency (SCAA)—created trend-setting advertisements, and they became leading agencies in China.[12] As a general rule, Chinese ad professionals respected Japanese and Western ad practices and viewed foreign ad agencies as well-intentioned teachers.

In short, advertising in the 1980s experienced rapid changes, which were also accompanied by foreign influence. But China's experience did not testify to the cultural imperialism discussed in chapter one, since Chinese ad professionals were proactive in seeking foreign collaborations and adapting foreign practices. Western influence in China was channeled through regional centers such as Hong Kong, Singapore, and Taiwan. Although Western advertising did enjoy cultural and financial superiority, its influence was also limited because of the government control. With increasing liberalization and interactions among local, regional, and global forces since the 1990s, Western advertising's superior position has been both reinforced and challenged.

Advertising's Exponential Growth and Depoliticization in 1992–2001

In 1989, China violently cracked down on a student democracy movement, in turn stagnating economic and political reforms and setting off severe international sanctions. In 1992, Deng Xiaoping delivered a series of speeches in Southern China, calling for further economic liberalization. Deng's "Southern Talks" ended the ideological debate over whether China's economy was capitalist or socialist and ameliorated the psychological burden of ad professionals who previously had to justify their profession. What matters, said Deng, was not the ideology behind economic development but the success of it. With this pragmatic approach, money gradually became a main criterion by which to judge one's success (Rosen, 2004).

The year 1992 also marked a turning point for advertising development; a large number of private firms were founded that year. Anyone with a registered capital of 100,000 yuan (approximately $12,500 USD) could start an ad firm. Ad agencies nearly tripled in number—from 1,156 to 3,037—between 1991and 1992, and the number tripled again, to 11,044, by 1993. From 1991 to 1994, revenues generated by ad companies increased more than tenfold, from 692 million yuan (approximately $85 million USD) to 7.1 billion yuan (approximately $900 million USD), and total Chinese ad revenues grew from 3.5 billion to 20 billion yuan (Fan, 2009). While only 242 private ad firms existed in 1991, the number increased to about 134,728 in 2007, a five-hundredfold increase. By the late 1990s, China had transformed from a shortage economy to a buyer's market, characterized by an oversupply of most consumer products (He & Lu, 2004). Advertising had thus become increasingly important in differentiating products.

Foreign advertising began pouring into China. Western advertising in particular achieved dominance since the 1990s, powered by leading advertisers such as Proctor & Gamble (P&G), Unilever, Coca Cola, McDonald's, and Pepsi. At that time, China only allowed joint ad ventures between foreign and local partners, with Chinese parties required to hold the majority share. By 1996, all top fifteen foreign advertising agencies (except for Publicis) had established joint ventures in China, as shown in Table 2.2. Their Chinese partners included ad agencies, newspapers, foundations, manufacturers, and trade centers.

Contrary to China's intention, Chinese partners of joint ad ventures were often marginalized, either because they did not provide required investments or lacked expertise. Many foreign ad agencies used the names of Chinese partners for registration purposes only and paid them with administration fees or dividends. Secret contracts were often signed to bypass Chinese laws and regulations. Even when Chinese partners provided capital, they often only appointed general managers who merely oversaw public relations and legal affairs and were not involved in making core business decisions because of their lack of knowledge or willingness to let the foreign partners to take charge.

The authority of Western advertising practices was further rein- forced by the introduction of advertising and marketing theories

Table 2.2 Top 15 Multinational Advertising Agencies in China in 2005

Name	2004 Global Rank	2004 Global Revenue	Year Founded in China	Chinese Partner(s)
Dentsu	1	$1.9 billion	1994	Chinese International Ad Agency & Da Cheng
McCann	2	$1.4 billion	1991	*Guangming Daily*
BBDO	3	$1.3 billion	1992	China Ad Alliance Firm
JWT, BJ	4	$1.3 billion	1992	Zhong Qiao Advertising Agency
DDB	5	$1.0 billion	1992	Beijing Advertising Co.
Publicis	6	$1.0 billion	1998	Ad-Link
TBWA	7	$838 million	1993	Shanghai Chemical Factory (Rihua Chang)
Leo Burnett	8	$826 million	1994	Taofen Foundation
Hakuhodo	9	$802 million	1996	Shanghai Advertising Co.
O&M	10	$802 million	1991	Shanghai Advertising Co.
Grey	11	$753 million	1992	Guo-An Advertising Co.
Saatchi & Saatchi	12	$534 million	1992	Chang Cheng Guoji Gongsi
Euro RSCG	13	$528 million	1994	*Guangzhou Daily*
Y&R (with Dentsu)	14	$497 million	1986	China Trade Center (NY) & Chinese International Advertising Co.
Lowe	15	$413 million	1996	*Guangming Daily*

Sources: Interviews with advertising executives in Beijing, summer 2005; Information from agency websites; 2004 top ad network ranking from Advertising Age. December 1, 2005 <http://www.mind-advertising.com/agencies_index_adv.htm>; Lu, T. & He, J. (2000).
Notes: 1) DDB restructured its company ownership in 2001 and DDB China is now a joint venture between DDB Worldwide Communications Group and Beijing New Century Advertising Company.
2) Publicis entered China through purchasing Hong Kong-invested Ad-Link in 1998.

touting Western practices as universal practices. While their number was small, relatively large foreign ad agencies contributed to disproportional revenues.[13] Western ad agencies, such as O&M, Saatchi & Saatchi, McCann Erickson, J. Walter Thompson (JWT), and Leo Burnett, quickly occupied leading positions and became dominant discursively in the Chinese market.[14] O&M has developed into the most successful foreign creative ad agency in China. Foreign agencies started to localize, blurring the line between local and foreign ad agencies since the 2000s due to cross-ownership, purchases, mergers, the localization of multinational agencies, and the globalization of Chinese agencies. With increasing knowledge concerning foreign practices, Chinese ad professionals also began promoting Chinese culture and practices, thus making Chineseness a competitive business and cultural strategy.

ADVERTISING IN THE POST-WTO PERIOD

China joined the World Trade Organization (WTO) in 2001 and further loosened ad restrictions to comply with WTO regulations. Investors from Hong Kong, Macau, and Taiwan were first allowed to fully own ad agencies beginning January 1, 2004. Foreign investors were subsequently allowed full ownership on December 10, 2005. Policies, in conjunction with business and technological developments, have produced new changes. This section will discuss seven new trends related to these new developments.

First, capital has become a main driver for advertising development. In contrast to the 1990s when ad agencies mainly focused on design and creativity, since 2000 the capitalists' main purpose has been profit maximization. They coined the concept *ziben yunzuo* (capital manipulation or management) to promote the importance of capital and economies of scale. They predominantly focus on increasing business size through expansions, purchases, mergers, shared holdings, and strategic partnerships with other firms in the industry chain.

This trend of advertising consolidation is driven by at least three business rationales. First, consolidation restructures China's scattered advertising industry, which was characterized by a large number of small agencies, with about half being outdoor media agencies that either own media resources or specialize in design or production. Second, there is a general desire for a larger scale of business in the advertising industry. In the triangular relationship between media, advertisers, and ad agencies, ad agencies are always the weakest. Chinese ad agencies desperately need to scale up to offset the power of large advertisers and media groups.[15] Third, Chinese advertising managers, investors, policy makers, academics, and practitioners have been paying close attention to the formation of global marketing and advertising groups, which control worldwide networks of creative agencies, media buyers, research firms, and public relations firms through acquisitions, mergers, and strategic alliances, since the 1990s. They are conversant with major global ad groups such as WPP Group, OmniCom Group, Interpublic Group, Publicis, Dentsu, and Havas. In particular, WPP, controlled by Sir Martin Sorrell, who has a finance background, played an important role in consolidating the global advertising industry. Globally, fragmented media, together with clients' demand for accountability and quantitative data, have driven the formation of larger buyers and marketing groups (Turow, 2011). In 2011, WPP was reported to have revenue of approximately $15 billion USD and pre-tax profits of $1.5 billion USD (Sweney, 2012, March 1). Its revenue was expected to reach $1.3 billion USD the next year.[16] Further, the failed merger of OmniCom Group and Publicis in 2013 aimed to create the world's largest ad group with more than 130,000 employees worldwide. Facing these trends, Chinese ad professionals gradually accept the idea that capital is now the driver for advertising development.

The second trend, related to the first, is that ad firms often seek to be listed and traded in the stock market after forming ad groups or networks. Public listing provides capital for further expansion. As is shown in Table 2.3, these firms initially chose the Hong Kong Stock

Table 2.3 A Partial List of Public Offerings in the Chinese Advertising Industry

Company Name	Company Nature	Initial Ownership	Year of Public Offering	Location of Public Offering
Tom Media	Outdoor, Controlled by Li Ka-Shing	Hong Kong investment	2000	The Hong Kong Stock Market
White-Horse Outdoor Advertising	Outdoor, joint venture between White-Horse Advertising and Clear Channel since 1998	Local company with foreign investment	2001	The Hong Kong Stock Market
*MediaNation	Outdoor, founded in Hong Kong with business in mainland China	Hong Kong investment	2001	The Hong Kong Stock Market
*Media Partners	Outdoor, founded in Hong Kong with investment from JCDecaux	Hong Kong & Foreign Investment	2001	The Hong Kong Stock Market
Dahe Outdoor Media Group	Outdoor, Founded by He Chaobin in 1994.	Privately-owned Chinese company	2003	The Hong Kong Stock Market
*Focus Media	Outdoor, Founded by Jiang Nanchun in 2003	Privately-owned Chinese company	2005	NASDAQ Stock Market
*Target Media	Outdoor, Founded by Yu Feng in 2003	Privately-owned Chinese company	2005	NASDAQ Stock Market
Charm Media	Media buyer initially, later developed into a full-service agency	Privately-owned Chinese company	2010	NASDAQ Stock Market

Table 2.3 (Continued)

Company Name	Company Nature	Initial Ownership	Year of Public Offering	Location of Public Offering
Guangdong Advertising Company	State-owned agency later transformed into share-holding company	State-owned agency	2010	The Shenzhen stock market

* 1) JCDecaux later purchased both MediaNation and Media Partners and strengthened its position in China's outdoor media market.
2) Focus Media purchased Target Media in 2006, creating a nationwide commercial-location advertising agency. The company purchased more firms later.

Market, but after 2005 there was a general preference for the NASDAQ largely because public listing in the United States generated more free news coverage. Yet, as China concepts stocks are becoming common, listing locations become more diverse. Furthermore, outdoor media agencies with foreign investments went public first, followed by Chinese media agencies and creative ad agencies. Outdoor media went public first because they were less controlled and more capital-driven. In comparison with creative ad companies, Chinese outdoor media companies' competiveness mostly relied on their exclusive media resources. However, media agencies with foreign investments enjoyed other advantages: larger networks, more resources, and more knowledge. After state-owned company GAC was successfully transformed into a shareholding company, it was offered publicly in the Shenzhen stock market in 2010. It was the first Chinese creative agency to be publicly traded and its traded businesses included digital advertising and media buying services.

Public listing enables these firms to obtain capital, acquire other businesses, and advance international collaborations. For example, after

Dahe went public in 2003, it collaborated with a few former ad professionals of the American ad agency Grey and founded West-East Marketing Group in order to serve a growing number of global and Chinese brands. As another example, the largest Chinese outdoor media network, Focus Media, purchased Target Media in 2006 after being publicly listed and subsequently created a location-ad network of over 60,000 displays in more than 30,000 commercial locations in 75 Chinese cities ("Focus media to merge with Target Media," 2006, Jan. 6). This media group purchased additional firms such as Cgen Media, Frame Media, E-Times, and Skyvantage.[17] Its founder Jiang Nanchun sought to set market price for outdoor media through economy of scale and he was widely reported as an expert in capital management. The expansion of outdoor media agencies in China is often called the "enclosure movement," a figure of speech referring to the private enclosure of public land during England's Industrial Revolution.

Global investment firms play an active role in pushing Chinese ad agencies' public listings, and accordingly, Chinese ad agencies often shift their corporate headquarters to foreign sites to facilitate global investments.[18] Actions such as these highlight the strategic maneuvers of Chinese ad firms in a post-WTO world.

Third, the post-WTO era has witnessed a more rapid expansion of multinational ad agencies, which have consolidated and expanded their businesses from first-tier cities to second- and third-tier cities in China. Their key strategy is to establish partnerships with competitive Chinese firms or purchase those with strong networks, talents, and clients. For example, WPP's O&M purchased Fujian-based Aohua Advertising in 2004. Since then, there has been a long list of foreign acquisitions, strategic partnerships, and cross-ownerships. Foreign ad groups generally purchase two types of Chinese firms: competitive agencies that specialize in an industry/region or agencies that diversify their portfolio. For example, in 2007 OmniCom Group purchased and controlled Kangsi Taike, a consulting agency established in 1995 that specializes in medical and pharmaceutical services. At the time of the purchase, Kangsi Taike already had large clients including Novartis, Novo Nordisk, Xian-Janssen Pharmaceutical, Ipsen, and Huarun Group. In 2006, JWT purchased Shanghai-based Always Marketing Services Company, which had seventy-five offices in China, to increase competitiveness in event marketing, store displays, and survey research. In addition to purchasing Chinese firms, foreign ad agencies also intensified collaborations with other foreign agencies in China. For example, Omnicom Group's TBWA and Japan's second-largest ad agency, Hakuhodo, formed TBWA/Hakuhodo China in 2006, on the foundation of their former Japan-based joint venture G1, to manage Nissan's global business.

Fourth, the line between leading Chinese and multinational ad firms has been blurring due to cross-ownerships, the localization of multinational agencies, and the globalization of Chinese firms. While multinational ad agencies predominantly or exclusively served global clients in the 1990s, since the 2000s they have attracted a large number of Chinese clients. Even though Chinese ad firms generally conduct foreign clientele's below-the-line advertising and promotional events that are less profitable than above-the-line marketing businesses,[19] some Chinese ad agencies such as GAC and BAC have successfully attracted large accounts such as Honda and Hyundai.

Fifth, Chinese ad agencies expand their scale using such strategies as adding branch offices and partnering with foreign agencies. They are generally willing to collaborate with foreigners to improve reputation and access to foreign partners' global networks and knowledge. Chinese ad agencies also aggressively seek to obtain exclusive or partially exclusive rights to powerful media. Affiliation with powerful state-owned media helps them become competitive. For example, Charm Media (formerly Charm Advertising), founded in 1995 as a CCTV media brokerage, has grown into a full agency that now provides media buying, creative, branding, and digital services. As an agency aspiring to become China's WPP (Yang, 2010, June 12), Charm formed additional strategic relationships with provincial satellite TV stations such as Oriental TV, Hubei TV, and Tianjin TV. It also established a partnership with London-based Aegis Media, one of the largest global media buying agencies, now fully controlled by Dentsu.

Sixth, large media buying agencies and service alliances have appeared. Since the first media buying agency Carat (Centrale d'achats Radio Affichage Television) was founded in France in 1966, media buying has gradually developed into a gigantic global industry (Turow, 2011). While media buying was formerly part of an ad agency, the function has become independent largely because consolidated media buying provides negotiation leverage with clients and media. Media buyers develop their own clients and also serve the clients of the communication groups they belong to. They typically negotiate for large amounts of media time and space and then fit the inventory into their clients' plans. New tracking technologies now enable media buyers to become more powerful and respectable.

The top ten global media buyers have already established branches in China. Among them, Zenith Media landed in China in 1996 as the first foreign media agency, and Mindshare was established in 1998. Although China initially permitted media agencies to operate, The State Administration of Industry and Commerce issued a notice on September 28, 1998, requiring its nationwide branches to stop issuing new licenses to media buyers and cancel existing permissions, largely because of the government's concern that media buyers may threaten the country's media and advertising industries (Liao, 2011). As a result, foreign media buyers now operate through the advertising licenses granted to their parent companies, and these buyers have not achieved independent legal status in China. For example, Zenith Media uses Saatchi & Saatchi's license. Starcom uses receipts of Leo Burnett, and Mindshare, formed on the basis of JWT and O&M's

media and planning divisions, and still uses receipts of O&M (personal communication with Chen Gang, Professor of Advertising in Peking University, January 2, 2016). Despite their ambiguous legal status in China, media companies expand rapidly in the Chinese market. Now Mindshare belongs to WPP's GroupM, which also consists of other media agencies such as MediaCom, MecGlobal, Maxus China, and Baolin Outdoor Advertising.

According to the Research Company Evaluating the Media Agency Industry (RECMA), a global reference company assessing media agencies, GroupM's media buying reached $3.3 billion USD in 2008, equal to the total revenues of all top ten media organizations in China (Liao, 2011). These agencies often have a presence in Beijing, Shanghai, and Guangzhou as well as in second- and third-tier cities. While the Publicis-owned media buyers ZenithOptimedia and Starcom Media-Vest Group now operate independently, the unsuccessful formation of Publicis OmniCom Group has provoked discussions about whether these buyers will bundle their media business. These gigantic media buyers have caused anxieties in China because of their enormous negotiating power in setting and manipulating media prices. Media buyers generally specialize in media planning, buying, and market research. They purchase media metrics from third parties and also collect their own consumer data in China. Some have also produced influential media contents in the form of branded entertainment, which will be discussed in chapter seven.

Finally, digital communication technologies have been influential in shaping advertising in post-WTO China. While TV advertising still dominates the Chinese market, Internet advertising is the fastest-growing ad sector. As stated before, Chinese internet research firm iResearch (2015) reported that in 2014 online advertising surpassed television and became the largest advertising sector in China. Although Chinese ad professionals hope that the Internet will flatten the playing field, multinational advertising and media corporations still dominate in digital advertising. Many leading digital advertising firms were founded and purchased by global marketing and advertising groups. For example, among the top ten most popular digital media agencies, selected at the Fourth Annual iResearch Marketing Conference in 2009 through popular voting, six are fully or partially owned by global media buyers, including WPP's MEC Media, hdtMedia and Maxus, OmniCom's OMD, Publicis's VivaKi/Starcom MediaVest Group, and Dentsu (Damn Digital, 2011, Dec. 19). [20] In 2012 alone, multinational advertising groups purchased six competitive digital agencies in China.[21] In short, advertising in China has become more diverse and complex: while global ad agencies have become more powerful, Chinese ad agencies also use their resources to expand. These trends in the post-WTO era suggest the immense influence of globalization as well as the convergence between local advertising and global advertising, which may be analyzed by the concept of *glocalization*, discussed in chapter one. While glocalization glosses over the issue of power, it does capture the essence of how local, regional, and global players actively collaborate with each other to explore the expanding consumer market in China. Chinese players are aware that global ad agencies may be more powerful, but they are generally optimistic about their capacity to catch up with them. Indeed, with the rapid expansion of Chinese ad groups, foreign ad firms have gradually lost their prestige and attraction. A few large Chinese ad groups can play on a more equal footing with foreign players.

THE GOVERNMENT'S SUPPORT FOR CONSUMERISM AND CHINA'S MIDDLE CLASS

The Chinese government has played an important role in promoting consumption, regulating advertising and nurturing the middle class. Since advertising began with a lowly image in China, a key issue was how to professionalize the industry. Developing advertising into a reputable profession happened in conjunction with rising consumer culture and the growing middle class.

Advertising Professionalization

Under the government's guidance, China established two influential advertising associations: the Foreign Economic and Trade Advertising Association (founded in 1981, and now called China Advertising Association of Commerce, or CAAC) and Chinese Advertising Association (CAA, founded in 1983). These two associations played a crucial role in educating ad professionals, introducing foreign practices, arranging international exchanges, shaping Chinese advertising practices, and helping implement advertising regulations. Their members include ad agencies, advertisers, and media. Those who hold leadership positions are often current or former government officials, suggesting the political clout of these associations.[22] While CAAC's influence has been dwindling, it still operates the influential industry magazine *Global Brand Insight* (previously called *International Advertising*).

China joined the International Advertising Association and Asian Federation of Advertising Associations in 1987. In 2005, the China Association of National Advertisers (CANA) was established and in 2006, it joined the World Federation of Advertisers (WFA). In 2011, CANA, CAA, and CAAC worked in consultation with the WFA and established China's first cross-industry self-regulatory advertising code, the "China Responsible Marketing Code." While the code was celebrated by the WFA as a milestone for Chinese advertisers to bring their practices in accordance with Western norms, industry experts and CANA officials believe that the code will not significantly affect China's practices (Tong, 2012).

In the late 1980s and early 1990s, China also attempted to set the commission rates at 15 percent, following a general practice in the United

States where ad agencies charged 15 percent commissions based on media that ad agencies bought on behalf of clients in which to place the ads created by the creatives.[23] In addition, China followed the US practice and promoted the agency system, attempting to create more transparency and regulate the relationship among media, the advertiser, and the ad agency. Specifically, it called for advertisers to avoid dealing with the media directly and channel media buying and planning through ad agencies. However, the initiative largely failed because it received little support from the media or advertisers. With a large group of creative boutiques to choose from, advertisers either commissioned creative boutiques to do the designs or creative work, or handled the media business in-house. They preferred to negotiate with media directly because they sought to establish a long-term relationship and get better rates in China's murky media market. In-house handling of media business was also more flexible and less expensive. Chinese media were willing collaborators and many founded their own ad agencies in the 1990s. Most often, the media's advertising departments and their ad agencies' personnel were the same people. In this way, Chinese media could retain more profits. Further, Chinese ad professionals or the government did not notice, largely because of limited information, that the US advertising industry was also experiencing huge changes, resulting in the elimination of the commission model. Similar to current practice in the US, fees in the Chinese advertising industry are often project-based.

China now has a regular presence in events such as Cannes Lions International Festival of Creativity, One Show, CLIO Awards, the Mobius Advertising Awards, London International Awards, and Effie Awards. The country has also created its own festivals, including China Advertising Festival (which originated from the Exhibit of China's Excellent Ads in 1982), the Great Wall Awards, Longxi Awards (Hong Kong), and Shibao Awards (Taiwan). Award-winning ads, disseminated through various media channels such as television, magazines, newspapers, and the Internet, enable aspiring Chinese ad professionals to access the best advertising ideas and practices. Specialized bookstores dedicated to selling advertising books have also been set up.

Facing market chaos and various kinds of corrupt practices, leading Chinese ad professionals, especially those working in foreign agencies, formed 4A clubs to self-regulate the industry and prevent unfair competition.[24] The first 4A club was established in Guangzhou in 1996 and 4A membership required strict entry criteria.[25] Since most of the first 4A members were multinational ad agencies, this created a (mis) perception that 4A membership was restricted to multinational ad agencies. Further, 4A membership connotes prestige. Beijing and Shanghai subsequently established their own 4A Associations, which later were consolidated with Guangzhou into China 4A Association. Although there was resistance against blindly adopting Western advertising practices (Wang, 2008), 4A firms, most of which are Western, were considered role models in China. Recently, China formed a local 4A club for ad agencies of Chinese origin to further promote the professionalization of the industry. These efforts have improved advertising's reputation and made it one of the most lucrative and attractive professions for talented college graduates in China.

The Government's Promotion of Domestic Consumption

In the last three decades, China has gradually transformed into a consumer society, where consumption plays an important role in shaping one's identity. Many surveys indicate that pleasure in and pursuit of consumption has become a dominant value among Chinese youth (Zhang 2000; Rosen 2004). While role models for pre-reform China were revolutionary heroes, model workers, and military officers, Chinese youth are now inspired to become white-collar professionals, private entrepreneurs, and rich celebrities. While receptive to branded goods and eager to project their status through consumption, Chinese consumers simultaneously demonstrate a sense of anxiety because of the lack of security networks, rocketing housing prices, education costs, and inflation. According to Tom Doctoroff (2012), a leading American ad professional in China, any successful brand has to skillfully handle Chinese consumers' simultaneous desires to project status and to retreat to a familiar comfort zone.

In the past two decades, the government has made great effort to expand domestic consumption. China has institutionalized protection of consumer rights by such measures as observing Consumer Rights Day (March 15) since 1986, establishing the Chinese Consumer Association and its nationwide branches, passing laws for consumer protection, launching educational media campaigns about consumer rights, and prosecuting producers of substandard products.

The protection of consumer rights, together with the government's promotion of domestic consumption, has greatly boosted consumerism in China. For example, immediately after the 1997 Asian Economic Crisis, Premier Zhu Rongji called for the expansion of domestic demand, which was followed by the issuance of 510 billion yuan (approximately $61 billion USD) government bonds for development infrastructure in 1998–2001. A number of policies to increase consumption and promote exports were also introduced. Most important, reforms in three areas, including housing reforms (transforming houses from welfare to commodities), medical reforms (pushing medical expenses to consumers), and education reforms (commercializing higher education), have been implemented to promote domestic consumption. Starting in 2000, China established three golden-week holidays (International Labor Day, the National Holiday, and the Chinese Spring Festival) as official holidays,[26] leading to a holiday economy associated with shopping, entertainment, and tourism. Now the months between November and the Spring Festival in January or February (depending on the lunar calendar) are a celebrated shopping season. In particular, 11/11 (Singles

Day) has been transformed into a retail holiday. Encouraging singles to indulge themselves with holiday presents, Alibaba began to promote products to singles in 2009. On November 11, 2015, Alibaba brought in more than $14 billion USD in sales in twenty-four hours.

During the 2008 global economic recession, China issued a stimulus package estimated at 4 trillion yuan (approximately $577 billion USD) and took measures to loosen credit conditions, cut taxes, and embark on a massive infrastructure spending program to further increase domestic demand. Recently, sectors of private housing and private automobiles experienced rapid growth. The current administration of Xi Jinping and Li Keqiang continued to rebalance China's economy toward more consumption-driven growth, leading many global companies to produce for China.

In China's recent effort to restructure its economy and revive the cultural industries, advertising has been further elevated as a core cultural and creative industry, receiving the state's financial, policy, and taxation support.[27] Since 2011 advertising has been listed as one of the "encouraged cultural industries," making "advertising creativity, planning, design and production" eligible for preferential treatment in credits, tax, and other benefits.[28]

THE RISING MIDDLE CLASS

The rapid growth of advertising is contingent on the rising middle class in China. There are varying definitions of what constitutes the middle class, and there is no agreement about its size or its measurement in China.[29] The percentage of Chinese seen to be in the middle class can vary from less than 5 percent to 47 percent of the population.[30] Some researchers define the Chinese middle class as purely economic, using a benchmark of 30 percent of income being discretionary, while others argue that factors such as level of education, profession, political attitude and participation, lifestyle, self-identification, and cultural values should be included.[31] A 2011 report by the Chinese Academy of Social Sciences put the number at 230 million, with the prospect of 47 percent of the population entering the middle class by 2020 ("Half of China's urbanites to become middle class by 2023," 2011, Aug. 5). Alternatively, a 2012 McKinsey report estimates that only 8 percent of the Chinese population (equivalent to 18.26 million households) belong to affluent and mainstream consumers whose yearly household income is more than $16,000 (Atsmon & Magni, 2012, March). China uses the phrase "the middle income stratum" (as opposed to "middle class") to avoid discussions about class and unequal power and access to resources. In addition, terms such as "white collar" (*bailing*), "gold collar" (*jinling*), "bohemians" (*bobozu*), "yuppie" (young urban professional), "hippie," and "little bourgeoisie" are often used in media to refer to middle-class consumers.

The Chinese middle class is linked to China's urbanization. From 1978 to 2011, China's urban population increased from 19.7 percent to 51.27 percent, marking the first time in history that urban population has exceeded rural population ("Zhongguo chengshi fazhan baogao bianweihui," 2012). About 700 million residents in China now live in the city. Wang (2013) argues that the Chinese middle class, who often harbor conservative political values and support the current political and economic arrangements,[32] desperately seek status through conspicuous consumption in housing, home furniture, art, and leisure activities. Also, middle-class identity is increasingly defined by access to resources (Davis, 2000, 2005; Tomba, 2004). Ownership of a house, an automobile of a good brand, and access to good education are often used to define one's middle-class membership.

Meanwhile, China's distribution of wealth is polarized. The 100 richest Chinese on the Forbes list in 2012 have garnered 220 billion USD (Dou, 2012, Oct. 13). This is in sharp contrast to China's egalitarian society in the pre-reform era. China's Gini coefficient, an indicator of wealth disparity, increased from less than 0.20 in 1978 to 0.511 in 1994 (He & Lu, 2004). Since 2000 China's Gini coefficient passed the internationally accepted warning line of 0.4 and reached a shocking level of 0.61 in 2010 (He, 2012, Jan. 19; Hu, 2012, Dec. 10). A McKinsey report points out that China will account for 20 percent (approximately $27 billion USD) of global luxury sales in 2015 (Atsmon, Dixit & Wu, 2011, April). In contrast, around 50 million urban residents still live in poverty (those whose average per capita income falls below 7,500–8,500 yuan ($1,166-$1,321 USD)) ("Half of China's urbanites to become middle class by 2023," 2010, Aug. 5). Sun (2003) argues that increasing inequalities have produced a "fractured" Chinese society. Hu (2004) contends that there exist four worlds in China based on the gross domestic product (GDP) per capita, with the coastal areas and large cities being prosperous and the inland areas and outlying areas remaining poor. The geographical distinction is only a rough estimation, because even within the same area, enormous gaps exist between the rich and the poor. Thousands of millionaires in big cities coexist with tens of millions of the poor who are struggling with basic survival needs, thus complicating advertising culture in China.

CONCLUSION

The development of Chinese advertising has corresponded with the growth of the market economy, the expansion of global capitalism, and the acceptance of neoliberalism as an ideology in China. State policies played a huge role in shaping the structure and practices of advertising in China. The state's economic liberalization provided the necessary condition for early ad professionals to spearhead the growth of advertising, which also made media commercialization possible and provided an alternative source of income for Chinese media. In conjunction with these transformations, a consumer culture has developed: Chinese people now consider what to consume and how to consume it to be important ways of defining their identity, and they also accept the new freedom that is often associated with consumer choice.

With a generally interventionalist approach to economic development, the Chinese government plays a privotal role in guiding the advertising industry and supporting consumption through resource distribution, policies, and various notices. The government has recently been active in promoting the Chinese Internet industry. Like any consumer market in the West, Chinese advertising is also strongly influenced by the development of communication technologies: in the 1980s newspaper was the largest and most important advertising medium; television advertising then dominated the Chinese market from the early 1990s to 2014; the Internet now becomes the largest advertising sector. The rapid technological development requires marketing practitioners to constantly adapt to new practices. In 2015, the buzzword in China is "Internet plus," meaning that enterprises should center their business on the Internet and that other types of business are additions.

While early advertising was a progressive force and symbolized modernity, advertising since the 1990s has been simultaneously depoliticized and politicized because of its inherent association with capitalism. Now capital has become a major driver in advertising, with Chinese media, advertisers, and ad agencies all actively pursuing economy of scale.

The emerging middle class provides a solid basis for advertising and consumer culture. Because of the wide disparities between coastal and inland regions, urban and rural places, and developed and outlying areas, however, advertising practices effective in one region may not be effective in others. Sophisticated and unsophisticated advertising strategies coexist in the Chinese market.

The Chinese market has been strongly influenced by regional and global forces. Ad professionals from Hong Kong, Taiwan, Japan,

Singapore, and the West had great influence in China. Ad practitioners from Asian countries and regions not only brought with them ideas associated with their own cultural background but also channeled Western influences, given that advertising in these regions were more developed than mainland China. Thus, foreign advertisers and agencies enjoyed a special clout in the Chinese market in the past, despite the rising influence of Chinese ad agencies and practices. The competition between Chinese and foreign ad agencies intensified after 2000. Since then, there have been more discussions about Chineseness and various strategies to build the competitiveness of Chinese brands and Chinese ad agencies, which will be analyzed in chapters three through five.

3 | Chinese Advertising Agencies: Dancing in Chains?

The previous chapter discusses the rapid development of advertising accompanied by China's drastic internal transformations and increasing interactions with the outside world. The growing significance of the Chinese economy in general and advertising in specific for the global market goes together with China's growing assertiveness in Chineseness (Zhang, 2001). With China's effort to revive traditional culture since the 1990s and a surging nationalism, a key issue for advertising professionals is how to reconcile Chineseness and universality.

In this chapter, I will specifically focus on the construction of Chineseness as a business strategy. Chineseness emerged in the advertising industry at the turn of the twenty-first century when Chinese ad professionals strongly experienced the loss of their discursive power (*huayu quan*) facing Western influence. While globalization was generally framed as a win-win solution in China (Mittelman, 2006), advertising professionals felt anxious and uncertain about how China's WTO membership would affect advertising. In particular, prior to the country's entry into the WTO and during the subsequent grace period until 2005, admen and adwomen actively articulated their views to shape the future of Chinese advertising. Their voices helped us understand how Chinese ad professionals understood themselves, their competitors, and China's global positioning and identity.

This chapter emphasizes how neoliberal policies and the imagined West-China relations shaped advertising ideas and practices by further developing the diagram identified in chapter one. I specifically focus on how Chinese admen, adwomen, and ad agencies deployed their business strategies and rhetoric and how they dealt with new policies facilitating global influence and neoliberalism.

CONTEXTUALIZING THE CONSTRUCTION OF CHINESENESS

As established in chapter two, foreign ad agencies entered China in the 1990s and gradually became dominant despite their small number. Because of their global networks and support system, these agencies focused on longer-term strategies, unlike typical Chinese agencies. More important, Western agencies' *natural* association with modernity gave them an advantage in China. From the very beginning, Western ad agencies have promoted scientific modernity, exemplified in their standardized procedures, management, rationality, transparency, and the use of media metrics. Professional business relationships and the use of marketing and branding tools further evidence modernity. Professionalism has been promoted as a pinnacle of Western practice through seminars, trade journals, books, conferences, and informal conversations. Through branding toolkits such as Ogilvy & Mather's 360 Degree Branding Stewardship, J. Walter Thompson's Total Branding, and the integrative model of Foote Cone & Belding, Western firms claim expertise in both science and creativity and promote advertising as both an art and a science.

As was discussed in chapter one, Chineseness includes not only the official discourse centered on one's relationship with the state but also popular nationalism. Chineseness now combines elements of Western modernity, the legacy of Communism and Confucianism, and other aspects of traditional Chinese culture (Wang, 1991). Since the 1990s, market-driven nationalism, together with geopolitical interests and safety concerns, have become part of the discourse concerning the responsibility of Chinese citizens, largely due to an ideological shift that replaces Communism (Chow, 2009; Gries, 2004; Hughes, 2006).

A notion of universal chauvinism supported by a Han-centered ideology of "us vs. them" is central to Chinese nationalism.

Specifically, in Chinese advertising, a key question is how to develop the Chinese economy in the midst of globalization that has both strengthened and challenged China's status. A combination of top-down and bottom-up approaches is proposed to support China's economic nationalism and modernity. The neoliberal individualized approach—cultivating development that stresses privatization—is thus married to China's collective ideal and cultural norms. Therefore, developmentalism compromises the tensions between nationalism and cosmopolitanism to support nationalistic economic growth. Such a commercialized version of Chineseness is an important way of making China into a global leader in terms of economy, culture, and geopolitical status. China as an economy, nation, and state—both old and young—is thus becoming one. Unsurprisingly, leading Chinese ad professionals view themselves as guardians and promoters of Chineseness. The promotion of Chineseness also reflects China's uneasy relationship with global capitalism, given that "the Chinese state looms so large in its past and future imaginings" (Reid, 2009, p. 197).

The discourse of Chineseness in advertising also emerged at a time when foreign ad agencies stressed their local connections and Chinese identity as part of their strategy to localize their personnel and clientele.[33] Foreign agencies also appealed to China's desire to build global brands at home and abroad. At the same time, the Chinese government launched initiatives urging Chinese companies to go global around 2000. There were several goals, but two focused on increasing China's overseas investment and promoting Chinese brands and exports in the global market. As a result, China's total investment abroad increased from $0.9 billion USD in 1991 to $56 billion USD in 2009 (Huang & Wilkes, 2011). The "going global" policy was also accompanied by China's strategic shift in upgrading its industry structures from low-end products to value-added commodities, technologies, and services. The new industrialization model emphasizes innovation, sustainability, and information with a focus on high technology, high return, and less resource depletion and environmental damage. Advertising became a site for cultural identity negotiation, making Chineseness both a business and cultural strategy. Both Chinese and foreign ad agencies actively supported China's restructuring from "made in China" to "created/branded in China" (Wang, 2008). The new policies provided opportunities to Chinese ad agencies, but Chinese ad agencies also felt threatened by foreign agencies that were considered superior on both an ideological level and a practical level, as discussed in chapter two. Private ad agencies, which were often equated with unprofessionalism, were especially challenged. Even state-owned ad agencies, which normally had more resources, faced similar threats. As a result, their responsive strategies looked similar and different, reflecting individualistic as well as collective sentiments.

Chineseness is generally shaped by two powerful narratives: one views China as a victim due to foreign imperialism and the other sees China as a victor under the leadership of the Chinese Communist Party (Gries, 2004). Chineseness is thus defined in relation to China's tradition, the Communist legacy, and the imagined West. It demonstrates a remarkable sense of continuity, but it is also living and changing, reflecting how non-Chinese people view China as well as how Chinese citizens define the country (Wang, 1991). Specifically in advertising, Chinese ad professionals use Chineseness as a strategy—cultural as well as commercial, proactive as well as reactive—to develop and maintain competitiveness in the Chinese market.

THE TRANSFORMATION OF STATE-OWNED AD AGENCIES

State-owned ad agencies in China experienced tremendous difficulties in the late 1990s during the country's transition to a neoliberal economy.

At the Fifteenth Party Congress in 1997, China announced a plan to massively transform state-owned enterprises into shareholding companies. Equality, social justice, and full employment in socialist enterprises were replaced by the considerations necessary for profits, competitiveness, and efficiency. State-owned ad agencies faced special challenges from more competitive private and foreign ad firms. Their outdated business model that relied on privileges granted by administrative orders or personal relations was similarly challenged.

What was more, foreign advertisers no longer used China's state-owned ad agencies to handle their media placements, since top foreign ad agencies had already established their offices in China by 1994, as discussed in chapter two. As a result, state-owned ad agencies such as GAC, BAC, and SAC lost their major source of income. For example, GAC's foreign commissions at peak times were 40 to 50 million yuan, but this dropped to approximately 3 million yuan in 1995, a more than 90 percent decrease.[34] Criticized as inefficient and noncompetitive, state-owned ad agencies were forced to change their culture and personnel structure. For example, in 1992, 50 percent of BAC's employees consisted of foreign language experts (China Advertising Yearbook of 1994, 1995), but the loss of foreign clients made its labor force unsuitable for the market. Many state-owned agencies started personnel reforms, implementing tactics such as severance packages, open competition for management positions, layoffs, and job transfers. By promoting more transparent business practices, they began to change their past practices, which mostly relied on guanxi (relationship).

During this period of time, state-owned enterprises lost talented employees to rapidly growing foreign ad firms and private Chinese firms. For example, in 1994 BAC was ranked sixth in China Advertising Yearbook's list of the top 100 agencies, with revenue totaling 150 million yuan (about $17 million USD), but it was dropped from the top-100 list in 2002 (China Advertising Yearbook of 2003, 2004).[35] In line with a general trend of marketization, Chinese media were also gradually commercialized and began to prioritize profit maximization. As a result, powerful media requested advertisers or their agencies to prepay for ad space or airtime.

Consequently, Chinese ad agencies implemented ownership reforms and privatization and also funded joint ventures with foreign agencies in compliance with neoliberalism. GAC, for example, loosened its ownership in the late 1990s and established several joint ventures with Japanese ad firms, including ADK, Hakuhodo, and Delphys. It further expanded businesses nationwide by establishing branch offices in Beijing, Shanghai, Chengdu, and Wuhan and by purchasing other firms or forming strategic alliances with other media agencies. As a result, GAC has become one of the most successful Chinese ad agencies. Since 1999, GAC has been consistently ranked as China's best "local" (meaning "Chinese") ad agency based on revenue.[36] In 2008 GAC was transformed into a shareholding company. In the same year, China's Ministry of Culture recognized the agency as an "exemplary cultural industry base," making it the first ad firm to receive special support from the Ministry. In 2010, it did an IPO in the Shenzhen stock market.

GAC's success lay not only in its quick response to the changing ad environment but also in its insightful and timely entry into business sectors that experienced or are still experiencing quick growth, such as the electric appliance, automobile, real estate, and telecommunication sectors. Unlike most Chinese ad agencies, which had only short partnerships with advertisers, GAC maintained long-term partnerships, some of which have lasted more than a decade. Its success also lay in its flexibility and quick response to clients' needs, its long-term relationship with CCTV and provincial and city media, and its ownership of outdoor media resources. GAC sometimes buys out the airtime of a popular TV program or the ad space of a magazine. The exclusivity of media resources allows the company to establish a competitive edge. Additionally, it has made aggressive efforts in digital innovations. GAC has actively learned from foreign ad agencies and adjusted to rapid economic development by using their local knowledge and connections. Aiming to provide effective advertising, the firm has claimed to be the "flag-bearer of local advertising," thus linking its business to the destiny of Chinese advertising in general.

In the company's history, its victory in winning the Honda Accord account in 1998 was generally viewed as a landmark (Liu, 2007). This event enabled GAC to engage in the rapidly growing automobile industry and establish a new form of collaboration with foreign agencies. At that time the Japanese agency Hakuhodo was serving Honda Odyssey. Because both GAC and Hakuhodo were serving the same company, they decided to merge four years later and establish GAC Hakuhodo to jointly provide services to the Guangzhou Honda account. Following the same model, GAC Hakuhodo and Delphys formed a special agency in 2005 to serve the Guangzhou Toyota client. Furthermore, GAC collaborated with Japanese agency ADK to provide service to Japanese and Chinese clients. Keen on globalization, the company aimed to seek "global capital, networks, talents, knowledge that Chinese ad agencies often lack" (p. 72).

Chinese media widely celebrated GAC's winning of the Honda account in 1998 as symbolizing its increasing competitiveness—and a new beginning for Chinese ad agencies in general. At that time, most Chinese ad agencies only gained less profitable below-the-line advertising businesses from multinational corporations. Critics also argued, however, that Honda gained the business because of its connection with the Guangdong municipal government. Not coincidentally, Korean automobile producer Hyundai also chose BAC as its ad agency a few years later. This deal was again viewed as Hyundai's interest in capitalizing on BAC's connection with the Beijing municipal government.

SAC, another important state-owned agency, experienced similar structural and ownership transformations. SAC was among the first Chinese agencies to form a joint venture with a foreign ad agency

(Ogilvy & Mather), in 1991. Roughly one-third of the company's investment came from WPP and two-thirds from the government-backed Shanghai Eastbest International. Its major clients include automobile companies and banking services. Despite SAC's new ownership structure, it still claims to be a "local" ad agency in order to gain public support. Further, managers who successfully transformed state-owned ad agencies often gain important political or professional positions, which broaden the agencies' networks and attract businesses.[37]

While GAC and SAC were successfully transformed, BAC is in a more difficult position largely because it has been slower to respond to market shifts and to establish joint ventures with foreign ad agencies. At the time of writing, BAC had only established a joint venture with a South Korean corporation to serve the Beijing Automobile Group and Hyundai, suggesting that foreign connections provide advantages. Nevertheless, state-owned ad agencies generally have more resources than private Chinese ad firms. Advertising professionals in private firms have experienced a stronger sense of loss in discursive power, which will be analyzed in the following sections.

LOCAL EXPERIENCE VS. WESTERN THEORIES

In 1992, private firms were officially allowed to enter the field of creative advertising beyond production and design. Within two years, the number of agencies tripled from approximately 3,000 to more than 11,000; most of these newcomers were private firms (Fan, 2009). While most Chinese ad firms could not directly compete with foreign agencies, many gradually became competitive in their specialty, such as media planning, outdoor media business, or media buying. Notable among these firms were the Guangzhou-based Black Horse Ad Agency, White Horse Ad Agency, and Pingcheng Ad Agency, the Guilin-based Meikao Ad Agency, and the Beijing-based Yemaozhong Planning Agency and Li Guangdou Planning Agency.

Founders of these firms accumulated intimate local knowledge and experience through years of relationship with Chinese clients, media, and governmental agencies. These entrepreneurs were skilled in cultivating and maintaining a good relationship with government officials and Chinese media. For example, the Beijing-based Charm Advertising Agency, founded in 1995, was repeatedly ranked among "CCTV's top 10 media agencies." Its founder Dang He worked in several government institutes before founding the ad agency. He was also a member of the standing committee of the Beijing City Youth Union and the Chinese Youth Union.

CELEBRATING LOCAL KNOWLEDGE
AND CHINESENESS

Leading Chinese ad professionals promoted local knowledge while simultaneously emulating foreign practices. Both positions were in line with China's modernization objective and the goal of integration with global capitalism. Many ad professionals took the position that promoting Chinese products into global brands was significant for China's comprehensive power. This position underscored advertising's strategic importance for China as a competitive nation. It also worked in the interest of multinational ad agencies: their global networks and professional image put them in a better position to globalize Chinese companies. Not surprisingly, Chinese advertisers tend to dump their Chinese ad agencies and hire multinational ad agencies once they grew larger or planned to expand overseas.

In response to the potential threat, after 2000 leading Chinese ad professionals began to celebrate their Chinese knowledge, Chinese identity, and patriotism at professional conferences. For example, Li Guangdou, a well-known ad planner, shared his experience in building Chinese brands at CCA's annual Advertising Conference on May 21, 2005, which had participants from the media, ad agencies, and companies producing consumer goods. He stated, "We cannot surpass Westerners in theorizing....Our biggest strength lies in our experience." According to him, foreign firms had "inoculated" the Chinese with Western theories that were not necessarily useful because the Chinese economy developed at a different pace and was on a different stage. Citing Japan and South Korea as successful examples, Li remarked that if "Chinese companies follow the regular path of global brands or 4A [meaning "foreign"] models, China will never have its own global brands."[38]

Gao Jun, founder and president of Meikao Ad Agency, expressed a similar view at the conference, and called for Chinese media and ad professionals to treasure China's "five-thousand-year civilization," Confucian culture, and patriotic feelings. He stated,

> Chinese culture requires...everyone to have strong national feelings, especially when Chinese companies expand to the world or when they face foreign competitions in the Chinese market. I think the Chinese government and policies makers should be concerned with China's economic security....When Chinese companies expand to the world or compete with American companies, how can decision makers trust American ad agencies to help them? They can only trust Chinese ad agencies....Patriotism becomes a way for Chinese agencies to compete with multinational [ad] agencies.

Gao expressed similar concerns on various occasions and argued that Chinese companies could only depend on Chinese ad agencies. Many vocal ad professionals expressed similar suspicions toward foreign agencies by essentializing cultural differences between China and the West. For example, Cheng Chun, BAC's former general manager, remarked, "No matter how trendy or fashionable on the surface, all Chinese essentially follow Confucianism and harbor a strong respect for old ancestors and national dignity....Only when

China becomes strong can individuals raise up their heads in other countries" (personal interview, July 19, 2005).

From these examples, we can see that Chineseness was celebrated as a way to serve China's economic status and vice versa. Such an attitude reflects how the Chinese used "geopolitics, the national interest, and sometimes cultural conflict" as "some handy frames of reference" to discuss international issues (Zhang, 2001). These statements invoked nationalism and naturalized differences between Chinese and foreign ad agencies and Chinese and foreign corporations. Through discursive construction of Confucian heritage, economic insecurity, and cultural identity, various sets of binaries were established, thus making patriotism a competitive tool in China's late capitalism that disrupted conventional boundaries centered on the nation state. The ultimate purpose was to ground competition on an ideological level.

Chineseness was also based on the idea that foreign ad agencies' theories, practices, and toolboxes were not suitable for China because Chinese corporations developed at a different pace. For example, Jiang Shaoxiong, founder and CEO of Landao Advertising remarked, "The Ogilvy's 360-degree Brand Stewardship is useful for managing adults…but Chinese enterprises and products are still infants wearing diapers. How can you use the same method to treat them?" (phone interview, June 18, 2005). To infantilize Chinese companies endorsed the idea that advertising developed in a linear fashion, with foreign ad practices being more progressive.

In China, there was a general perception that ad professionals working in Chinese ad agencies were less skilled and more likely to use "dining and wining" to win business, in comparison with those in multinational ad agencies. Aware of such a negative perception and their inferior status, many Chinese ad professionals were eager to seek recognition from those working in transnational firms.[39] Because of the chaotic Chinese advertising market, some even argued that Chinese advertising could not maintain its autonomy. A Taiwanese executive creative director, who had worked in several multinational ad agencies and was working in a Chinese firm at the time of the interview, stated, "discussing independence of Chinese advertising…is like asking a five-year-old to have a speech floor. While he can do it, his lack of experience…affects the performance" (personal interview, June 16, 2005).

Consequently, Chineseness was viewed as simultaneously desirable and undesirable, thus posing challenges to Chinese ad agencies to legitimize Chineseness. While Western advertising practices were considered better, more rational, progressive, and modern, Chinese practices were treated as insufficient and lacking. Eager to promote Chineseness, ad professionals also endorsed discriminatory practices and treated Chinese culture as inferior and less advanced, thus reflecting both Orientalism and self-Orientalism (Said, 1978). Years of exposure to Western modernity and advertising theories humbled Chinese ad professionals. China's lack of theories and knowledge of capitalism reinforced ad professionals' sense of insufficiency. In order to enhance their competitiveness, Chinese ad professionals rallied around the state, attempting to rhetorically create a profession/business different from the West, one that was not purely driven by self-interest but by collective national pride. Increasing global pressure made the Chinese identity a convenient instrument to unite ad agencies, media, and advertisers. However, in reality, Chinese advertisers chose to work with Chinese ad agencies not because of their shared identity but because of Chinese ad agencies' lower prices and greater flexibility. While foreign ad agencies often followed standardized work procedures that required more time in advance, Chinese ad agencies reportedly completed TV commercials—from the concept stage to production and media placement—within a week, even in 2005.

To a large extent, the discourse of Chineseness reflected a general dilemma when China dealt with the West. On the one hand, the rhetoric of Chineseness was related to China's use of the West "as a contrasting Other in order to define whatever one believes to be distinctively 'Chinese'" (Chen, 1995, p. 39). Gries (2004, p. 35) also argues that the West "has become China's alter ego." Thus, Chinese ad agencies had a desire to develop the Chinese version of whatever was considered "the West." But on the other hand, Chineseness was also associated with labor exploitation, bribery, corruption, kickbacks, and other dubious practices, which delegitimized Chinese ad agencies' support for the Chinese practice. Thus, the reputation of Chineseness was tarnished by under-the-table transactions and digression from professional norms. For example, a Beijing University graduate and deputy media director of the Beijing office of a large Japanese advertising firm remarked,

> Localization in China means downward localization, which has a beautiful name, but in essence sides with the corrupt....Localization means inviting bad habits and societal practices to [multinational] companies....It concerns kickbacks, interests, personnel conflicts, low efficiency, and high external transaction costs. (Personal interview, July 14, 2005)

A critical view of Chinese ad agencies was shared among the majority of Chinese ad professionals I interviewed who worked at multinational advertising agencies. While those working in Chinese ad agencies tended to be more receptive, many still felt dubious about the lack of professionalism or standardized management in Chinese ad agencies.

THE YE MAOZHONG PHENOMENON

Chinese adman Ye Maozhong has been celebrated as a maverick genius, a creative swordsman, a master planner, and a celebrity. He entered the ad profession in 1988 and has masterminded more than 600 TV commercials. As an iconic adman, Ye received The State Administration of

Industry and Commerce's "Outstanding Contribution Award in China's Thirty-Year Advertising History" in 2008, and was recognized as one of China's top ten marketing experts in 2005, one of the top twenty-five marketers of 2004, one of the top ten ad professionals in 2003, and CCTV's ad adviser, among other awards and titles. He was a regular speaker at advertising conferences, a frequent contributor to ad magazines, and a prolific writer on advertising, marketing, and planning. While his popularity was confined to the advertising profession, major TV stations recently conducted lengthy interviews with him, suggesting that his influence went beyond advertising. Most coverage celebrated his success and ideas of advertising, which further promoted Ye and his firm.[40]

What distinguished Ye from other Chinese admen was his strongman image, unique style, and successful strategy in branding himself. When he worked for an ad agency in Shanghai in the early 1990s—his first job in the ad industry—he was among the first ad professionals to publish books and articles to attract business. His first book, titled *Notes of an Adman*, published in 1997, reportedly sold more than 10,000 copies in a month and more than 200,000 copies over years. Celebrating his knowledge, experience, and advertising philosophy, he included his phone number in several places in the book draft. While the book editor eventually deleted almost all his contact information, he surreptitiously placed his phone number on the copyright page. His first client reportedly called him three months after the book was published (Dongnan Satellite TV, 2013, Nov. 27). Ye claimed that the book changed his fate; since its publication he no longer had to look for clients. Ye founded a planning agency in Beijing in 1997 bearing his name, intertwining his personal brand and corporate brand. He became one of the most influential ad planners in the 1990s, a time when "idea masters" and "idea companies" flourished as a primitive form of consulting services.

In public presentations, he freely mixed his personal style, expertise, and character in a way that molded him into a unique brand. His most powerful assertion was that his ideas could produce quick sales. This statement was attractive to small and medium-sized Chinese companies mostly concerned with immediate sales. Considering that growth was often the most important goal, small and medium-sized Chinese companies prioritized quick actions, even when these actions were based on instincts, over a detailed analysis of a rapidly changing market.

Ye was flexible in responding to market changes and his agency's structure was also compatible with small to medium-sized Chinese companies managed by risk-taking entrepreneurs. Of Ye's more than 200 clients, most were small to medium-sized Chinese companies. His clients were from a wide range of industries, and he created ads for an eclectic variety of products, including tobacco, air conditioning, beer and wine, drinks, food, cell phones, apparel, strollers, pharmaceuticals, furniture, lubricant, and motorcycles. Ye never asserted his specialty in any industry, but instead highlighted his general expertise in marketing, planning, and business strategy. He offered an appealing solution to struggling clients willing to stake everything on a single throw. A prominent Beijing-based advertising scholar remarked,

> Ye has powerful abilities and is very skilled in using media and past cases for publicity. While there are exaggerations, [he provides] immediate solutions to Chinese companies. If Chinese companies use 4A firms, [these 4A firms] will do the analysis first, which probably takes at least a month. But things will change after a month. Instead, Ye Maozhong promises to give them drugs that may have an immediate impact....Although his drugs sometimes are ineffective, they are simple, obvious, bold creative ideas, which sometimes produce effective results. (Personal interview, July 11, 2005)

Ye skillfully packaged his brand as rooted in Chinese culture as well as the recent Communist tradition. He consistently reiterated his admiration for Mao Zedong and the Red Army. He always wore a black cap with a red star in public and repeatedly stressed the applicability of Mao's military strategies, culminating in phrases such as the use of "concentrated force to fight annihilation battles," "the dialect of major conflict and minor conflict," and "the philosophy of coming from the mass and going back to the mass." His headquarters in Shanghai included a sculpture of Mao in the yard and a large red star at the top of a glass wall. In using Mao's language as a rhetorical strategy, Ye not only linked the market to a smokeless battlefield, but also associated himself with the Communist legacy. He repeatedly and publicly expressed how the Red Army's Long March motivated him. His association with Mao not only endorsed him as a strongman and a lone fighter for an extraordinary cause but also implied his anti-foreign stance and support for a military-style management, a popular trend among Chinese companies at the time of my research.

Ye celebrated the "spirit of a wolf" in himself and in his organization. According to him, a wolf was the only animal able to think while running at high speed. A wolf's qualities, such as aggression, diligence, and unyielding character, became part of his own celebrated personality and corporate culture. In line with China's totemic wolf culture, he promoted his philosophy on his website: "We refuse to be tamed. We refuse to be submissive....We'd rather be wolves than beautiful tigers caged in zoos....You are doomed if you have no creative ideas."

Ye expressed little self-sympathy or sympathy for his employees. He applied strict disciplinary practices and overworked his employees to extremes, requiring them to develop strong self-discipline, stating, "Man should be hard on himself." He stated in interviews how he and his employees slapped their own faces in front of others for failing to deliver creative ideas on time. He also promoted the Chinese cultural concept "shede" (referring both to "sacrifice" and "give and take"), by stating that "one can only gain after one gives: one gains little when giving little, and one gains big when giving big."

Unlike typical Chinese agencies, Ye stressed that he never worked to please clients or showed servility to them, and he expressed dislike for advertising pitches. On the website (yemaozhong.com) he published thirteen books. In his books and published interviews, Ye constantly referred to his relationship with clients as "fate" (*yuanfen*). Ye stressed his integrity, reflected in the name of his meeting room: "Hall of Righteousness." He didn't allow "his clients to rape his creative ideas" and "would rather be a shattered vessel of jade than a complete piece of pottery." Further, he would never "lower his head for five deciliters of grain." His practice of requiring clients to prepay one year in advance was in sharp contrast to other Chinese agencies, which often had difficulty collecting fees after providing services.

While difficult to verify, his statements and his assertions were interesting rhetorical strategies. Various legends about him were circulated online and in traditional media, celebrating his idiosyncrasy, pride, straightforwardness, adventurousness, and unyielding personality. In a way, Ye engaged in a two-front fight that simultaneously challenged foreign and Chinese practices. Attacking Chinese agencies' servility and unprofessional practices asserted his professionalism. Attacking 4A firms underscored his Chineseness. His Chineseness and global knowledge were mutually reinforced through constant references to influential global communication theories (such as positioning, differentiation, branding, corporate identity systems, and integrated marketing communication), marketing techniques (SWOT analysis, market analysis, survey research, and consumer insight), admen (such as Ogilvy and Bates), business figures (Bill Gates, Steve Jobs, and Warren Buffett), theorists (Al Ries, Marshall McLuhan, Philip Kotler, and Don E. Schultz), and Chinese and global politicians (Theodore Roosevelt and Mao Zedong). Mediated messages including media reports, interviews, articles, books, speeches, blogs and microblogs on *Sina, Sohu, QQ*, and other sites produced Ye Maozhong as a distinctive personal and corporate brand.

Ye strongly preferred celebrity endorsement. He was well able to execute his creative ideas because of his local knowledge and media connections, and was skilled in using a "strong brand"—a celebrity, a media brand or an event—to promote a weak brand. He asserted, "A weak brand should lean on a strong brand" just as "a beautiful woman should lean on a rich man" (Ye, 2014, Nov. 7). His clients often advertised on CCTV, featuring celebrities in commercials. They also advertised products on popular TV programs such as *Super Girl*, *Happy Camp*, and *If You Are the One*, and during events such as the World Cup and the Beijing Olympics. For example, when Serbian national Bora Milutinovic, the coach of the Chinese national soccer team whom fans affectionately called Milu, led the team to China's first-ever entry into the World Cup in 2002, Ye signed Milu as a spokesperson for his client Jin Liufu, a Chinese liquor brand. In a commercial aired on CCTV, Milu dons a red traditional Chinese garment and holds a bottle of Jin Liufu, while the voiceover states, "Milu, for the first time he is coaching in China; for the first time he is leading the Chinese team to the World Cup; the first liquor he tasted is Jin Liufu; for the first time he is bringing happiness to Chinese fans." The smiling coach then announces, "Jin Liufu, the lucky liquor for the Chinese." Ironically, Milu was reported as rarely drinking any liquor, let alone Chinese liquor. Nevertheless, the Chinese company capitalized on his popularity.

Ye developed a strategy of concentrated media exposure because he largely worked with small to medium-size companies that often had limited budgets. His clients bombarded consumers with heavy exposure over a short period of time through powerful media such as CCTV or popular programs to "create an overwhelming local if not national dominance." Because of increasing media prices, the commercials he produced aired on CCTV for fifteen seconds or even five seconds, mainly aiming to increase name/brand recognition. Timing was especially important; his clients strategically chose important Chinese holidays such as China's New Year, the Moon Festival, and other events. Ye summarized his advertising formula in four stages: extracting the core values of the brand, visualizing the values, repeating the message again and again, and producing associations among consumers. He largely treated consumers as passive and believed that information could be nailed into consumers' heads. As will be analyzed in chapter six, the Chinese brand Naobaijin, which was Ye's client for a period of time, used a similar marketing strategy.

Ye and his team produced some of the most memorable slogans: "all earthmen know about it" in a commercial selling cold-proof underwear; "man should be harder on himself" in a commercial selling men's apparel; "a 30-year-old body, a 60-year-old heart" in a public service announcement; and "the farther our thoughts travel, the farther we can go" in a tobacco commercial. His strategy of concentrated media exposure further increased the possibility of the slogans being discussed and disseminated in a saturated media environment.

Ye often worked directly with the general managers who had the power to make immediate decisions, and was involved in his client's business development at a very early stage. Ye's advertising strategy partially depended on his intuitive knowledge and his clients' flexibility. For example, in 2004 when he worked for Double Seed, a growing fast-food restaurant cofounded by two Chinese peasants, Ye identified its core value as "steamed" food. According to him, steamed food in the Cantonese tradition implied natural taste, flavor, and nutrition. Based on his suggestion, Double Seed changed its business strategy by removing fried products and launching a rebranding campaign with a new logo, look, and name. The chain restaurant was renamed Real Kongfu in an attempt to capitalize on China's Kongfu fever at that time. Jet Li, a well-known Chinese Kongfu master and film star, was hired as the spokesperson. The campaign used the slogan "Kongfu will never fail anyone with determination; steamed food has better nutrition." It positioned the brand as "the chain restaurant for global Chinese" and attempted to link Jet Li's global appeal to the restaurant's ambition for future global expansion. In addition, the company sponsored the exhibition of a popular film called *Kongfu* starring Hong Kong actor Stephen Chou.

The brand expanded quickly and the number of its chain restaurants increased from a few dozen in 2004 to more than 400 in 2009. However, like a typical Chinese family business, the company later encountered difficulties. One founder was arrested and sentenced to fourteen years in prison in December 2013 because of the financial disputes. Ye's unstable clientele made it difficult to implement long-term growth strategies. Chinese enterprises survive less than four years on average, far below the eight years and twelve and a half years in the United States and Japan respectively (He & Lu, 2004). A survey conducted in 2004 showed that 53.4 percent of Chinese ad agencies work for less than three years with their clients; 32.3 percent have three-to-five-year collaborations; and only 12.4 percent have five-to-ten-year collaborations. Less than 1.9 percent have collaborations lasting longer than ten years.[41] Given rapid media changes and transformations, it is possible that the agency-client relationship is now even less stable.

Ye's good relationship with media, ad magazines, and websites led to celebratory media coverage. As an iconic figure symbolizing the triumph of local advertising, his popularity was associated with recent nationalism. Advertising scholar Huang Shengming remarked, "While Chinese media looked up to the West in the past, they now have become very critical of the West largely due to the changing popular feelings" (personal interview, July 11, 2005). To those ad professionals knowledgeable about Western ad practices, however, Ye symbolized unprofessional, undesirable, and idiosyncratic practices. He was often criticized for making exaggerated claims and misleading campaigns, especially in his early career.[42] In an interview, Ye apologized for his misleading early campaigns: how, in his past, he had advertised useless products in unethical ways (Dongnan Satellite TV, 2013, Nov. 27). He acknowledged that in his early days his main purpose was to earn money and that he sometimes cudgeled his brain to come up with a selling position. However, he now felt more responsibility to promote positive values to society.

His image as a fighter was significant in the losing battle between Chinese and foreign agencies. After 2000, foreign ad agencies in China were growing rapidly while Chinese ad agencies were in rapid decline. After China further loosened ownership restrictions in 2005, many foreign ad agencies were in a consolidation spree, buying many Chinese firms, as discussed in chapter two. In the creative business, the market share for Chinese ad agencies continued to dwindle despite the success of a few ad agencies such as GAC and Simei Media. In 2011, Chinese creative agencies totaling around 66,000 only took up about 20 percent of the advertising market, while agencies with foreign investment numbered at around 6,000 consituted 60 percent of the market. The remaining 20 percent was left to media agencies (Oriental TV, 2011, Sept. 20). While Ye may not be popular with large advertisers in first-tier cities, China's vast size, fragmented media markets, and varying consumer tastes and lifestyles meant that his ad strategies could still find a market. While his ads were criticized as vulgar by cosmopolitan consumers and ad professionals, they appealed to consumers living in small towns or rural places. The very fact that he won business, regardless of the underlying process or related ethical practices, was celebrated by China's pragmatic media.

Ye freely selected Western or Chinese elements for his campaigns and promotional materials, and his pragmatic approach and "patchwork" philosophy were reflected in contradictory claims that catered to the growth-oriented culture in China. For example, while he claimed dislike for the formality of multinational agencies, he simultaneously asserted that his firm used data and scientific procedures. Ye promoted juxtaposing values for his employees, such as the individual trait of "the wolf's spirit" as well as teamwork, and harsh discipline as well as genuine care. He stated that he treated consumers with respect while also making condescending remarks at various times, such as, "don't expect consumers to be smart," and "don't tell consumers the truth." Further, while arguing that media exposure was not the same as branding, he nonetheless advocated the use of "small money to achieve big results" and "explosive techniques" to bombard consumers.

Ye's contradictory views could be understood through Michel Foucault's notion of discourse. Foucault stated, "Discourses are tactical elements or blocks operating in the field of force relations; there can exist different and even contradictory discourses within the same strategy; they can, on the contrary, circulate without changing their form from one strategy to another opposing strategy" (1978, pp. 101–2). Ye achieved discursive power precisely because he spoke differently to different audiences. He maintained a professional image, and simultaneously attracted Chinese clients who cared about sales. The Chineseness constructed by Ye reflected a "collective habit of supplementing every major world trend with the notion of 'Chinese,'" a discriminatory practice largely produced by "the lingering, pervasive hegemony of Western culture" (Chow, 1998, p. 3). In conclusion, as a product of neoliberalism and developmentalism, the Ye Maozhong phenomenon was reactive to Western ad agencies' privilege and Chinese agencies' marginality. Despite (or because of) Ye's consistently contradictory claims, his unorthodox practices successfully shaped the image of Chinese advertising and enhanced his own status and that of his agency in the rapidly globalizing Chinese market.

A CASE STUDY OF A PRIVATE CHINESE FIRM: DANCING IN CHAINS

The following section analyzes a Beijing-based small ad agency that simultaneously promoted Chineseness and emulated Western practices. All names were pseudonyms and the data were drawn from my month-long participant observations in 2005, informal conversations while I was doing an internship there, and six semi-structured interviews. The firm (hereafter called Youbang International Ad Firm (YIAF)) was founded in 1999 by thirty-four-year-old Teng Shengyuan, a journalist who previously worked at a CCTV-affiliated ad firm. YIAF initially focused on media buying and gradually transformed into a full-service agency. In 2005, it had thirty employees (sixteen men and fourteen women), averaging twenty-seven years old, fifteen with bachelor's degrees, ten with associate degrees, and four with degrees lower than associate. Seven of the employees majored in advertising. These employees graduated from less prestigious programs than typical Chinese graduates in foreign ad agencies. YIAF had four divisions: Creative, Account, Media, and Comprehensive Services. While twenty-eight employees were from mainland China, the firm hired two division directors from Taiwan with international experience to promote globalization. A twenty-eight-year-old Taiwanese was director of the Creative department; he was educated in Canada, with six years of experience in multinational ad agencies in Taiwan. A thirty-one-year-old Taiwanese was hired as the director of the Account Services department.

Like Ye Maozhong, YIAF founder Teng was an ambitious man with a strong personality. What differentiated him from Ye was that he constantly stressed the importance of Chinese agencies to learn foreign business procedures, management styles, and practices. "Local ad agencies," he stressed, "must improve their standardized management in daily operations." Indeed, in client and proposal meetings, YIAF promoted the use of "unique selling proposition," a dated marketing technique that was the hallmark of U.S. advertising in the mid-twentieth century. The firm also standardized its work procedures and required the employees to sign various forms, including creative brief forms, task orders, task progress forms, and quotation forms. While all employees spoke Chinese and the firm did not serve any foreign clients at that time, the forms included both

English and Chinese languages to convey the firm's cosmopolitan image. Like many Chinese firms, this agency used two accounting systems—one for internal cost control and the other for charging clients—to evade taxation.

The firm was heavily decorated with Chinese and foreign cultural symbols, suggesting its Chinese roots and cosmopolitan inspiration/ connection. At the entrance was an artificial mountain, with water running from it into a small pool at the bottom, in which goldfish swam. The entrance was also ornamented with a small decorative sailboat, a winter plum tree, green bamboo bushes, joss sticks in a red jar, and a white Bodhisattva placed close to a blue flowery vase. Nearby was a small Chinese wine container and a jade sailing boat engraved with the Chinese words *Yi Fan Feng Shun* (meaning "smooth sailing"). A glass container, used to collect lucky money, was engraved with Chinese words such as *qifu shankuan* (goodwill money), and *kuan bu zai duo, xin cheng ze ling* (a small amount is enough; wholeheartedness makes good fortune). These items meant to convey good *fengshui* to bring fame and fortune. A newspaper rack near the entrance displayed publications such as *China Times*, *China Daily*, *China Advertising*, *International Advertising*, *Modern Advertising*, *Admen*, and *Sales and Marketing*. On a large neon-lit picture wall were Teng's photos with foreigners (mainly Westeners), surrounded by visitors' signatures. The glass-walled meeting room displayed a large Chinese map, posters, logos, paintings and calligraphy that celebrated "mutual communication and mutual benefits by helping others." Chinese paintings on the themes of peony and winter plum flowers were hung in the main office. A picture with the Chinese characters for good luck (*Jixiang ruyi*) was posted on the door of the HR office. Teng occupied a heavily decorated office, which was closed most of the time. The Chinese character for happiness (*fu*) was hung upside down on his door, meaning "fortune/ happiness has come home." Like typical small Chinese firms with limited resources, Teng's secretary also worked as a receptionist and, most of the employees worked in cubicles and had to share computers.

DISCIPLINARY AND PATRIARCHAL CULTURE

Employees were disciplined through countless rules, notices, sayings, pledges, and formal and informal talks. For example, a red board near the entrance stated, "You make Youbang proud. You make Youbang brilliant. Let's join hands and create our future." The "employee's oath pledge" hung on a wall, declaring,

> I promise to work hard, [and] strive for success. To realize my own values, I will work diligently and conscientiously to the best of my ability every day. Treat others with honesty and sincerity. Work selflessly for the public interest. Be faithful to my duty. Fight side by side. Co-create a great cause leading to a better life.

Such inspirational phrases were thrown together and linked individual success to the company's interests. Words referring to the battlefield created a sense of urgency. Every Monday morning, a meeting for manager-level employees was held, during which time Teng mostly lectured his employees and sometimes authoritatively pounded the table for emphasis.

The firm implemented a strict attendance policy. While the by-laws posted in the HR office specified the work time for weekdays as 8:30 am–5:30 pm, as well as Saturday mornings, the actual work time exceeded these hours. Being late meant financial punishment and employees had to pay by degrees of lateness: 10 yuan for being late for 10 minutes or less; 20 yuan for 10–30 minutes; and being late for more than 30 minutes was treated as a half-day absence. However, employee's frequent overtime work was not necessarily compensated: overtime work before 8 pm was not considered overtime; overtime work after 8 pm was acknowledged but not compensated; and only those who worked after 11 pm could take off work for the same amount of time the next day. Employees lost compensated time, however, if they had to work the next day and the firm could not afford to allow them the time off. Sensing resistance at times, Teng stressed repeatedly at meetings that the district government had approved the time schedule, although he referred to the officially posted schedule, not the one that was actually implemented.

Teng indoctrinated his employees to focus not on pay (which was usually lower than multinational ad agencies) but on their own contribution to the firm. He stated that one must transform one's ad career into a cause:

> Strictly speaking, we make a career into a cause. One should not care about monthly salaries of the few thousand yuan, but rather about how many things one can do in an entire life or how much money one will earn for the company....Only in this way can a firm develop, lead the profession, and eventually attract others. But China badly lacks such people. (Personal interview, June 24, 2005)

Through invoking a sense of selfless devotion, Teng hoped that his firm would become the best Chinese firm in two decades. He constantly referred to general managers and executives in multinational agencies, especially those ethnic Chinese from Hong Kong, Taiwan, and Singapore, as his role models. Teng was goal-driven, meticulous in details, and worked hard. He also set up role models among his managers who internalized his values. Because of the high turnover rate, he only trusted employees who had proven their loyalty. Viewing new employees merely as "interns," he remarked, "I will never consider new employees as *my* employees [my emphasis]. I constantly select them and use my own ideas to influence them" (personal interview, June 24, 2005). Teng's heavy-handed indoctrination made it easier to exploit his employees. Constant assessment and job insecurity forced employees to outperform others.

This agency was run like a typical family business, with the boss as the father and the employees as children. The boss enjoyed absolute authority and the employees were expected to provide service and be submissive. While Teng had unlimited access to his employees' time and space, he instructed his secretary to keep his doors closed all the time. He vented his anger when he perceived challenges to his authority. The employees always referred to him as "Teng Zong" (meaning Executive Teng), a respectful way to address superiors in Chinese companies. In contrast to Western agencies' relatively relaxed work environment, Teng referred to his style as "military management."

His tactics produced some impact. For example, an account manager remarked, "Local firms need cohesion and a sense of cause…for people to come together to…develop the Chinese advertising industry, expand it globally, and win credit for the Chinese." Another female worker, who just started in the firm as the only English translator, called her mother and repeated Teng's words, stating, "Teng Zong said that we should not focus on the 2000 yuan monthly pay, but on what we have done or will do for the company." She asked her mother to support her pursuit. A few employees also agreed that primitive accumulation of capital was necessary. For example, the twenty-six-year-old female HR manager remarked in an interview, "The advertising industry is still at the stage of primitive accumulation. Many employees here are not well paid, but they do not complain because they view their work as a good learning experience." While the future was uncertain, according to her, the employees expected to benefit financially and symbolically as the company grew. However, the co-creation of a common cause was an empty slogan, and at times, lower-level employees sometimes pretended to be occupied when Teng was present and killed time when he was not around.

The three mid-level managers and role models who had worked in the firm for more than three years all internalized Teng's sense of mission and idea of sacrifice. A twenty-five-year-old female media manager stated in an interview, "To me, the learning experience is the most important and the title and personal benefits do not matter." The production manager and account manager, who had worked in the firm for five years, stated that he was proud that people rarely complained about overtime work. While "people might not work full-heartedly for their own advertising life and the firm at first," he stated, the constant removal of unqualified employees means that "a few elites willing to sacrifice for the firm and for their own advertising life continue their work and become role models." Another production manager and account services manager expressed a similar view: "Everybody has a sense of mission.... Working harder increases our value.... We have a mission to copy the ideas of the leader and spread them to other people. Such a centripetal force creates the company's direction." An account manager and production manager in the firm disclosed three reasons for staying at his job: his identification with the organizational culture, the boss's trust, and the company's continuing growth, which had already attracted an increasing number of large clients. The company became a good platform for his development. These managers obviously were instrumental in implementing Teng's ideas and management style. A production manager in the firm stated that his biggest problem was to make others work as hard as he did without complaint. Teng exploited the Communist heritage (i.e., individuals were expected to be fully devoted to social causes without considering their own benefit) as well as the market logic (i.e., many graduates had difficulty finding jobs). While Teng owned an expensive Volvo, the monthly salary of an entry-level employee was only a little more than 1,000 yuan (approximately $140 USD) at that time. Salaries were sometimes delayed for months, but employees dared not ask to be paid for fear of leaving a bad impression.

China's widespread neoliberalism and developmentalism decreased concerns over social justice and egalitarianism. The idea that a company's sole responsibility was to maximize profits was generally accepted. For example, the production manager cited previously remarked, "An enterprise is like a boat. Once you board someone's boat, you should behave according to that person's rules." Youbang's patriarchy was also accompanied by a close collegial bonding. Young employees, many of whom were the single children in their families, called co-workers brothers and sisters. They ordered lunch boxes, ate together, shared food, and made fun of each other, but the two Taiwanese directors never ate with them. This social bonding was also a reason why some employees chose to stay, despite other difficult working conditions.

BALANCING POPULAR NATIONALISM AND COSMOPOLITANISM

YIAF linked popular nationalism (Gries, 2004; H. Wang, 2003; Zhang, 2001) with its corporate objectives, and employees sometimes reluctantly internalized this relationship. For example, an account executive stated, "a dog should not dislike its poor family, and a son should not despise his ugly mother." Her position (a Chinese, a woman, an employee, etc.) involved a particular way of thinking. As an employee, she felt obligated to endorse YIAF. After discussing her poor pay, however, she continued, "it would be noble not to become a traitor if there is no food after you have battled an enemy."

Like most Chinese agencies, YIAF sought international collaborations, but as a newly established firm, it had few choices. Because influential multinational agencies had already established their operations in China, YIAF turned to foreign agencies that had not yet entered China. In 2005, during the time of my participant observations, it was negotiating a joint venture arrangement with a Swedish ad firm and a Swiss cultural agency. Teng was flexible with collaborative terms and hoped that foreign partners would provide some clout when his firm pitched for Chinese clients. The advantage of a joint venture, stated Teng, was that "foreign clients recognize this [international collaboration] and pay higher service fees." Teng also hoped to gain "advanced international experience" and to share his partners' cultural capital. Teng stated, "Having a foreign partner improves the image of a Chinese firm and also attracts Chinese clients." He also invested in the communications program of a vocational college in Southern China. The company had expanded quickly and established a branch in Shanghai and Wuhan. More recently, it invested in TV productions because of the dwindling profits from creative advertising services.

Like many Chinese agencies, this firm desperately needed resources to produce a cosmopolitan image. The hiring of two Taiwanese managers was in line with a general trend in the Chinese advertising industry, which recruited experienced ad professionals from Taiwan, Hong Kong, and Singapore for leadership positions. Ad professionals with experience in foreign agencies were paid more by Chinese firms than they could earn in foreign agencies because such a move was considered a downward move in the hierarchy of prestige in the Chinese advertising market. At client meetings, Teng frequently mentioned, sometimes with exaggeration, the two Taiwanese managers and YIAF's collaboration with foreign firms in an effort to promote his firm's cosmopolitan image.

Like a typical Chinese agency, YIAF was in a weaker position in relation to advertisers. YIAF had to simultaneously stress its willingness to serve and stretch its resources to project a professional image. Because Chinese advertisers constantly shopped for new agencies, YIAF always risked losing its current clients. For example, after rounds of competition, YIAF was chosen as one of four agencies (two Chinese and two foreign) for a large bank (hereafter called Bank A). Any new project from this bank was pitched among these four agencies. During the time of my research with YIAF, Bank A planned to launch a new financial management program. Before the formal proposal meeting, the bank sent a representative to each agency to preview their proposal. After the preview at YIAF, the bank's representative Mr. Chen commented on the ad and made suggestions for improvement. He also stressed, however, that it was only his personal opinion and that he had no intention of influencing the creative idea or direction. Based on Chen, what Bank A wanted to see "is whether the agency perceives the target audience the same way as the bank does." Interestingly, Bank A only provided a short description of the program, without giving information about its consumers or competitors. YIAF's creatives thus researched Bank A and its competitors online. With no consumer data, the proposal could only speculate on what Bank A really wanted.

YIAF only had two weekend days to revise the proposal. Two days later, I attended the on-site presentation together with the creative director, account director, media director, account manager, and Teng. The account director first discussed the strengths and weaknesses of recent campaigns of other banks, Chinese and foreign, providing images and statistics. After discussing the strengths and consumer characteristics of Bank A, he proposed that the campaign focus on "high-end clients, local competitiveness, and international vision." Afterward, the creative director stated that the campaign should highlight the Bank's "professionalism, talented employees, and extended branches," themed on "worth being together" (*zhide zai yiqi*). Storyboards for several TV commercials and ideas about marketing, promotion, and events were presented. Teng concluded the presentation,

> I believe your financial management program will do very well no matter whose strategy you choose. In some sense, the purpose of an ad firm is to gather intelligence. Many of our ideas and intelligence come from communicating with clients, marketing people, colleagues, and other ad agencies....Youbang International has attracted many international

advertising elites. The evening party and the branding seminar we did for you have proved that Youbang can do things well. We are unique in that we will work diligently on all projects, no matter if it's an ad painting job worth 150 yuan, a conference event costing 3,000 yuan, or an event budgeted at 10 million or even 50 million yuan. As a founding institute of the Beijing local 4A club, we will perform things very well.

Following Teng's remarks, a bank representative stated that the concept was too general and could be used in any campaign for any product. Another person added, "In a Chinese consumer's mind, financial management was about using an abacus, but now we use computers. We should use this [historical transition] to differentiate ourselves from foreign banks since Bank A strongly embodies the characteristics of the Chinese nation." A third person was also concerned about how to differentiate Bank A from foreign banks and wanted to highlight the bank's Chineseness. All the commenters stressed that these were merely their personal opinions.

Understandably, these employees stressed that their views were just personal opinions. Because of the bank's hierarchical structure, to get a campaign idea approved was very difficult. Any campaign proposal had to first be approved by department directors (chuzhang), which was then reported to the general managers of large branches (fenhang hangzhang), and finally to the general director (zonghang hangzhang). An idea could fail at any level. Unlike many large foreign companies that empowered the marketing directors, the general director with no marketing experience had the final say. Interestingly, the general director did not attend the meeting. The participants were lower-level employees who handled daily operations with no power to make final decisions. YIAF thus had to speculate what the client really wanted. Teng later remarked that if he had known their preference for the abacus, his proposal would have included it.

Teng's remarks during the proposal simultaneously showed his modesty—praising Bank A's strong position and wise judgment—as well as his agency's qualifications as a local 4A firm. As one of the ten founding agencies of the Beijing local 4A club, YIAF's 4A membership redrew the boundary between a Chinese agency and a foreign agency. Teng's claim of being a "4A agency without 4A prices" asserted his firm's professionalism and the advantage of lower prices. Given that Chinese agencies were generally perceived as unprofessional, with wining and dining as a major way to attract business, grouping YIAF with 4A firms uplifted its image. To charge lower prices was a benefit associated with Chinese agencies in comparison with foreign 4A firms. In 2005, the charge for a typical Chinese agency's services was 20–30 percent lower than that of a multinational corporation. Teng's remarks highlighted the firm's professionalism and competitiveness in comparison with multinational agencies' general unwillingness to work on small laborious projects.

This example showed the challenges that Chinese agencies faced in the Chinese market. YIAF had to stretch its resources to create business opportunities. Teng actively participated in associations and made personal connections with noted academics, officials, media workers, and business managers. He was also a board member of trade journals, including *International Advertising*, *China Advertising*, *Advertising Guide*, and *Advertising Panview*, which helped promote his firm. Also, winning awards was a strategy to enhance YIAF's reputation. Framed award certificates were hung in the firm's meeting room, including a certificate for "The Top 100 Most Influential Local Ad Agencies in 2004–2005" issued by the ad magazine *Sales and Marketing*, Teng's certificate for "The Top 100 Most Influential Advertising Executives in 2004–2005" from the CCTV Advertising Department, and another certificate issued by the Advertising Department of the Communication University of China. As a small firm, it utilized every opportunity to boost its fame in the chaotic Chinese ad market. For example,

CCTV created the Gongyi Guanggao (Public Service Ads) award in the mid-1990s. Despite the lack of any material incentive, Teng pushed his creative team to participate in this competition, which required weeks of intensive work. China's increasing demand for awards also led to the creation of numerous awards and advertising festivals. A communication scholar viewed this phenomenon as Chinese ad professionals' "collective defense strategy" (personal interview, July 11, 2005). Winning an international award was considered even more prestigious. Trade magazines had numerous articles that discussed how far Chinese ad agencies still lagged behind. In short, this case study suggests that Chinese agencies had opportunities but also faced many challenges in China's opportunistic market.

CONCLUSION

Chinese ad agencies' responses to economic, cultural, and political challenges and opportunities have changed after China's entry into the WTO. Chinese agencies competed with foreign agencies on an ideological level, and with other Chinese agencies on a practical level. How Chinese ad agencies responded to the developing situation depended on their resources: while some state-owned agencies formed joint ventures and became shareholding firms, private firms generally had fewer choices and were more aggressive in constructing Chineseness and cosmopolitanism as a competitive strategy.

In the triangular relationship that involved the ad agency, the advertiser, and media, the agency was often the weakest of the three. It could thus be heavily influenced by the changing media and business environment. Given that Chinese advertisers rarely committed to long-term relationships and were mostly interested in quick sales, Chinese agencies catered to them by making quick decisions based on experience rather than on scientific data and careful research. Chinese ad agencies were at the lower end of the food chain in comparison with foreign ad agencies. Their competitiveness generally relied and still relies on lower prices and flexibility, which in turn meant a "race to the bottom." Because of the dwindling profits from creative services, many Chinese ad agencies have been diversifying into media buying and ownership, TV productions, and other businesses.

On an ideological level, Chinese ad agencies faced the challenges of foreign ad agencies and of their own unprofessional image. They thus used Chineseness as a symbolic competitive instrument. By constructing the Western Other, Chinese agencies were united on an ideological level. However, as some researchers (e.g., Chen, 1995; Ma, 2000) argue, Asian values and Oriental essentialism have often been used against Asians as justification for social control and monitoring. While the discourse of Chineseness enhanced local knowledge and problematized Western modernity, it also re-inscribed patriarchy, self-Orientalism, and labor exploitation. It further endorsed the hegemony of a "market economy and its monopolization of social resources" that placed economic, cultural, social, and political activities under its logic (H. Wang, 2003, p. 182). In this sense, Chineseness did not provide an alternative solution; rather, it endorsed inequality and new types of exploitation.

During the time of my research in 2005, regardless of whether Chinese ad agencies collaborated with or contested the practices of foreign agencies, their strategies were predominantly reactive to foreign agencies' privilege and their own marginalized position. Chinese ad professionals were othered in the midst of a wide celebration of Western capitalism, modernity, and neoliberalism. Chinese advertising practices were treated as less desirable and ad agencies had to use opportunistic tactics when competing with Western ad agencies. At the same time, the revival of traditional Chinese culture made it possible to construct Chineseness as a legitimized cultural and business strategy. Thus, supporters of Chineseness simultaneously occupied a position of "will and power" and of marginality

(De Certeau, 1984). Chinese ad professionals demonstrated conflicting ideas about advertising practices because they drew resources from different places to remain relevant across situations. Even though Chinese business people are more confident as China is becoming increasingly important in the global market, the underscoring Western hegemony is still predominant in shaping the discursive power of Chineseness. Since the 2007–8 global financial recession, there has been increasing skepticism toward the Western model of modernity, which may change how Chineseness and Western advertising practices are perceived and received in the future in China.

4 Branding Chinese Products: Between Nationalism and Cosmopolitanism

Models for understanding the relationship of advertising to national identity historically focus on the selling of patriotism in a landscape of industrial and global capitalism. In the United States, for instance, the equating of brands with patriotism has been a strategy since the early twentieth century. It is common to relate nationalism to consumption and citizenship (McGovern, 2006). In addition to American consumer society analyzed by scholars such as Richard Fox and Jackson Lears (1983), Jackson Lears (1994), William Leach (1993), and Roland Marchand (1985), the United States since the mid-twentieth century has also been described as a "consumers' republic," where civic-minded citizens and social policies are replaced by consumer citizens and practices of consumption (Cohen, 2003). For example, in the weeks after 9/11, not only did the US President George W. Bush urge citizens to consume as a civic duty but numerous advertising campaigns also capitalized on patriotism and linked buying American brands to national pride. Consumption, to some extent, has become a basis of "a reconstituted modern citizenship" (McGovern, 2006, p. 5). In a nation such as China, however, in which capitalism has emerged through a different hybrid model characterized by a decentralized economy and a centralized one-party political system, the selling of nationalism and cosmopolitanism takes on different meanings. The broader question is: how does advertising function as a site for different ideas about the Chinese nation, its relationship with the imagined West, and China's response to globalization?

This chapter analyzes how contemporary Chinese advertisers sell nationalism and cosmopolitanism through an in-depth examination of advertisements—in particular, TV commercials and print ads that were created by Chinese ad agencies to sell Chinese products. These ads were important because Chinese advertisers and their agencies often claimed to represent more "genuine" Chinese feelings and values when competing with foreign brands and agencies. Thus an analysis of these ads helps us understand how Chinese advertisers produced "Chineseness" and conflicting understandings of China as a nation and state in an increasingly globalized market.

Chinese advertising is an important field in which we can study China's varying responses to globalization and its ambivalent relationship with the West, as discussed in chapter one. Considering that globalization means increasing interconnectivity as well as disconnectivity (Giddens, 1990; Castells, 1996a, 1996b; Held, McGrew, Goldblatt, & Perraton, 1999), globalization breaks down traditional boundaries centered on the nation state and sets up new boundaries. Most of the ads analyzed in this chapter come from *Zhongguo Guanggao Zuopin Nianjian* of 2000, 2002, 2003 (*Yearbooks of Chinese Advertisements*). Ads included in the *Yearbooks* were published or aired in China from 1997 to 2002, a period of rapid changes for advertising. The ads were submitted by ad agencies or advertisers and evaluated by a committee of media experts and academics for inclusion in the publications. Arguably, these texts can be viewed as representative of upscale Chinese ads in terms of their creativity, trend-setting styles, and social influence for that period.

CHINESE ADVERTISING AND MODERNITY

Advertising reflects many of the desires of the society in which it operates; it also helps to shape social values, preferences, attitudes, and even behaviors of consumers (Jhally, 1987; Pollay & Gallagher, 1990).

Through advertising, an object may lose any real connection with its practical utility, and be reduced to a signifier of abstract and changing qualities that make products worth purchasing for consumption (Jhally, 1987, p. 11). Products take on social and emotional meanings through reification (Sturken & Cartwright, 2001), a process in which products are awarded magical power, promising to make consumers more patriotic, desirable, sexy, human, young, and beautiful. While Chinese advertisers sell a variety of values, such as individualism, family, heterosexual love, youth culture, happiness, and coolness, this chapter focuses on nationalism and cosmopolitanism as a way to advance the understanding of the diagram identified in chapter one, which identifies four major factors that influence advertising practices: market, technology, culture, and policy. These four factors further shape three sets of relationship: advertisers and consumers, the state and media, and the local and the global. The negotiation between nationalism and cosmopolitanism symbolizes China' changing conception about the West and itself.

On the one hand, researchers (e.g., Jian Wang, 2006; Jian Wang & Z. Wang, 2007; Li, 2009; Shirk, 2007) have documented rising consumer nationalism in contemporary China. Calls for boycotting Japanese goods in 2005 and the French retailer Carrefour in 2008 are just two of many cases that bear witness to consumer nationalism in China.[43] On the other hand, export products from other countries continue to enjoy a high level of popularity. Western cultural symbols in China have functioned as what Pierre Bourdieu (1984) called "symbolic capital" and "social capital." Products and services produced in the United States and other Western countries, in particular, are often fetishized in China as symbols of modernity. Even the association of products with Western symbols gives the impression that such products are more modern (Li, 2008; Zhou & Belk, 2004; Zhou & Hui, 2003; Zhou, Yang & Hui, 2010; Zhuang, Wang, Zhou & Zhou, 2008). Lianxi Zhou and his colleagues (Zhou & Hui, 2003; Zhou,

Yang & Hui, 2010; Zhuang, Wang, Zhou & Zhou, 2008) argue that consumers in developing countries, including China, often worship products made in Western countries. A range of studies support the idea that perceived foreignness is desirable in the Chinese market and that Western products have an influence that local brands find difficult to match (Alden, Steenkamp & Batra, 1999; Batra, Ramaswamy, Alden, Steenkamp, &Ramachander, 2000; Eckhardt, 2005; Ger & Belk, 1996; Zhou & Belk, 2004; Sklair, 1994). Zhou and Belk (2004) argue that "global brands, advertising techniques, brand names, and models were effectively associated with status, modernity, cosmopolitan sophistication, and technology" (p. 67). In addition, women perceive fashion and beauty products as "more fashionable" and "beautiful" when their ads use Western models. However, "nonluxury and noncosmopolitan" goods such as Chinese medicines, foods, and nonalcoholic beverages are found to resonate well with consumers when their ads use Chinese cultural elements and values.

There has thus been an increasing convergence between the marketing strategies of global brands and those of Chinese brands in China. For example, Chinese brands increasingly adopt advertising and marketing strategies to associate themselves with Western images. Cosmopolitanism (used interchangeably with transnationalism), nationalism, and the convergence of the two can be understood as responses to the three modes of cultural globalization often conceptualized as cultural homogenization, heterogenization, and cultural hybridity (and glocalization in the business arena), as was discussed in chapter one. While nationalism can be viewed as an obstacle to globalization, transnationalism celebrates the commonality that transcends national boundaries. Nationalism and transnationalism are not mutually exclusive concepts, but rather complement each other in that transnationalism can be an extension of nationalism and nationalism can be expressed in the rhetoric of "hierarchical universality" (Duara, 1993, p. 4). While glocal advertising often refers to how global brands tailor their advertising messages when they move to a foreign market, however, glocalized practices by Chinese advertisers mean the inclusion of foreign elements in their advertising campaigns in order to engineer a cosmopolitan image for the domestic market. In the following sections, I will first discuss how Chinese advertisers sell nationalism. I will then discuss the selling of cosmopolitanism, which is followed by an analysis of the convergence of the two strategies. This will enable us to draw some tentative conclusions.

SELLING NATIONALISM

Nationalism has multiple meanings but is often understood as a form of collective identification with a nation and people who share a common origin, ancestry, language, religion, and geography. As discussed in chapter one, Chinese nationalism should be understood as a dynamic process that has been complicated by the historical relationship between China and the West. Many studies on Chinese nationalism (e.g. He & Guo, 2000; Zhao, 2000; Zhang, 2001; Gerth, 2003; Shirk 2007) focus on state or official nationalism, which is often reactive to internal and external pressures and has been instrumental to the Communist regime. China's dealing with international affairs demonstrates both a responsible and rational dimension as well as an irrational reactive dimension (Shirk, 2007). These two sides have a lot to do with how China is perceived and how the country perceives itself. Gries (2004) argues that nationalism in twentieth-century China is a combination of a victory narrative against imperialism, and a victimization narrative attributed to foreign powers. These two narratives work together to create Chinese national consciousness toward the West. However, nationalism also concerns the proactive production and reproduction of China's history and contemporary events and the reinterpretation of China's changing global position. Chinese advertising that sells nationalism thus concerns the reconstruction and reinforcement of traditional images, symbols, rituals, myths, and customs at a time when China's national identity is increasingly challenged in an increasingly globalized world.

SELLING NATIONALISM THROUGH APPROPRIATING CHINESE HISTORY AND HEROES

Chinese advertisers can use nationalism because the Chinese market has been shaped by years of patriotic education that provides fertile soil for it. Hughes (2006) provides a detailed analysis of how the Chinese regime has, at various times, manufactured and shaped different discourses of nationalism and especially patriotism in the last few decades. Patriotic education, with historical humiliation as a recurring theme, is typically closely linked with nationalism and national pride. Patriotism emerges as a banner with potential to unite different Chinese ideologies (Hughes, 2006; Zhao, 2000).

One mode of Chinese advertising sells nationalism through Chinese symbols, images, rituals, historical heroes, and China's anti-imperialist history, to create a narrative of patriotism, loyalty, and national glory. An analysis of three campaigns can help unravel how nationalism intertwines with China's history and its search for modernity.

In July 2000, a Sichuan-based software company launched an ad campaign for its new domain Chinese.com, aiming to create a web-based franchise to compete with existing Chinese portals including Sohu, Sina, and Netease. The creators positioned the domain as an umbrella for all Chinese-language websites throughout the world. The campaign, created by Guangdong Advertising Agency, aimed to produce brand recognition in the shortest amount of time with the lowest investment. When the domain Chinese.com was launched on July 3, 2000, the operators held press conferences in Beijing, Shanghai, Chengdu, and Guangzhou with the slogan "the Chinese have stood up."

The event was covered by CCTV prime-time news. The word "Chinese" here refers to the website as well as the Chinese people. The company's Chinese name, Tuopu, is the phonetic translation of its English name "Top," as if the company had an international origin. In addition, the website's Chinese name, Yanhuang Zaixian, was placed in a smaller font to highlight the company's global connection.

Nationalism was a selling strategy from the beginning. The slogan, "the Chinese have stood up," is a famous announcement made by Mao Zedong in his speech on Sept. 21, 1949, at the First Political Consultation Meeting of the Chinese People. Mao made the same remark on Oct. 1, 1949, when he announced the founding of the People's Republic of China in the Tiananmen Tower. Mao's phrase has been endlessly circulated in Chinese media as a denouncement of Western imperialism. The ads construct "Chineseness" in conjunction with China's history of anti-imperialism. In addition, the ads also claim the website to be "our name, [and] our net," thus inviting all Chinese to claim ownership and identification in this commercial venture. Two other prominent ads use the images of a Chinese dragon and five arrows (resembling the Chinese national flag) to associate the website with China as a nation and the Chinese as a people and culture.

After the first wave of marketing, the company immediately placed another "explosive" ad that features the image of the womb of a pregnant woman, symbolized by a fattened "@" sign. Its slogan "let us nurture it [Chinese.com] big together" constructs China as a gendered nation, reinforcing the cultural framing of "mother China." The copy reads,

> Yesterday, descendants of Yan and Huang Emperors were famous for the "four inventions"! Today, the Chinese website alliance Chinese.com sets sail, allowing descendants of Yan and Huang to stand up in the world! Tomorrow, Chinese people of the entire world will connect hearts and join hands to establish [our] own beautiful homes together!!!

Legend claims that Chinese people are all offspring of Yan and Huang Emperors. Phrases such as "descendents of Yan and Huang," "race or nation of Hua and Xia," "the Chinese race or nation" or "the ancestor's country," carry a strong emotional connection to China as a nation (Dikotter, 1996; see also Sautman, 1997). The four inventions, referring to paper, the compass, gunpowder, and printing technology, allude to China's glorious past, and urge the Chinese to create a bright future.

In addition, the advertiser launched a nationwide campaign called "Red Express," inviting Chinese-language websites to join the cause of unity. The color red was predominantly used in the campaign, a color associated with China's national flag, the CCP, and luck and happiness in Chinese culture. Within four months, approximately 1,000 websites became members of Chinese.com and its stock was publicly traded.[44]

Aiming to earn a quick profit and produce name recognition in a short time, Chinese.com sold a pastiche of cultural symbols of the past and the present through selectively including and reorganizing elements of Chinese history. It dictated a nationalistic narrative. Even though the campaigns enabled Chinese.com and its parent company Top Group to thrive until 2002, Top's problematic expansion strategies and murky business practices bankrupted the company. Top's CEO fled to the United States in 2004 and was imprisoned for nine years for embezzlement in 2013. The website was shut down and sold to a Hong Kong investor in 2007 for 810,000 Euros.[45] This example suggests that nationalism as a business driver may work in the short term, but it does not guarantee long-term success. Various failures and nontransparent practices actually damaged the reputation of the Chinese style of advertising practices, as discussed in chapter three.

While Chinese.com ads construct nationalism without explicitly referencing Westerners, a commercial for Chan Li Chai (Chen Li Ji) Kidney-Strengthening Pill, created by the Guangzhou Lanse Huoyan Advertising Firm, uses a staged shadowboxing competition between a foreigner and a Chinese man to symbolize the pill's effectiveness. The commercial features Chinese spectators watching the competition between the Chinese and the foreigner and shouting, "Beat [him] up, beat [him] up." The competition scenes are cast in yellowed color, suggesting that the event occurred a long time ago. The ad ends with a color scene, leading to a Chinese man in a business suit and tie holding a bottle of Chan Li Chai and announcing, "Healthy waist, healthy kidneys, [and] good *kungfu.*"

The staged boxing competitions, allegedly common in the Republican period of China (1912–1949) between the Chinese and foreigners, aimed to stir up national pride. After a brief close-up of the white man, he is knocked down, while the Chinese man stands proudly. The ad thus conveys the idea that Chan Li Chai literally strengthens one's kidneys and figuratively strengthens Chinese men and, thus, the nation. The temporal shift stresses the product's historical linkage and its contemporary relevance.

The Republican period of China was essential for forming China's identity (Duara, 1993, 1997; Gerth, 2003). In contemporary cultural activities, it is a common trope to pit a foreigner against a Chinese. The presence, and eventual defeat, of a foreigner implies the superiority of Chinese culture. The ad analyzed here symbolizes a desire among Chinese advertisers to redress historical Chinese/Western relations. With limited knowledge about the West, Chinese copywriters often lump Westerners into the ghostly white Other as an undefined and ever-changing opponent and suppressor.

Such nationalism mixes the victimization and victory narratives (Gries, 2004). Chinese victories now appear more victorious precisely because of China's past suffering, effected by foreign powers. Thus, both the Chinese.com and Chan Li Chai ads produce and reproduce China's history of patriotism and heroics. Also notable, however, is that the foreigner is present only in the shadows, which to some degree dilutes the Chinese victory.

Chinese advertisers have a deep well of history from which to draw material for narratives of patriotism. Even legends and heroes from ancient China can be used to produce an essentialized Chinese identity. Ancient legends are often associated with contemporary tales to produce an unchanging Chinese history of loyalty to the state. For example, the Chinese hair brand Ao Ni Honey Locust created a series of ads that celebrate the Chineseness of the product (*guo huo*). In a commercial in 1997 before the turnover of Hong Kong to China, various historic heroes and events are juxtaposed to convey a sense of unchanging loyalty and patriotism in China's civilization. Created by Guo-An Advertising Agency, the commercial features historical figures such as Su Wu working as a shepherd in exile in the Han Dynasty (206 BC–220 AD), Guan Tianpei knocking at a clock as a signal to start firing at the British army in the Opium War (1839–1842), brave Chinese soldiers on horseback fighting against Japanese soldiers, and so on.[46] A Chinese boy and the Great Wall are shown at the end of the commercial, with a voiceover and subtitle reading, "In a moment of talk and laughter, powerful enemies are blown out like ashes and extinguished like smoke."[47] The commercial ends with a male voiceover stating, "The Great Wall will never fall down. Chinese products should be self-strengthening."

The commercial celebrates China's long history of heroism against foreign invasions. Su Wu working as a shepherd is a quintessential example of Chinese loyalty to the Han Dynasty in particular, and China in general. Guan Tianpei, who was killed by the British army in the Opium War, conveys an unconditional devotion to both the Qing Dynasty and China. Ao Ni is thus made into a product of national pride through such associations. The tagline on a red flag connotes confidence, power, and strength, qualities that Chinese enterprises badly need to compete with foreign products. In the sector of hair products, P&G took up the biggest chunk of the market share in China in the late 1990s, followed by the British brand Unilever and the Japanese product Sofina. The space of Chinese products was dramatically cramped. Ao Ni was supported by the ad directors of many satellite TV channels, who hoped that the brand would eventually beat P&G. At that time, P&G also had a tense relationship with many satellite TV channels because P&G attempted to lower their advertising prices by first negotiating with the less powerful city stations and then going back for price reductions.

While in previous commercials Ao Ni also used the slogan "black hair, China's national product" to promote nationalism, this commercial goes one step further in explicitly appropriating China's anti-foreign history. It also forgoes the brand's long claim of the benefits of its natural plant ingredients. Even though Ao Ni is a hair product for men and women, the message here predominantly celebrates masculinity, which provides an interesting contrast with the pregnant woman in the Chinese.com ad (strong versus nurturing).

The Great Wall is often portrayed as *the* symbol of national pride in an orthodox sense. The Ao Ni commercial appeared just before Hong Kong was returned to China in 1997, an event that symbolizes the Chinese triumph over British colonialism. The commercial also appeared on CCTV-2 right after the U.S. bombing of the Chinese Embassy in 1999, which caused widespread anti-American demonstrations in China.

Interestingly, such a branding strategy backfired. According to Liu Yanming, general manager of Guo-An Advertising Agency, "many consumers said that they would not purchase this brand any more. It is sad that many consumers felt that foreign products always had better quality than Chinese products."[48] Liu also mentioned that the product was actually produced by a joint venture, with investment from Hong Kong.

However, when context changed, the brand also changed its advertising strategy. For example, in 2002, Ao Ni completely changed its branding position and celebrated foreign culture and cosmopolitanism.

It aired a commercial on multiple TV stations featuring exotic Indian women, music, and culture. This was done because after Miss India won the title of Miss Universe, the brand sent a group of researchers to India to see the "origin of Indian women's beauty," and it found that it came from the natural garden of plants, thus leading the brand to incorporate Indian cultural elements in its advertising campaigns. While the commercial continues Ao Ni's previous claims regarding its plant ingredients, it gives up its claim of "black hair, Chinese product" (Tian, 2008). Both nationalism and cosmopolitanism are merely different selling strategies used to maximize profits.

CELEBRATING CURRENT CHINESE ACHIEVEMENTS

Chinese advertisers also celebrate China's current achievements, such as its entry into the WTO, the Olympic Games, its launch of a series of space shuttles, and other accomplishments. For example, the milk brand Meng Niu conducted a three-stage advertising campaign centered on the launch of the Chinese space shuttle in 2003. The campaign first used outdoor billboards and bus ads with the slogan, "Raise your right hand, [and] cheer for China." The ads feature a boy, a young man, a young woman, and an elderly woman, wearing space outfits with their right hands and arms raised, shouldering the image of the Temple of Heaven, a fifteenth-century shrine located in Beijing. The ads state, "Meng Niu Milk cheers for the Chinese aerospace cause." The ads symbolize Chinese citizens' support for space exploration, whether they are male or female, old or young, and show that they are shouldering the future through literally carrying tradition. The ads' celebratory tone was restrained because they were released prior to the launch. According to the advertising agency, the ads use "cheer for China" rather than "celebrate the launch" as a hedge against the possibility of an unsuccessful launch.[49] After the successful launch, the advertiser bombarded consumers with outdoor billboards, double-deck shuttle body ads, and store displays. Again, the ads feature the four models, with the headline stating, "Meng Niu Milk, strengthen the Chinese. Specialized milk for the Chinese spaceflight." Meng Niu also placed TV commercials featuring happy Chinese families. Chinese families are thus made part of the national cause, uniting individuals with the nation.

Indeed, the celebration of China often blurs the line between the regime and citizens, as if what is significant for the regime benefits all Chinese citizens. In particular, the Beijing Olympics was celebrated as an event that enhanced the well-being of the Chinese government, the nation, and all citizens. The association of the Olympics with happiness and success was a common theme in Chinese media prior to the Olympics. For example, a commercial of Xinhua Insurance Company celebrates a variety of Chinese national events as if these events were the most significant for ordinary Chinese. The commercial begins with a tranquil morning. Chinese citizens of various backgrounds talk with each other or to themselves:

> An elderly man: So many good things have occurred this year.
> Another elderly man: [I've] heard that our country will enter the world (ru shi).[50]
> A boy: Grandpa, it is called the WTO.
> A barber: What a soccer team! This year we will compete for the World Cup.
> A young woman: Our Olympic bidding has been successful.
> An elderly woman: Tomorrow is our National Day. We should all hang our national flag.
> Voiceover: Wish our motherland prosperous and powerful forever.
> An elderly man: When our small families have become rich and prosperous, how can the big family not?
> Caption: Wish our motherland everlasting prosperity and more richness.

The commercial presents an optimistic picture of China by using words of ordinary Chinese and mixing significant national events. China becomes "our China" and "our motherland." Phrased as such, the commercial renders common ownership of these events and implies that they carry equal significance for all ordinary Chinese, old or young, men or women. Nationalism bonds the country together. The WTO, the Olympic Games, the World Cup, and the National Day are made significant nationally as well as relevant on a daily basis.

Here, China represents a large family consisting of numerous smaller families. In Chinese, the word "country" consists of *guo* (state) and *jia* (family). *Guo* is ambiguous and often refers to the nation state, the government, the land, and "the nation." Although China has a collectivistic tradition that emphasizes the state before the family, this commercial reverses relationship and states that when smaller families become prosperous, the large family will become rich. While this reversal gives a sense of newness, the ultimate goal of the Chinese family is to enrich the country. To some extent, the celebration of China also implies China's denial of the perceived threat to its national sovereignty in the process of globalization. Even though China's entry into the WTO means the weakening of China's sovereignty, it has been celebrated as part of the nationalist cause and essential for the country's economy.

PROMOTING THE CHINESE HEART IN A FOREIGN COUNTRY

Nationalism also means that the Chinese continue to love China while abroad. A popular song called "My Chinese Heart" by a Hong Kong singer in the 1980s proffers the idea that an overseas Chinese always has a Chinese heart, even though the Chinese land can only appear in their dreams. Accordingly, Chinese advertisements construct nationalism and identity by describing and prescribing what is desirable and what is not. Nationalism shares these characteristics: "belonging as the only right, loyalty as the supreme duty; dignity as basking in collective glory; self-interest as partaking of collective welfare" (Bauman, 1995, p. 147).

A commercial of Confucius Mansion Wine (Kong Fu Jia Jiu), for example, sells the idea of the Chinese heart. Liu Huan, a Chinese popular singer, travels to perform in the United States. He receives a bottle of Confucius Mansion Wine from his wife. The lyrics follow, "One cup of Confucius Mansion Wine. Songs of tens of miles away expect [your] return, Confucius Mansion." Liu's wife writes him a note stating, "Huan, I wish your performance a great success. We bring you a bottle of Confucius Mansion Wine, and expect you to return home as early as possible. Your Wife." Liu's performance is portrayed as a great success, surrounded by admiring Westerners, who kiss him, take his picture, and shake hands with him.

This commercial suggests that despite his success in the United States, Liu still misses his Chinese home and culture. Liu's wife represents Mother China and Chinese culture. The ad implies that the Chinese who have achieved international fame are still rooted in Chinese culture. The United States is used to represent the quintessential Western country to which China aspires. Gries (2004) says, "the West is central to the construction of Chinese identity; it has become China's alter ego" and "As the sole superpower of the post-Cold War world, America symbolizes the West for China and for much of the rest of the non-Western world" (p. 35). By portraying the brand loyalty of a Chinese celebrity situated in the United States, the product has gained an international aura and an image of supreme quality and modernity. Using the United States, in particular, and the West, in general, as the Other to define whatever is considered Chinese, has been an entrenched practice in China (Chen, 1995). In this sense, nationalism is a controlling mechanism and ideology that sets the limits for Chinese consumers.

SELLING COSMOPOLITANISM

While it is common to view nationalism and cosmopolitanism as dichotomous, Duara (1993, 1997) argues that all nationalists hold transnational ideals. Chinese culture has long contained cosmopolitan components, which can be seen in the particular forms of Confucian, Marxist, and neoliberal ideologies. Confucianism promotes the Chinese nation as a "culture nation" and any non-Chinese possessing knowledge of Chinese civilization and Han rituals can be considered Chinese (Duara, 1997). Joseph Levenson (1969), a renowned Sinologist, pointed out that the moral values and high culture of Chinese Confucian elites strove for the morals and values of universalistic civilization. Only after China encountered repeated defeats by the West did it begin to adopt a more particularistic worldview about itself as a nation and state and about the Chinese as a race. Chinese Communism also harbors universal components.

As discussed in chapter one, cosmopolitanism can be understood as the third space; as hybridity, creolization, bricolage, or pastiche. Cosmopolitanism is not only about flows of material and nonmaterial goods but also about imaginings. Appadurai's (1996) theory of five scapes suggests that the current cultural landscapes always have the capacity to create new possibilities for new cultural identities and spaces.

The following sections examine how Chinese advertisers sell cosmopolitanism, and explain the implications with an emphasis on the unequal power relations between China and the West. Even though the concept of cosmopolitanism often has a strongly positive connotation, the concept here is used in a neutral sense to examine how Chinese advertisers invoke the West as a form of transnational imagination.

MARKETING CONTRIVED WESTERNNESS THROUGH WESTERN MODELS AND SYMBOLS

Western cultural symbols serve to elevate the social status of an advertised product, and foreignness is associated with prestige in consumption (Schein, 2001). Indeed, Western images have become ubiquitous in Chinese media, and advertisers use these symbols to sell an imagined West that Chinese consumers should aspire to. Advertisers tend to appropriate Westernness in two ways: one is to contrive links between their products and the West through the appropriation of Western symbols, including languages, Caucasian models, architecture, sculpture, and famous tourist sites such as the Louvre Museum and the Eiffel Tower, or cities such as Cambridge, Paris, or Rome. The second way is to sell values associated with Western modernity, such as individualism, freedom, newness, and pleasure. Indeed, modern values such as newness and individualism are among the top values sold in Chinese commercials (Zhang & Harwood, 2004).

Another strategy that advertisers often use is to give Chinese products exotic names. Real estate projects, for example, include names like the Vancouver Forest, the Victoria Harbor, Yosemite, the Laguna Garden, and the California Garden. Foreign-sounding names are especially common in China's apparel industry. For example, in 2006 a survey found that over half of the 200 leading Chinese clothing brands reportedly used foreign-sounding names and in Shanghai's main popular shopping stores, over 80 percent of clothing brands use exotic names (*Xinmin Wanbao*, 2006, March 2). Brand names such as Youngor (雅戈尔 in Chinese), Romon (罗蒙), Jodoll (乔顿), Aige (艾格), Captaino (凯普狄诺), Metersbonwe (美特斯邦威), Rouse (洛兹), Casablanca (卡莎布兰卡), and Semir (森马) all sound exotic to ordinary Chinese. Names of these brands use both Roman letters and Chinese characters, with the Chinese characters sounding phonetically similar to foreign names. The same survey cited above found that 53.3

percent of Chinese consumers tended to purchase a clothing brand with a foreign image if they could afford it, and that only 16.7 percent preferred a Chinese brand. Another reason for brands to use foreign names is that they plan to expand to the international market in the future. The clothing brands using foreign names often sell at a relatively higher price.

Some Chinese producers also make false claims about Western origins. This sort of fabrication was so prevalent that Chinese media, including CCTV, launched a campaign to disclose misleading information about product origins. For example, Oudian floorboard claimed to be produced in Germany and to have a hundred-year history, but it was revealed in 2006 by CCTV that it was actually produced in Jiling Province and branded in Beijing, with only six years of history. The scandal caused a dramatic decline in its sales ("Oudian diban shijian quancheng jiexiao," 2006, Sept. 26).

Other products rely on a detoured strategy: they are first registered in Europe and then registered in China as European brands, even though their productions and designs are completely done in China. For example, Captaino advertises on its website that this brand was imported into China in 1998 from Italy. It claimed to be a joint venture with Mauro Mazzocchi, founder of a little-known Italian brand by the name of Gammatex. All available sources suggest that the brand was managed and made in China. Captaino used an alligator logo, almost identical to Lacoste (France), IZOD (America), Cartelo (Singapore), or Crocodile (Hong Kong). This evidences the prevalence of copying in the Chinese clothing industry, which will be further discussed in chapter five. It is also possible that Captaino is a misspelling of Capitano. Its website introduced the product with sentimental poetry and manufactured "Italianness."[51]

The tide of the Adriatic Sea brings,
Captaino's ship from faraway places.

Captaino's ship brings the Italian spring wind!
Probably because of the historical sediment of the Renaissance,
Italians love beauty so much.
Probably because Michelangelo so successfully created David without
precedent, David has become a symbol of male beauty.... There comes
Captaino.
It brings in real male beauty.
It is the blueprint of a successful man.

The models on its website were all Western in appearance, with European-style architecture visible in the background of some print ads.

The ad sold its contrived Italian origin through a discursive connection to stereotypical Italian icons such as the Renaissance, Michelangelo, sculpture, the Adriatic, and European models. In turn, the producer aimed to sell "real male beauty" derived from its associations with Italian high culture. Chinese firms commonly manufacture the foreignness of their products by appropriating foreign models, European architecture, and other symbols. Western models are commonly featured in Chinese advertising to represent product quality, social status, cosmopolitanism, taste, and modernity.

The foreign-sounding brand Eenor Western Suit (*eenor* meaning "a promise") placed an ad featuring a European man wearing the company's product. He is standing next to a luxury car in a corridor lined with sculptures and Roman-style columns. Using Italian opera as background music, the commercial juxtaposes sculptures, a car, and close-ups of the thoughtful-looking European model. The voiceover states, "let the thought have wings; thought creates fortune; Eenor weighs more than one thousand pieces of gold." The last scene features the name "EENOR Classics" in conjunction with the name in Chinese characters, phonetically "*yi nuo xifu.*" Word play is common in Chinese advertising because Chinese characters of the same sound can have totally different meanings. Here, the suit is used to symbolize trust; consumers wearing the suit are considered trustworthy.

The commercial constructs an imagined West using highbrow European cultural symbols: Greek sculptures, European-style architecture, and Italian opera. *"Yi nuo"* is the phonetic translation of "Eenor," and can mislead unsuspicious consumers to believe the brand is of foreign origin. Using a European male model associates the product with success, good taste, and modernity. Western products such as Italian shoes, Swiss watches, and German automobiles have long been advertised in China as symbols of success. Middle-class consumers are familiar with images of European tourist sites.

The use of foreign models is also gendered. White men included in the ads are businessmen and are depicted in association with technology, science, cars, and sports, and other themes that imply an authoritative position. In contrast, Western women are often used for products such as skin whiteners, breast implants, luxury spas, bras, and undergarments. They are generally portrayed as more sexualized than Chinese women (Johansson, 1997).

SELLING MODERN WESTERN VALUES

Another strategy associated with cosmopolitanism is to sell Western values that are disassociated from locality. Values such as freedom, individualism, happiness, mobility, and pleasure are especially common. For example, a commercial for a small Chinese shoe brand, Voit, starts with a driver listening to an English radio program. The camera then switches to a foreign policeman awed by a Chinese basketball player shooting a ball high up into the sky in an urban setting. The caption reads in English, "Why?" Then, the camera changes to a close-up of the word Voit. The Chinese player catches the ball and the caption reads, "Who?" The player is then shown playing basketball on the street. He nimbly moves among cars, with American rap music in the background. The caption reads in English, "It's Voit," which is followed by the caption and voiceover in Chinese, "Voit basketball shoes, unlimited freedom."

The commercial predominantly uses English, which conveys a sense of "foreignness" and cosmopolitanism. The English words are short and simple so that Chinese consumers with middle-school educations can easily understand them. Even if the target audiences do not understand English, they at least recognize that the words are not Chinese. The foreign urban setting conveys cosmopolitanism and street culture. The commercial seems to be influenced by Nike commercials that sell street basketball culture. An unsuspecting consumer will have difficulty telling whether the brand is Chinese or foreign.[52] Appropriating stereotypical Western iconography, including the visual and social branding of Nike, the commercial conveys ultimate freedom and cultural power personified in the unknown Chinese player.

Many Chinese ads promise consumers endless freedom, unfettered dreams, individual choice, an expansive lifestyle, and individualism. Technology companies in particular like to sell freedom, endless possibilities, and unlimited imagination, supposedly provided by their products. Such commercials celebrate the single-child generation, whose members have more choices and material abundance than their parents. Society views them as demanding autonomy and individualism, in contrast with upholding traditional values of saving and producing in pre-reform China. For example, China Mobile in its 2001–2002 campaign used the slogan "Connect with freedom, unlimited possibilities" to promote its cellphones. Bu Bu Gao Electronics sells its home theater equipment using the tagline, "my brilliance, my decision" (*wo de jingcai, wo zuo zhu*). Haizhu Beer announces, "[My] happiness is the most important; don't bother me" (*gaoxing jiu hao, ni guan wo shenme*). Auldey digital camera uses the slogan, "Youthful is playful." Li Quan Beer uses the lyrics, "You are happy. I am happy. Cheerful Li Quan, cheerful hearts" (*ni kaixin, wo kai xin, huanle liquan huanle xin*). The Xurisheng drink brand has the following lyric: "Everyday, I am my own boss. I know what I should do. It is good to enjoy myself." Given that Chinese consumers often demonstrate a desire to simultaneously project their status through consumption but also seek protection in collective ideals, advertisers address individual pleasure and collectivity at the same time. For example, China Mobile M-Zone used the slogan, "Let's play together" (*yiqi wan ba*). Because of their association with Western cultural values, notions of individualism, self-fulfillment, and freedom also convey cosmopolitanism and global thinking; Chinese advertisers seek to use these qualities, but often temper them with suggestions of collective life.

To some extent, the construction of Westernness endorses a particular understanding of the relationship between China and the West, and between Chinese brands and foreign brands in global capitalism. A Taiwan-born account director working in a large Japanese firm stated:

> I think this [the appropriation of foreign elements] has something to do with the confidence of our nation. After all, the living environment in foreign countries [read, industrialized Western countries] is very progressive.... The big price difference between foreign and Chinese brands further produces the worship and blind faith in foreign things. Of course, it has something to do with brand [qualities]. After all, foreign brands have a history of over 100 years. (Personal interview, thirty-two-year-old Taiwanese account director of a large Japanese firm, Aug. 16, 2005)

The remarks were representative of the views of Chinese ad practitioners. Western brands were generally perceived to be better in quality and higher in status than Chinese brands. In addition, Western products benefit from Western modernity, and China's recent acceptance of capitalism and frequent product scandals greatly damage the reputation of Chinese products. Chinese manufacturers, therefore, attempt to associate their products with Western symbols and values in order to achieve a higher status. European symbols and American images have different meanings in China: the former stand for history, romance, taste, art, culture, aristocracy, and nobility, while the latter stand for technological advancement, individualism, freedom, and consumeristic pleasure.

THE CONVERGENCE OF NATIONALISM AND COSMOPOLITANISM

The fusion of foreign and Chinese advertising strategies leads to a convergence of nationalism and cosmopolitanism, similar to the construction of the cosmopolitan–patriotic image discussed in chapter five. These ads generally support the idea of the grand unity and universal humanity, and they celebrate China's economic development and culture as being comparable with the West. They further market their products' global popularity to Chinese consumers to celebrate China's integration into the world market.

MARKETING THE GRAND UNITY AND UNIVERSAL HUMANITY

Chinese ads celebrate dreams of a grand unity and universal humanity. For example, China's largest wireless service operator, China Mobile, aired a commercial featuring children of various ethnicities desiring to know more about the world. With music adapted from Beethoven's Ninth Symphony as the background, the commercial starts with a Chinese boy wearing a red scarf, singing in a royal court, and expressing his hope to know more about other cultures. Children from other parts of the world are also included: a Chinese in San Francisco, an African American boy in New York, Islander boys, Egyptian girls holding pots on their heads, an Indian girl, a French girl in beret playing the violin, and a child wearing a Saudi Arabian headscarf. Some children are swimming in a blue ocean, while others are ice-skating. Various cultural symbols appear, including the Great Wall of China, the Eiffel Tower, and towering urban buildings. The last few scenes portray a group of children, smiling and running toward the Great Wall and the Temple of Heaven. The last scene is shot from above, with all children holding hands and looking up. The image is vague and the camera is positioned in a particular way to hide the fact that they are probably Chinese children dressed up exotically. These lyrics follow:[53]

> Can I tell you the hope in my heart? Listen to my voice flying to faraway places. Ah…I want to know what the tide spray is like on the other side of the sea. I want to meet the same curious look as mine. Let me walk to your corner. Let me hold your hands, my friends on the other side of the world. Do you have the same heartbeat as I do? Can you push open a window for me? In the future we will not have unfamiliarity any more.…Just like this, please hold my hand. Just like this.

The commercial ends with a male voiceover, "Communication starts from the heart. China Mobile." On the one hand, the ad celebrates the idea that all children, no matter their gender, race, and locations, have a similar curiosity about the others and desire a more harmonious world, a significant rhetoric in the Chinese model of nationhood. The commercial suggests that China Mobile can help the children transcend language, cultural, class, and racial boundaries. But on the other hand, such a harmonious world is created when all the children are running on the Great Wall, and toward the Temple of Heaven, suggesting China's central position. The Chinese boy's red scarf, an identifier of a Young Pioneer in China's Communist Party system, represents childhood as well as his party affiliation. Targeting global Chinese consumers, the commercial constructs other cultures in relation to

China's leadership role, and thus expresses cosmopolitanism and nationalism. The universal dream of connecting to the world is thus accomplished through Chinese culture and especially through China Mobile, making the nation a unifying factor in creating a global harmony.

Many other Chinese advertisers also celebrate global harmony. For example, Wondial telephone uses the slogan "the entire world is one family" and the sports clothing brand Lanshi asserts, "there is no distinction between foreignness and Chineseness." In these ads, the grand unity of the world echoes an influential Confucian belief that there is "*the* way of understanding the world" (Pusey, 1983, p. 234, emphasis original). For example, in *Da Tongshu*, Kang Youwei, a prominent Confucian scholar in the Qing Dynasty (1644–1912), made a plan for world unity and for an ideal society where all people would use *ren* (compassion, love, or benevolence) as the main way to resolve world problems.

Duara (1993, 1997) points out that Confucianism's universal claim often includes compromise between Chinese culture and other cultures. Unsurprisingly, the idea of grand unity was often promoted when China experienced rapid transitions. In Kang Youwei's time, China was repeatedly defeated by Western and Japanese powers, leading Chinese scholars to blame Chinese culture for the country's weakness. In the last few decades, China has been experiencing rapid economic development and rising global status. Globalization has greatly benefited China but it has also created anxiety and uncertainty. Marketing universalism thus offers a solution that helps China soothe this anxiety and regain confidence. Chinese corporations now have to compete with multinational corporations in the Chinese market and globally. They thus have to produce a distinctive identity and voice. While Chinese corporations' expansion in the world market further enhances China's global position, these companies have also encountered tremendous challenges. Thus, it is common to see Chinese companies sell the concept of "dream": dreams of reaching out to the world and of inviting the world in.

CHINESE LANDSCAPE ENDORSED BY WESTERN TOURISTS

An award-winning commercial for China Unicom features an elderly Western traveler in China. The ad starts with him riding a horse on a muddy road lined with poplar trees. He speaks with his friend over his cell phone in English, "I am having fun; I am a Chinese cowboy." He is then depicted with a group of Chinese children on a country road. A montage portrays scenes symbolizing Chinese culture: red curtains, the traditional art of paper cutting, and an old Chinese driving a flock of sheep. The man is then singing a Chinese opera near a red wall, riding a bicycle, and telling his friend over the cell phone, "I am king of China; I am coming." He enters a Chinese temple, plays shuttlecock with Chinese citizens, watches a Peking opera, and tries on a traditional Chinese long gown. Again, he speaks into his cell phone, "It's so beautiful and classic here!" He is back on the street and encounters scenes of modern buildings, speeding cars, and urban Chinese. He says over his cell phone in English, "I am confused. Where am I? New York? Shanghai!" He is walking in a rice field, where Chinese farmers are transplanting rice seedlings. He dances with exotically dressed women of Chinese ethnic minorities in Yunnan. Again, he speaks over his cell phone in English, "It's beautiful anyway. China, a fantastic place to be!" The caption reads in both Chinese and English, "Enjoy it anytime, anywhere!"[54]

Mixing Chinese and English, the commercial intends to simultaneously convey nationalism and cosmopolitanism. It juxtaposes concepts and images—ancient and contemporary, urban and rural, Han people and the minorities, economic and cultural, royal and mundane—to showcase China's vast landscape, rich cultures, and mixture of tradition and modernity. The Western traveler is not only a tourist but also someone who is capable of evaluating and judging Chinese culture and development. He constantly announces over his cell phone that China is beautiful, classic, and fantastic. Kaviraj (1992) writes that counting of citizens, territories, and resources is an inherent part of a nationalist project. Gries (2004) also argues that "Enumerating 'China'—its vast geographic and demographic size—has long been central to the modern Chinese nationalist project of creating the psychological strength necessary to mobilize the Chinese people" (p. 80).

The commercial not only endorses nationalism but also implies that China's development and tradition become more meaningful when a Western tourist appreciates them. The image of an elderly Westerner implies that he is experienced and wise. Comparing Shanghai with New York, a quintessential place that captures the Chinese imaginary about modernity, elevates Shanghai's status and makes it more modern. The Western tourist symbolizes the West on the road: the West travels to meet the East and is amazed. The Western traveler's endorsement implies the universal attraction of Chinese culture as well as China Unicom's lack of confidence in its ability to claim the values of Chinese culture by itself. The cultural critic Fredric Jameson (1993) argues, "The First World does not have to know the Third World, while it is quite obvious that it is impossible for the Third World not to be aware of the First World" (p. 31). This commercial is a symbolic representation of such an unequal power relation.

While the ads of China Mobile and China Unicom invite Westerners in, ads of other Chinese brands market their success in reaching out to the West. Haier, for example, conducted a series of campaigns featuring foreign media praising its product quality and foreign retailers eager to carry the products. Haier's ads also proudly announce, "Made in China."

Haier highlights its international reputation in the Chinese market not only to assure its product quality but also its modernity.

As we have seen, Chinese consumers often view foreign products as having higher status and better quality, so Chinese products that have already achieved international success repackage and sell their global achievement back home. For example, a series of Haier's print ads from the late 1990s celebrate its extraordinary success in foreign countries, especially in developed Western countries. Large sales numbers and successful development in Australia, Germany and America are featured. The ad about Australian success depicts two koalas up on a Haier fridge. The copy reads, "The Australian national treasure koala gives Haier a warm hug." The ad about US achievement claims that the combined height of all Haier fridges sold in America has surpassed the height of New York's Empire State Building 2,500 times over. An image of the Empire State Building is placed next to a wall made of Haier refrigerators. The copy explains, "The Empire State Building is located in New York. [It] is a famous building in America." The headline in the ad about Germany states, "Haier in Germany has genuinely convinced German counterparts [of its quality]." Recognition by Germans is significant because Germany has been known for producing products of supreme quality. A picture of Cologne Cathedral is placed next to a wall made of Haier refrigerators as well as a flying flag with the Haier logo. The ad copy reads, "The Haier flag is flying high together with national flags of the European Union at the Cologne Bridge over the Rhine River."

The portrayal of Haier's success in Western countries, symbolized by recognizable tourist icons including a koala, the Empire State Building, and Cologne Cathedral, enhances Haier as a brand of supreme quality and a symbol of national pride. These ads celebrate Haier's global success and educate Chinese consumers about Western cultural symbols. Acceptance by a foreign country, in the context of China's go-global movement, means that Haier implements China's national strategy and conquers foreign lands on China's behalf.

CONCLUSION

Chinese advertisers use varyious strategies to sell nationalism and cosmopolitanism. These imply complicated and contradictory constructions of China as a people, a culture, and a nation in the broad context of China's search for modernity and the historically unequal power relationship with the West. Selling cosmopolitanism invokes the West as a locale of transnational imaginaries, while selling nationalism reproduces Chinese history as a continuing narrative of patriotism. Selling the hybridity of the two offers a solution to the tension, conflict, and anxiety caused by globalization.

Nationalism and cosmopolitanism, as social constructions, reflect China's ambivalence toward tradition and modernity and its anxiety in a global economy dictated by the United States in specific and the West in general. On the one hand, China's rapid economic development has made Chinese producers more assertive in claiming Chineseness. But on the other hand, there remains a pervasive feeling that Chinese products have lower quality and are less desirable and modern, leading to a general trend that Chinese products often sell at lower prices than global brands. Thus, Chinese brands have to associate themselves with Western modernity to enhance their image and reputation.

In many cases, these promotional strategies are based on intuition rather than careful market analysis or research. They are not necessarily long-term strategies but rather idiosyncratic response tactics. As sales vehicles, both nationalism and cosmopolitanism are merely unifying strategies aiming to achieve larger market shares and more profits. These sentiments are appropriated to satisfy Chinese consumers desiring both Chineseness and global connections.

Ad professionals in the Chinese market were very keen on catering to Chinese middle-class consumers' simultaneous desire for a collective sense of belonging and a unique experience associated with other cultures in China's rapid societal transformations. For example, an ad professional described China's middle-class consumers as "small pota-toes with big dreams who experience a lot of pressure and need others' recognition" through consumption (interview with a general manager of the Beijing office of a Western advertising firm, Aug. 2, 2005). Thus, consumers have to wear expensive watches and drive high-priced cars. He pointed out that their advertising can "satisfy their needs and help them stand out from the crowd." Their research further indicated that when these consumers purchase home appliances, they often purchase Chinese brands because these brands are not visible to others; but consumers prefer foreign brands of cellphones because others can see the products they carry. Therefore, the advertising strategies reflect the anxiety of consumers and the solutions to it provided by advertisers and their ad agencies in the rapidly changing Chinese market.

5 | Chinese Sportswear Brand Li-Ning: Selling a Cosmopatriotic Image

On August 8, 2008, during the spectacular opening ceremony of the Beijing Olympics, China's "prince of gymnastics" Li Ning was running in the air inside the Beijing National Stadium. Wearing an Adidas outfit, Li Ning lighted the cauldron, triggering a dazzling fireworks display that set the night sky over Beijing ablaze. About 90,000 spectators watched the opening ceremony on site, while billions around the world viewed it on television and over the Internet. Generally considered by the business world to be one of the most successful ambush-marketing events, Li Ning's stunning performance made the Chinese sportswear brand bearing his name one of the biggest winners. The share price of the publicly traded company rose 3.7 percent on the previous Friday, in the expectation that Li Ning would appear in the opening ceremony, and increased an additional 3.4 percent on the Monday after the event (Guppy, 2008, Aug. 12). Li-Ning's stock value increased by 80 percent within a year (Wang, 2012, July 27). In the second quarter of 2009, Li-Ning's profits outperformed Adidas, the official Beijing Olympic sponsor, and regained the second position in the Chinese sportswear market.[55]

After the Beijing Olympics, the company increased its global presence and the number of its retail stores in China. Only four years later, however, the brand encountered tremendous difficulties: the closing of hundreds of retail stores, the accumulation of a one-billion-yuan inventory, and a substantial decline of orders. The company's stock price dropped 76 percent (Tian, Fang, & Wang, 2012, Sept. 18). What is more, its semi-annual performance report in 2012 showed a profit of merely 44 million yuan (approximately $7 million USD), lagging far behind other leading Chinese brands such as Anta, 361° and Peak, let alone global brands such as Nike and Adidas.[56]

The brand's rise and fall over its twenty-year history symbolizes the growth path of China's sportswear industry, and its market economy in general. Its development illustrates the ways in which a leading Chinese brand negotiated its identity and adjusted to China's ongoing economic and cultural globalization. This chapter analyzes how Li-Ning competed with other sportswear brands, both global and Chinese, and discusses the intertwining business and political logics in the Chinese market. Predominantly focusing on the brand's Olympic strategies, my analysis complicates the previous discussion of nationalism and cosmopolitanism by looking at how the brand drew upon symbolic and material resources and engineered a cosmopatriotic image. Here we will expand our understanding of the diagram in chapter one—especially the complex local-global interactions and the policies' impact on business practices.

THE BRAND'S HISTORY

The brand was founded in 1990 by China's "prince of gymnastics" Li Ning, a successful athlete and winner of more than one hundred national and international medals. He won six Olympic medals (three gold, two silver, and one bronze) in 1984, the first time the People's Republic of China participated in the Olympics, which made him a national hero. However, his unexpected loss of the gold during the 1988 Olympics attracted overwhelming criticism from the Chinese media and the public. A year later, Li retired and joined soft drink company Jianlibao, a pioneer in sports marketing and Olympic sponsorship. With Li Ning as the manager and figurehead, Jianlibao founded the brand Li-Ning in 1990, making it China's first sportswear brand bearing an athlete's name, and the most successful brand in this category.[57]

When Li-Ning was founded, China's sportswear market was dominated by generic products of questionable quality. While there were a few branded products—Kangwei, Meihua, Lantian, Huili and Feiyue—they rarely used modern promotional strategies. Li-Ning, however, employed modern branding strategies from the very beginning. The company issued a public call for ideas for its logo in *Guangzhou Daily* and other newspapers on July 21, 1989, and got tens of thousands of entries (Yu, 2008). A submission from a middle school teacher was adopted, which juxtaposed the letter "L" and the English spelling of Li-Ning (see Figure 5.1). Even though Li-Ning was later criticized for copying Nike's "swoosh," it was unclear whether Nike influenced the logo design.

The founder Li Ning's celebrity status and extensive official and media connections, and Jianlibao's knowledge of sports marketing quickly ushered the brand into China's top spot in the sportswear market. As "red-hat merchants"—government-supported businessmen—Li Ning and his boss Li Jingwei enjoyed official and media support. For example, Li-Ning sponsored the 1990 Asian Games in Beijing, paying merely $500,000 USD, one-sixth of the amount that was originally requested by the Asian Games' organizing committee, reportedly because Li Ning's patriotism moved the committee members (Yu, 2008). The brand also opened the first *zhuanmaidian* (specialty store) in Beijing two days before

Figure 5.1 Li-Ning's Old Logo (left) and Current Logo since 2010 (right)

the Asian Games. The store, carrying only Li-Ning products and decorated with the Li-Ning logo and signs, initiated an unprecedented selling practice for China, where general stores sold almost all daily necessities. During the Asian Games, Chinese athletes wore Li-Ning clothing, and hundreds of millions of viewers were exposed to the brand. The flame-lighting ceremony, featuring athlete Li Ning in his own branded uniform receiving the flame from a Tibetan girl, also deeply impressed Chinese audiences. President Jiang Zemin officially greeted Li Ning and his boss and thanked them for their sponsorship, merging business practice with political significance.[58] Within months after the closing ceremony, Li-Ning experienced exponential growth and became "the one and only Chinese apparel brand."

Like Nike and other global brands, Li-Ning is mostly interested in manufacturing a brand image. It currently owns only one factory originally associated with Jianlibao; most of the products are sourced from other factories. The brand focuses on sports sponsorship. For example, Li-Ning sponsored the Chinese Olympic delegations from 1992 to 2004. It also sponsored individual sports such as gymnastics, table tennis, diving, and archery at the Olympics and at other major-league events. Media reports and promotional materials often celebrated Li Ning's dream of "clothing Chinese athletes in Chinese brands at the Olympic medal podiums" (Yu, 2008), making Li Ning and his brand interchangeable.[59]

FOREIGN COMPETITION IN THE 1990s

Initially, Li-Ning experienced little competition from foreign brands because foreign marketers generally treated China mostly as a place to find cheap labor. For example, even though Nike started buying from Chinese factories in 1981, it did not begin selling in China until 1988 (Fiddes, 1994, Dec. 8). A growing middle class and increasing disposable income, however, gradually made China a desirable consumer market. In 1992, Nike opened its first retail store in Shanghai, and by 1994 Nike had opened stores in Beijing, Shanghai, and Guangzhou. Nike's initial ads in China were mere translations from its American ads. Endorsed by sports icons such as Michael Jordan and Andre Agassi, Nike products were popular among Chinese youth. Nike also boosted Jordan's popularity in China at a time when the National Basketball Association (NBA) gained wide recognition. A survey found that Jordan was the most recognizable person in China after Deng Xiaoping (Weir, 1993, Oct. 7). Nike's intensive effort to seek and support mainstream youth sports programs also enhanced its brand image and loyalty (Low, 1994, Oct. 21). High school and college students strongly aspired to own Nike products, even though most Chinese then could not afford a pair of Nike shoes, which cost a few months' salary. At the turn of the twenty-first century, Nike had already became the coolest brand in China (Forney, Fonda, & Gough, 2004, Oct. 24).

Other foreign brands (Adidas, Reebok, and New Balance) began selling in China in the 1990s. While these global brands experienced rapid growth, Li-Ning's growth stagnated between 1997 and 2001, with its sales fluctuating around 700 million yuan (approximately $90 million USD), merely 1 percent of Nike's $9 billion USD revenue. Typical of family businesses, Li-Ning experienced difficulties because of nepotism and mismanagement. Its marketing and advertising strategies in its early days were based on intuition. Its advertising position shifted among athletics, fashion, and leisure. Its slogans also oscillated between collectivity and individualism, philosophical abstraction and worldly pursuit, and outward assertion and inward pursuit. Some of the slogans in the 1990s included: "the hope of China's new generation" (which sounds similar to Pepsi's slogan), "winning in each step," "leave excellence to yourself," "I exercise, I exist," "seasonal winds, new sports," and "excellence originating from Nature." Additionally, the brand faced challenges because of a pervasive counterfeit culture in China.

COUNTERFEITS, PASS-OFF BRANDS AND SHANZHAI PRODUCTS

The counterfeit issue in the Chinese sportswear industry is intricately related to the history of branded goods in China. Founders of many Chinese sportswear brands worked in sourcing factories for global brands. Jin Jiang, a county in Fujian Province, which is often referred to as China's shoe capital, had thousands of shoe factories and manufactured more than 80 percent of China's athletic and sport shoes (Quanzhou Footwear Association, 2006, June 28). These factories were original equipment manufacturers, producing shoes for global brands such as Nike and Adidas. Realizing that global brands were profitable while manufacturing had small profit margins, a few Chinese entrepreneurs founded their own brands, such as Anta, Peak, Xtep, and 361°. Often these entrepreneurs had little knowledge of brand protection or legal issues and simply copied well-known global brands in design, logo, and even name.

With loose legal protections, China has become one of the largest producers and markets for counterfeits in the last few decades. Chew (2010) documents that knock-off menswear brands have copied global brands' name, logo, ad image, packaging, and other visual elements as well as materials such as fabrics, tailoring, and design. The term "*shanzhai* culture" was used to describe this phenomenon. Literally meaning "mountain fortress," a place outside the jurisdiction of China's central authority, *shanzhai* initially described how small mobile phone production companies copied the features of established brands. The term now is applied to a wide range of goods produced by small workshops/studios that are either outright copies or knockoffs (Leng & Zhang, 2011).

The branded clothing industry—sportswear brands in particular—has long competed with *shanzhai* products. For example, logos of Chinese sportswear brands, such as Guirenniao, Xtep, Qipai,

Shuangxing, Fuling, Deerhui, Erke, are critiqued as looking "suspiciously similar to" Nike's swoosh (Doctoroff, 2012, p. 20). Foreign producers hoping to branch out into the Chinese market sometimes find that a third party has already registered their trademarks. For example, a Jin Jiang apparel company registered 别克, the U.S automobile brand Buick's Chinese name, in the 1990s. Not until the early 2000s did the Chinese company change its name to 361°. Another Jin Jiang company registered 乔丹, the Chinese translation of (Michael) Jordan. A company in Chendi, also in Jin Jiang province, registered the trademark of (David) Beckham, as well as Reebok's Iverson, completely copying Reebok's original shoes (Liu, 2006, July 16).

Specifically, companies either partially borrow Chinese characters used in foreign brands or use similar characters to name their products. For example, 别克 includes the same Chinese character (克) used by Nike's Chinese name (耐克), and both Chinese brands 特步and 耐步share the same Chinese character (步) as Reebok's Chinese name (锐步). The *shanzhai* brands Anmani, Adidos, Fuma, Pama, and Hike and Nake intend to confuse consumers with Armani, Adidas, Puma, and Nike respectively. These brands also copy the design and advertising images of established brands. Of course, Chinese companies also employ exotic foreign-sounding names to confuse Chinese consumers (as discussed in chapter four). While South Korea and Japan had to deal with pass-off products in the past, the challenge in China is more severe because of the country's ineffective regulations and fragmented and expansive Chinese market. While Li-Ning does not necessarily face the same threat in comparison with global brands, however, counterfeits and knock-off products cheapen the branding culture in general in the Chinese market. Facing such a chaos, Li-Ning is forced to produce a brand image that is both authentic and high-end. Consequently, the company chose to combine nationalism and cosmopolitanism, which I call cosmopatriotism here in this chapter.

LI-NING'S COSMOPATRIOTIC IMAGE

While Li-Ning was mainly a patriotic brand in the 1990s, it has been promoting a cosmopatriotic image since the turn of the century. This practice is closely associated with a general yearning among Chinese consumers for global knowledge as well as Chinese tradition. Producing a hybrid identity that mixes foreign and Chinese cultural elements is a common practice, and Chinese corporations generally aim to emulate and adapt other cultures' competitiveness to local contexts (Doctoroff, 2012).

Li-Ning's cosmopatriotism is reflected in its branding and global strategies. For one thing, the brand asserted its intention to become "the World's Li-Ning rather than China's Nike." Li-Ning's globalization started around 2000, a move often called *yuangyu yundong*, which referred to the Qing Dynasty Self-Strengthening Movement (as discussed in chapter one). Li-Ning implemented a two-pronged complementary approach: global expansion and an internal management transformation.

In 2001, the company commissioned Gallup China and conducted the first survey among Chinese consumers about their perception of Li-Ning and its competitors (Gallup, 2001, June). From thirteen Chinese cities, the survey gathered information from 3,963 consumers, aged fourteen to forty-five, who had purchased branded sports products. The survey found that respondents associated Li-Ning with national pride, vitality, easiness, and friendliness, while they associated Nike with excellence, fashion, and leadership. National pride was found to be Li-Ning's most salient image, and its low price its biggest advantage. The survey also found that respondents were willing to pay a higher price for Nike in comparison with Chinese brands Li-Ning and Anta. At the time of the survey, Li-Ning was attempting to target cosmopolitan fashion-conscious affluent urban consumers aged fourteen to twenty-eight, living in medium-sized and large cities. The actual demographics of Li-Ning consumers were different, however: the average age was 28.54 and 82 percent had family monthly income below $360 USD; the majority lived in second-tier cities and they were more concerned with product price than brand image. In response, Li-Ning chose to rebrand and attract a younger demographic in first-tier cities. In 2002, it signed a contract with the American ad agency Leo Burnett to produce a more professional athletic image. An advertising campaign was launched, with the new slogan, "Everything Is Possible," an inspirational statement that encourages consumers to dream big and be entrepreneurial and confident.[60]

At the time when Li-Ning was rebranding, it experienced increasing pressure from global brands, which had already established their presence in first-tier cities and were expanding into second-tier and third-tier cities. For example, Nike launched the World Shoe Project in 1998 to produce lower-cost products for emerging markets. In 1999, Nike was already selling two product series in China: Series 100 with a price range of $15–22 USD, and Series 400 with a price range of $40–45 USD (McDonald & London, 2002). Although Nike suspended the project in 2002, it continued to reach price-conscious consumers through promotional events. Indeed, from 2001 to 2006, global brands laid out their distribution channels in first-tier cities and used pricing strategies to attract more consumers in second- and third-tier cities (Huang et al., 2011). Adidas and other global brands further limited Li-Ning's market share. Nike and Adidas surpassed Li-Ning in China in revenues in 2003 and 2004, respectively.

Consequently, Li-Ning implemented a dual strategy for internal transformation and external expansion. Internally, it sought management professionalization, adopted the information management system widely used in the global sports and footwear industry, and recruited managers and financial officers with previous experience in multinational corporations. The company worked with global advertising and consulting firms and hired French, Italian, and Korean designers, some of whom had previously designed for Nike and other global brands. Li-Ning opened its first overseas retail store in Santander, Spain, in November 2001, aiming to increase its overseas revenue by 20 percent in five years. The brand also granted licensing rights to retailers in Spain, Greece, France, and other European countries. By 2004, when Li-Ning was publicly listed on the Hong Kong Stock Market, its corporation presentation listed "professionalism and innovation" as its two core values (Li-Ning, 2004, June 11). The brand also experienced rapid expansion in China in the 2000s: its retail stores increased from 2,516 in 2004 to 8,255 in 2011 (Li-Ning, 2012, March 30).

Li-Ning's global strategy also included the sponsorship of foreign sports. The first foreign sponsorship for Li-Ning was the French National Gymnastic Team (a third-tier global team) during the 2000 Olympics in Sydney, Australia. In that year, the brand aired a commercial in China featuring a French female gymnast dressed in Li-Ning dancing in the streets of Paris, incorporating images of iconic French symbols such as the Eiffel Tower, the Arc de Triomphe, and the Seine. According to Li-Ning's brand manager Zhang Qing, the commercial, produced by the Japanese agency Dentsu, aimed to shed Li-Ning's *tuqi* (rustic-looking or local) and make it more *yangqi* (foreign or cosmopolitan) (Da, 2005, Oct.). Yet many middle-class young consumers I interviewed in Beijing in 2012 associated the Chinese brand with *tuqi*. Some criticized its name, saying it was too old-fashioned and too Chinese. They would rather pay more to buy Nike and Adidas, suggesting the depth of Li-Ning's challenge in its competition with global brands.

Li-Ning's foreign sponsorship aimed for two complementary goals: foreign expansion and an even more important objective of image enhancement in China. Chinese media also celebrated the brand's global ambition. For example, at the International Basketball Federation's World Championship in 2002, the Spanish Women's Basketball Team sponsored by Li-Ning beat the Chinese team dressed in Nike, prompting Chinese media to celebrate Li-Ning's symbolic victory.

Li-Ning often chose to sponsor Chinese sports players who had already garnered global currency through their influence, location, or other connections. For example, in 2003 it signed soccer player Li Tie, who was playing for the Everton Football Club in the United Kingdom. Specially designed shoes were produced for Li Tie at the Premier League, and Li was quoted as saying, "I believe that China's specialty sports products can occupy a special position in international competitions and I am willing to grow with Li-Ning" (Sohu, 2003, Feb. 16). The company produced a series of shoes called the "Tie Series," claiming that Li-Ning shoes can better fit the "Chinese feet." In 2005, however, the company discontinued the series and shifted toward sponsoring NBA players.

Li-Ning's globalization encountered major failures. Its foreign revenue was only 2.4 percent in peak times and it dropped to 1.3 percent in the first half of 2005 (Yu, 2009). In recent years, its overseas market share is consistently less than 2 percent. Realizing the dim prospect of global expansion, Li-Ning shifted to the mere manufacturing of a global image in 2004, in response to the Beijing Olympics.

THE BRAND'S OLYMPIC STRATEGY

Li-Ning's Beijing Olympic strategy balanced nationalism and cosmopolitanism, a tactic that was in line with China's Olympic image in general.[61] Corporate sponsorship, especially that of global brands, not only provided economic resources but also alleviated the tremendous criticism that China faced from human rights organizations. Li-Ning offered a sum that was an "extravagant gamble" to become an official sponsor, but it was outbid by the German brand Adidas.[62] With a much higher bid,[63] Adidas was also arguably a more desirable choice for Beijing because China was anxious to appeal to a global (Western) audience. Li-Ning thus turned to sponsorship of individual teams and players, both Chinese and foreign. It collaborated with CCTV's sports channel, an official channel of Olympic coverage, and provided clothing for CCTV hosts and journalists. However, the Li-Ning's alternative marketing strategy was quickly blocked because Beijing implemented stringent measures to protect the sponsors' interests. Li-Ning willingly obeyed the rule. The brand was unlikely to openly implement ambush marketing and violate the state's policy, given its founder's reputation and status as a national hero. In fact, the brand aired a commercial prior to the Olympics featuring well-known sports players, each illustrating the scenario that if they deviate from the sports spirit, "please expel me from the field."

Li-Ning was at a disadvantage in attracting global and Chinese athletes during the Beijing Olympics. Although the Chinese athletes the brand sponsored had medal potential, many foreign athletes it sponsored had little chance to win (Balfour, 2008, May 12). For example, it sponsored the Vietnamese Football Federation and the US table tennis squad; neither had prospects to win medals. The Argentinian Basketball Team was the only foreign team sponsored by Li-Ning that won a medal. With limited choices, Li-Ning even sponsored Sudan's track and field team, despite global condemnation of Sudan's human rights violations. One explanation for this controversial sponsorship is that Li-Ning intended to gain free media coverage in China. Abel Wu, director of Li-Ning's foreign footwear division, stated, "We don't have as strong a brand" as Nike and Adidas and "our thinking is that as a local brand, we need to have an international image" (Balfour, 2008, May 12).

In addition, Li-Ning launched an ad campaign themed on "One Team, One Belief." In a commercial, European, African, South American, and Chinese athletes were featured standing in a stadium with their hands over their hearts, promising to "awake the hero in our hearts." The commercial includes various Olympic champions and athletes at key moments during competition. The Chinese gold medalist diver Xiong Ni states, "Never giving up is the greatest talent." Tanzanian marathon runner

John Stephen Akhwari remarks, "The strongest muscle is my heart." Paralyzed former Chinese gymnast Sang Lan says, "Smiling is my unyielding power." With Eric Lévi's song "The Champions" playing in the background, the commercial celebrates harmonious competitions between Chinese and foreigners and dares ordinary consumers to awaken the hero in themselves. Centered on the Olympics with a focus on TV advertising (in addition to outdoor, Internet promotion, and store displays), Li-Ning planned to spend 16 percent of its sales revenue on promotional activities in 2008 ("Sohu zhengjuan," 2007, Jan. 15). However, the brand's globalization was criticized as a "paper tiger" marketing strategy (Balfour, 2008, May 12; Leibenluft, 2007, July 25). Given that more than 98 percent of its products are sold in China, the brand's global image was produced for Chinese consumers. Tom Doctoroff, JWT's chief executive officer in Asia, stated, "helter-skelter messaging" is an ineffective way to establish brand loyalty (Balfour, 2008, May 12).

While Li-Ning's previously mentioned sponsorships and promotional activities may seem irrational, they were implemented largely because of the fierce competition the brand has experienced in China. In comparison with global brands, Li-Ning has less cultural, symbolic, social, and economic capital to sign global and Chinese superstars as spokespersons. For example, before the Beijing Olympics, gold medalist Liu Xiang and soccer player Yi Jianlian were signed by Nike. Yao Ming was a spokesperson for Reebok (now part of Adidas's operation). And rising Chinese soccer player Sun Yue was recruited by Adidas. A leading sports-marketing consultant claimed that prior to the Olympics foreign brands signed every starter on the national basketball team (Leibenluft, 2007, July 25). They also recruited many players as spokespersons from other mainstream sports. With limited opportunities, then, Chinese brands were forced to create sponsorship deals. For example, when Reebok signed a $100 million contract with Yao Ming in 2003, Li-Ning immediately signed Yao's little-known Houston

Rockets teammate Chuck Hayes, aiming to capitalize on the popularity surrounding Yao. Peak followed suit and offered a seven-figure deal to Yao's other teammate Shane Battier in 2006.

Chinese sportswear brands commonly used such detour strategies. For example, Peak sponsored the little-known Iraq Olympic team for the Beijing Olympics and the 2012 London Olympics, and Erke and 361° supported the North Korean team for the Beijing Olympics and the London Olympics, respectively. Given that these brands do not sell in Iraq or North Korea, the only explanation was that they aimed to gain media publicity at home.

SELLING PROFESSIONALISM AND CHINESE CULTURE

Li-Ning's Beijing Olympic marketing included not only the specific tactics discussed above but also a broader goal of reinforcing its professional and athletic image. Realizing that global sportswear brands often created a strong affiliation with major sports—such as Nike's association with basketball and Adidas's association with soccer—Li-Ning sought to develop a strong athletic image through affiliating with major sports. However, there was a (mis)perception that Li-Ning's association with gymnastics was not good enough. Facing pressure from both domestic and global brands, Li-Ning collaborated with NBA and global athletes. The China launch for the NBA's premiere interactive touring program "Jam Van Tour" was in 2005. This is a marketing mechanism that consists of a portable basketball court, a video game section, and a giant screen showing classic NBA moments. Li-Ning sponsored the event from 2005 to 2007. In March 2008 Li-Ning launched its own "Hero Van Tour" ceremony at the Chaoyang Park, where the Olympic beach volleyball competitions were scheduled. The company timed its ceremony in conjunction with the lighting of the Olympic flame in Greece. The ten-month tour proved to be very successful and allowed consumers to interact with past Olympic medalists and present players.

Prior to the Olympics, Li-Ning also signed several NBA basketball players, including Damon Jones, Shaquille O'Neal, Evan Turner, Baron Davis, Jose Calderon, and Hasheem Thabeet. This was a direct challenge to global brands, but the NBA players Li-Ning signed often were fading in popularity—and sometimes Li-Ning did not gain the full sponsorship advantage. For example, NBA player Shaquille O'Neal endorsed Li-Ning in China, but in the US he wore Li-Ning shoes without the brand logo (Balfour, 2008, May 12). This example illustrates Li-Ning's lack of resources and symbolic capital in the global market.

In order to enhance the company's professional image, Li-Ning also designed special shoes to raise its profile and reputation as an innovator.[64] They made a Shaquille O'Neal signature shoe, a Damon Jones signature shoe, and a Dwayne Wade signature shoe. These limited editions incorporated traditional Chinese culture and quality design, and used new materials. Corresponding commercials were aired to promote them: a commercial selling the Shaquille O'Neal "flying armor" shoe features O'Neal playing basketball in slow motion while his shoes paint brushstrokes, creating a traditional Chinese ink painting.[65]

Li-Ning has a strong association with Chinese national pride not only because the founder was a most well-known and respected Olympic medalist but also because of the brand's marketing and business strategy. The brand was marketed as a quintessential Chinese brand of national pride. The company emphasized this even further prior to the Olympics by drawing upon traditional and contemporary Chinese culture and legends in product designs. For example, in 2006 the company developed a sneaker called "Lei Feng 001," which incorporates cultural elements to commemorate Lei Feng, China's revolutionary hero and role model soldier during the Mao Zedong era. The green shoe (the color symbolizing the Chinese military) features a red star (symbolizing the People's Liberation Army) and the Chinese words *fu wu wei min* (meaning "serve the people"). Only thirty-five pairs with serial numbers and sixty-six pairs with no serial numbers were produced, to commemorate the 66th anniversary of Lei Feng Day on March 5 (Yu, 2008). With a memorable name and cultural cues that cater to the public memory of Chinese people, the shoe aimed to produce nostalgia and invoke devotion in pre-reform China. Another sneaker, called "The War of the Red Cliff," is based on a famous war in China's Three-Kingdom Period (208–280 AD). The sneaker, made with laser technology, features historical scenes such as a debate among Confucian scholars, and *cao chuan jie jian*—a legend of the military mastermind Zhuge Liang who led his disadvantaged army to victory against the enemy. The company also freely drew upon Chinese tradition to enhance consumerism. For example, on the Chinese Valentine's Day in July 2007, Li-Ning produced the male and female versions of "Double Seventh Day Legend" shoes, featuring two fictional lovers, Niu Lang and Zhi Nu, who were cruelly separated along the Milky Way by the goddess Wangmu Niangniang, based on Chinese legends. These efforts won acclaim, and Li-Ning was praised as an innovator and promoter of Chinese culture. A fan community for the sneakers was also developed, and Li-Ning sponsored online and offline gatherings of these fans prior to the Olympics.

In addition, Li-Ning produced collectible shoes that incorporated Western culture. For example, in 2007 it produced "Christmas Lovers' Boots" featuring red and green shoelaces, and images of bells, reindeers, and Christmas trees. Further, Li-Ning designed a pair of shoes featuring a slogan from the American reality TV game show *Jailbreak*, but the production was stopped, possibly because of copyright issues (Yu, 2008).

Like a typical Chinese business, Li-Ning could act quickly and flexibly in response to crises. Right after the Sichuan Earthquake, a devastating tragedy that killed tens of thousands of people three months prior to the Beijing Olympics, Li-Ning provided immediate relief money and aired a TV commercial within two weeks celebrating China as a nation that was destined to rise again from tragedy.[66] The ad plays in rewind and shows scenes such as a young boy opening and re-closing a pomegranate, Chinese people and athletes running backward, and people wiping off red face paint. The color red is predominant in all the scenes and the background music features the lyrics "I still believe in love." A caption reads, "the same heart; the same blood; restarting; anything is possible." Chinese consumers, especially Internet users, were deeply moved by Li-Ning's relief effort and by this commercial, and many claimed to provide greater support in the future for Chinese products as a result.

Li-Ning's marketing strategy, together with the founder's lighting ceremony performance, provided the company with expansive media exposure. These activities also earned consumers' goodwill. A survey conducted after the Beijing Olympics by China's largest media research institute, CVSC-TNS Research, found that approximately 40 percent of the respondents thought that Li-Ning was an official Olympic sponsor ("Zhongguo pinpai weilie waizi jutou," 2008, Aug. 19). While Li-Ning was not considered a serious competitor in the past, in 2010 the director of Adidas acknowledged that his company paid more attention to the Chinese brand than previously (Knowledge @ Wharton, 2010, Aug. 18). Li-Ning also diversified its portfolio through acquisitions and strategic alliances with multiple brands such as Z-Do (mid- to low-priced goods), Aigle (outdoor sporting products), Lotto Sport (fashionable sporting goods), Double Happiness (table tennis products), and Kason Sports (badminton-related products), thus aiming to reposition the brand in the Chinese market.

However, major problems emerged. First, Li-Ning's marketing strategy was scattered. It stretched its resources to compete globally and locally. Because of its negligence, Anta and other Chinese brands quickly established a strong presence in second-tier, third-tier, and rural markets. Li-Ning's failure to globalize also cost it opportunities at home. Many of my interviewees pointed out that Li-Ning's growth was much slower than other brands. According to them, Li-Ning's development was largely due to the rapid development of the sportswear industry. Once the industry slowed down, the brand's problem became more obvious.

REBRANDING IN THE POST-OLYMPIC ERA

Following the Beijing Olympics, Li-Ning furthered its effort to become a professional athletic brand. It narrowed down sponsorships to a few key sports, such as basketball, soccer, field and track, tennis, and fitness. It also intensified marketing to women by launching the "inner shine" campaign. One commercial, for example, features a Chinese woman practicing yoga, dancing, and running, while whispering words such as "fly high," "the purpose of moving is to calm myself down," "take a deep breath," "slow exhalation," and "listen to your heart." The campaign encourages women to have peace with their bodies, thus celebrating a different kind of femininity. Some ad professionals hailed this campaign as fresh air for the Chinese advertising field, but others viewed it as ineffective for Li-Ning's target consumers: fourteen- to twenty-eight-year-olds, the self-centered single-child generation, "little emperors and empresses" who value outer appearance and materialism over inner beauty and spiritual pursuits.[67] The campaign gradually faded, and Li-Ning later shifted back to celebrating external beauty by hiring the Taiwanese supermodel Lin Chi-ling as a spokesperson.[68]

Li-Ning's significant move was its 2010 rebranding campaign, launched on its twentieth anniversary, attempting to rejuvenate its image among China's "post-90s"—the generation born after 1990 who grew up with material abundance.[69] With a new logo and a new slogan—"Make the Change,"—Li-Ning aimed to transform the brand into a premium one comparable to global brands.[70] (See Figure 5.1.)

Li-Ning also launched a series of ad campaigns for the rebranding, which celebrate *balanced* individualism by encouraging consumers to stand out while simultaneously fitting in. For example, a commercial features sports players Baron Davis, Lin Dan, and Yelena Isinbayeva, who make statements such as "Please don't compare me with others"; "You can't find a new world with an old map"; and "I believe change is power." But Li-Ning was careful not to celebrate extreme individualism. Instead, its ad imagery and statements were confined within the parameters of social acceptance. Believing that major brands charge premium prices, Li-Ning also raised its prices three times in a year, dramatically narrowing its price differences from major global brands: while Li-Ning products traditionally sold at prices 30–40 percent lower than Nike and Adidas, and 50 percent higher than most other Chinese brands ("Li-Ning: Pinpai Jiema," 2011, Dec. 5), the price increases brought the Li-Ning brand to just 10 percent less than Nike and Adidas. Further, because of global brands' frequent promotional sales, Li-Ning's prices could be even higher than global brands sometimes.

While some analysts expected that the rebranding could help Li-Ning develop into a major global brand, the campaign largely failed, resulting in excessive inventory, a dramatic decrease in stock price, lower profit, and the closure of hundreds of stores.[71] There were various reasons for the failure. First, Li-Ning missed the target consumers while alienating its current consumers in their thirties and forties. Li-Ning used celebrity endorsers born in the 1980s, who did not resonate with the post-90s generation. Second, Li-Ning had little control over their distribution channels, and scattered distributors and retailers. The lack of communication and coordination between the company and the distributors caused confusion when the company was attempting to upgrade the stores to the newest version. Limited resources allowed only some stores to be upgraded in the rebranding process, while others continued to carry off-season products. Third, its pricing strategy backfired. Many young consumers would rather spend more on Nike and Adidas than similar Li-Ning products. Last, Li-Ning aimed to target young consumers in first-tier cities and large second-tier cities. However, only about 160 stores existed in first-tier cities during the rebranding campaign. In contrast, Nike and Adidas had tripled the amount in the first-tier cities during the same period of time. For example, the brand was invisible in Shanghai's prime business locations such as Huaihai Road, resulting in a mismatch between its new look and its actual distribution to consumers who had access to the products (Knowledge @ Wharton, 2010, Aug. 18).

Following Li-Ning's failure, Chinese brand Anta surpassed Li-Ning in revenue in the Chinese market. Anta also became the official sponsor of the Chinese Olympic delegation for the 2010 Winter Olympics and 2012 London Olympics. Many price-conscious consumers in second- and third-tier cities switched to Anta, Peak, and other Chinese brands. Furthermore, a wave of layoffs, income reduction, and resignations of high-ranking managers forced Li-Ning to reconsider its marketing strategies. Starting in 2012, it limited its international business. Partnering with the Chicago-based digital marketing firm Acquity Group, Li-Ning opened a retail store in Portland in 2010 as a symbolic gesture toward conquering Nike's backyard, but the store was closed in 2012. In July 2012, its licensed partner in Spain also filed for bankruptcy.

Attempting a comeback, Li-Ning's London Olympic strategy stressed persistence, self-confidence, and enthusiasm. Featuring various Chinese sports players, Li-Ning's ads include slogans such as "Everyone fails themselves, but with courage, one can be a new self," and "Trying does not mean success, but giving up means failure." This campaign shifted Li-Ning's previous focus on the post-1990s to an attempt to reposition itself as a Chinese product of national pride.[72]

Typical of Chinese advertisers who target mass consumers and expect advertising to enhance sales immediately, Li-Ning made some irrational decisions recently. For example, in 2012 Li-Ning signed NBA player Dwayne Tyrone Wade, paying $100 million USD plus dividends and shares over ten years. This contract was comparable with Adidas's thirteen-year contract with Derrick Martell Rose for $185 million USD. While Adidas can also profit from the sponsorship in other markets, Li-Ning can only utilize the players' influence in China, making its global contracts more risky. Li-Ning continues to rely on mass advertising even as media prices and sponsorship fees increase; its digital and social media marketing are still underdeveloped. In contrast, advertisers such as Nike and Adidas are more skilled in engaging consumers using fact-based algorithmic bidding systems, social media, and other digital technologies.

COMPETITION FROM GLOBAL BRANDS

As top global sportswear brands have been operating in China for decades, they have already acquired local knowledge and localized their personnel and management. Many of their advertising campaigns appropriate Chinese cultural symbols. For example, while Nike previously implemented its global strategy in China, it now markets specifically for this nation. Even though Li-Ning is an iconic brand of national pride, it does not own national pride. During the Beijing Olympics, almost all Olympic sponsors of Western origin cheered for China in their advertising campaigns. For example, McDonald's launched an ad series supporting China, with the slogan "I'm loving it when China wins." Coca-Cola launched an extensive marketing campaign called *changshuan aoyun* (smooth and invigorating Olympics) and developed a popular ad anthem called "Red Around the World," which attempted to show China's global influence. Adidas promoted Chinese national pride and culture. For example, one ad portrays countless hands holding in the air the Chinese basketball player Sui Feifei, soccer player Zheng Zhi, diver Hu Jia, and Chinese volleyball players, illustrating support for these athletes and linking Adidas to China's collective culture and national victory.[73]

Global brands who were not official sponsors for the Beijing Olympics also appropriated Chinese national pride. For example, Pepsi launched the "Go Red for China" promotion and painted its blue cans red (Barboza, 2008, July 20). Nike used ambush marketing and produced a documentary called *Chong* (meaning "Dare"), which celebrates China's Olympic success from 1984 to 2008. It depicts world-record high-jump holder Zhu Jianhua, pistol shooter Xu Haifeng, and other contemporary athletes. To commemorate 1984 as the first milestone in China's Olympic history, Nike also sold specially designed products. These included a limited number of jackets with signatures of three Chinese gold medalists, and several throwback sneakers, one of which features patriotic red and gold Chinese characters *ling de tu po* (meaning "the breakthrough") and another features the shape of the Bird's Nest (China's National Stadium). Nike's sport shirts, in patriotic red and yellow colors, incorporate Chinese cultural elements such as terra cotta soldiers and feature the Chinese words "get up, advance," linking to China's national anthem (Liao, 2008, July 29).

Nike's handling of the two crises related to Liu Xiang, China's star hurdler and gold medalist at the 2004 Olympic Games, represent its skillfulness in managing unexpected occurrences. Called "China's flying man," Liu was celebrated as a Chinese and Asian hero who successfully challenged the stereotype that Asian men cannot succeed in field and track. Nike made full use of Liu's influence in 2004 through TV commercials, print ads, outdoor advertising, store posters, the Internet, and public relations activities. Nike also sold a Liu Xiang signature sneaker called "flying man" (*tiansheng wo xiang*). It placed an even bigger bet on him in 2008, with many commercials repeatedly showing Liu's classic hurdle jumping and his determination to conquer his own hurdles and motivate others, young and old, male and female, athlete and amateur players.

Realizing that Chinese people and officials had high expectations for Liu, Nike doubled down on its bet in 2008, creating a campaign that considered two scenarios: Liu Xiang either winning or losing the gold medal. Liu's last-minute withdrawal due to injury, however, was a devastating blow to his fans and the sponsor. Nike managed to turn the crisis into an advantage. It immediately issued an official statement praising Liu as "one of the greatest field and track players." It stated that Nike "is very proud" of "a close collaboration with him" and expects "him to come out to play again after his recovery" ("Liu Xiang turan tuisai," 2008, Aug. 19). Within hours of his withdrawal, Nike produced a new print ad stating, "[I] love games, love with all my self-respect, love winning it back, love commitment, love honor, love setbacks, [and] love sports, even when it hurts." Nike's timely new ad, placed in prepurchased newspapers as well as newly purchased spaces and store displays, appeared side by side with the news about Liu Xiang's withdrawal. Nike's continuing collaboration with Liu Xiang was highly praised in Chinese media, suggesting that Nike was a trustworthy friend.

In 2012, Nike again created a calculated campaign. As part of its global "live your greatness" campaign, the ads featuring Liu Xiang use taglines such as "1.3 billion are watching you closely," but "[there is] no need to answer others. Live your greatness." However, Liu Xiang crashed through the first hurdle and limped to the finish line. Nike's Olympic team responded immediately and it posted the first *Sina Weibo* post within fifteen minutes. It stated, "Who dares compete with all one's might? Who dares start all over again in one's prime, despite the pain. ... 1.3 billion people all hopped on one foot to the finish. Live Greatness." This entry was forwarded 130,000 times and received more than 26,000 comments. Nike has been skilled in handling crisis, which enables the brand to continue to expand in the Chinese market.

CHALLENGES FROM OTHER CHINESE BRANDS

Li-Ning also faced challenges from other Chinese brands. Generally speaking, Chinese brands tend to implement similar advertising and marketing strategies: once a branding strategy becomes successful, other brands copy the strategy immediately, resulting in many undifferentiated ad campaigns. In the sportswear industry, endorsement by athletes and celebrities is now commonly used. As was discussed before, both Chinese and global brands are very keen in signing Chinese athletes as their spokespersons. With a common perception that opinion leaders are extremely important in influencing Chinese consumers' purchasing decisions, advertisers often throw lots of money at sports stars and celebrities for endorsements.

Many of Li-Ning's competitors come from Jinjiang, Fujian Province. Anta, one of the fastest-growing sports brands, is Li-Ning's most formidable competitor. Anta was founded in 1991 as a manufacturing sourcing company for global brands. The company began marketing its own brand in 1994. Anta's breakthrough came in 1999 when it spent 800,000 yuan (approximately $100,000 USD), a quarter of its annual profits, hiring China's rising table tennis player Kong Linghui as its spokesperson. After signing Kong, Anta also spent its entire annual profits of 1999 on CCTV advertising (Lin, 2012, April 27). Kong won a gold medal at the Sidney Olympics in 2000, which greatly boosted Anta's name recognition. Its market share in China increased from a negligible portion to 13.4 percent in two years after the Sydney Olympics (Netease, 2004, April 23).

Anta's bold move is common among Chinese advertisers, who are often willing to take risks for higher returns. Many view advertising as the last resort and a magic instrument to promote sales. Anta's formula for success, which was often summarized as celebrity endorsement plus CCTV platform, attracted many imitators. In two years, more than forty sportswear brands from Jinjiang spent hundreds of millions of yuan on CCTV and placed ads featuring sport or entertainment stars. The CCTV sports channel was then jokingly called the "Jin Jiang Channel" by observers and analysts.

For many Chinese brands, a central strategy was to strengthen their positions by creating brand association with opinion leaders, which mostly meant celebrities and sports stars. Because Li-Ning's global expansion meant that it directed fewer resources toward development and maintainance of its domestic market share in second- and third-tier cities, Anta and other Chinese sports brands such as Tebu and Peak managed to grow and strengthen their position in the Chinese market. In particular, Anta signed highly desirable resources such as the Chinese Basketball Association (CBA), the Chinese University Basketball Association, and the Chinese Volleyball League as well as individual sports players. With its slogan "Anta, keeping moving," and its proclamation, "[We are the] champion's backbone, made in China," Anta inspired to be a Chinese national icon.[74] These brands are also successful in selling to the lower-end market of the first-tier cities.[75] Anta's CBA sponsorship deal, which ran from 2003 to 2012, was rewarding and allowed Anta to have access to the huge basketball fan base. Desperate to gain influence in the Chinese basketball market, Li-Ning obtained the CBA sponsorship deal in 2012 after CBA's contract with Anta expired. However, the fees skyrocketed. Li-Ning had to pay 2 billion yuan (approximately $320 million USD) over five years, ten times the amount paid by Anta. Given that Li-Ning's profit in 2011 was only 44 million yuan (approximately $7 million USD), the contract was considered an "unrestrained gamble" (*haodu*). Li-Ning responded and stated that the contract aimed to "make Chinese basketball better" (Liao, 2013, Feb. 25).

Like Li-Ning, Anta also began working foreign advertising agencies after it gained more economic capital and influence. It partnered with J. Walter Thompson in 2006, launching a new campaign with their slogan "Anta, keep moving." The ads celebrate Anta's grassroots spirit, underdog status, an upbeat attitude, and a more rugged and authentic Chinese identity; the campaign also establishes Anta's Olympic associations through imagery, promotional events, special timing (such as its one-year countdown to the Olympics), and its sponsorship of individual medalists and inspiring music (e.g., "We will rock you"). Anta ads encourage people to strive for greatness and fulfill their dreams (the notion of dream has become a fad after Chinese President Xi Jinping originated the "Chinese dream" concept). These ads worked because Chinese consumers were obsessed with inspiring ideas and concepts encouraging individuals to achieve success.

Many of Anta's strategies were similar to Li-Ning's. For example, Chinese brands often seek to be publicly listed in order to gain capital and prestige. Public listing is also used to transform a company's management, making it modern and professional. A massive number of Chinese corporations were publicly listed in the Shenzhen, Shanghai, Hong Kong, and New York stock exchanges. Chinese sportwear brands are no exceptions. For example, Li-Ning was publicly traded in Hong Kong in 2004. Following in Li-Ning's footsteps, Erke was traded in Singapore in 2005. Anta was listed in Hong Kong in 2007. Xtep, 361°, and Peak were publicly traded in Hong Kong in 2008 and 2009 respectively. Finally, Naibu was listed in London in 2012. Most strategies employed by Li-Ning were quickly emulated by other brands.

Anta also responded to the Sichuan earthquake in 2008 in a way similar to Li-Ning. Like Li-Ning, Anta celebrated Chinese patriotism and unity. In a commercial aired immediately after the earthquake, images of yellow earth and a montage of Chinese athletes striving for success were included. The ad made such statements as "Are the setbacks too much to bear? Are the challenges too daunting? We're Chinese. Let's prove ourselves. Sweat will awaken our courage. Grit will power our spirit. Stand up, China, tall and proud." Once again,

Anta's move produced similar images and sentiments, which made Li-Ning's strategy less distinctive.

Undifferentiated bombardment advertising also forces Chinese brands to compete on pricing and focus more on economy of scale and efficiency of production and delivery (Doctoroff, 2012). Chinese advertisers and consumers believe that "bigger is better" and equate size with product quality and safety.[76] Consequently, most Chinese sportswear brands dramatically expanded their retail store numbers. Like Li-Ning, Anta stressed the establishment of a national network of chain stores. Its first retail store opened in 2001. The number of stores, both self-owned and licensed, increased to approximately 10,000 stores in ten years, allowing Anta to have a strong presence in the third-tier, fourth-tier, and small-town markets. Its rapid expansion posed a huge challenge to Li-Ning's national strategy. While Anta has an advantage over Li-Ning because of its lower prices, it faces similar competition from other Chinese brands such as Tebu, 361°, Erke, and Peak, which sell at even lower prices. Some of the brands also aimed to produce a similar cosmopatriotic image.[77]

Li-Ning recently diversified its business strategy and is now working with global investors, hoping to gain capital and stage a comeback. This will be a difficult task, however, as Chinese consumers are becoming increasingly selective in brand choices. Electronic retailers such as Alibaba and Jingdong also pose challenges to Li-Ning's retail-store strategy. Furthermore, Chinese consumers have also been shopping directly from sellers in the United States and Europe through Chinese citizens in the West, a practice that further influences market needs in China. With increasing labor costs, Chinese products are becoming less competitive in price. While following global practices has arguably made Li-Ning competitive in the past, its future success depends on a strategy that considers changing consumer tastes, the technological environment, and business culture and competition in China.

CONCLUSION

Squeezed between global brands and the nationalistic push from Chinese brands, Li-Ning is forced to engineer a cosmopatriotic image that combines nationalism and cosmopolitanism. The brand's challenges in the Chinese market concern not only its economic capital and global knowledge but also its cultural and symbolic capital. While global brands are often associated with quality, status, and modernity, Li-Ning, as a Chinese brand, does not enjoy such benefits automatically. Many ad professionals I interviewed pointed out that Chinese consumers often preferred foreign brands for public consumption and Chinese brands for domestic consumption. As a Chinese brand for public consumption, Li-Ning is forced to engineer a cosmopatriotism that simultaneously satisfies cosmopolitanism and Chineseness. While foreign brands can use Chinese images without worrying about the loss of their global image in China, Li-Ning's global image seems to be more contrived. Other Chinese brands' nationalistic push, bombarding advertising, and low-price strategy also pose challenges to Li-Ning.

The analysis of Li-Ning helps us revisit the theory of cultural imperialism. Though many argue that cultural imperialism is outdated, my analysis suggests that modernity itself functions as a way to endorse cultural imperialism. While Chinese consumers are generally ethnocentric and prefer to identify with Chinese values and celebrities, they also endorse the superiority of foreign goods. Even though Chinese brands can produce a hybrid image of nationalism and cosmopolitanism, they are in a disadvantaged position because cultural imperialism privileges certain positions, naturalizes cultural distinctions, and creates competitive hurdles for Chinese products. In this sense, cultural imperialism is still alive not only in the global political economy but also in the minds of consumers. I contend that we should combine the strength of cultural imperialism and hybridity, and consider power relations when analyzing commercial culture in emerging economies.

As consumers become more sophisticated, other factors also play an important role in determining their consumption choices. For example, Chan, Cui and Zhou's (2009) survey finds that consumers in Beijing are now less likely to buy foreign brands of fast-moving consumer products than those in second-tier cities such as Chengdu and Xi'an. Second-tier cities are now repeating some of the early consumption practices characteristic of first-tier cities. Also, a report released by accounting giant KPMG found that while 46 percent of luxury purchases by Chinese consumers were driven by "status" in 2006, only 33 percent were so in 2011; while values such as connoisseurship and self-reward scored at 8 percent and 21 percent in 2006, respectively, they increased to 18 percent and 26 percent in 2011 (Chow, 2011, May 17). Consequently, marketers need to design campaigns that cater to a wide range of consumer motivations.

In the future, Chinese consumers may stress the emotional benefits of brands. In order to become successful, Chinese brands such as Li-Ning have to cater to changing consumer tastes in China through innovation. Holt (2004) argues that an iconic brand has to provide resolution to a deeply felt anxiety in a society. While Li-Ning in the past partially captured China's desire to globalize and localize, it was not successful in making the position an inherent part of its brand. As Chinese consumers become more assertive in claiming Chineseness, Li-Ning has to be more confident in innovating its marketing practices and identifying a unique position that resonates with Chinese society.

6 | Controversial Advertising in China

The nature of controvery in Chinese advertising has changed over the last three decades. In this chapter I will explore what types of advertising are controversial in China, and how advertising controversies have changed over time. Is there a pattern regarding how controversies unfold? How do controversial advertisements of foreign products differ from those of Chinese products? Finally, how does the changing communicative environment shape controversial advertising practices?

It is important to see how changing market, technologies, policies, and culture—the four key factors established in chapter one of this work—have an impact on controversial advertising. I also look at how increasing global information flows controversialize advertising practices that are otherwise noncontroversial. This analysis is situated first in China's problematic regulatory regime. This understanding then leads to how advertising controversies have changed: from early concerns over advertising as a form, to recent concerns over specific products and advertising implementations. I will discuss specific Chinese controversial advertisements in relation to changing market, political, cultural, and technological contexts. I also investigate controversial foreign advertising by comparing and contrasting different challenges faced by American and Japanese marketers. Controversial advertising embodies the problematic relationship between citizens and consumers, the state and media, and global and local powers.

ADVERTISING REGULATIONS IN CHINA

Advertising in China is regulated in three ways, some explicit, some implicit or non-formal: formal regulations through laws, policies, and circulars; self-regulations; and ethical and moral values. When China resumed advertising in 1979, there were no regulations. Initially, the authorities approved advertisements on an individual basis, as discussed in chapter two. In 1982, the State Council issued "Provisional Regulations for Advertising Management," which was revised and formally adopted in 1987. The 1987 regulation specified that advertisements "must be truthful, healthy, clear, and unequivocal, and cannot mislead clients or consumers in any way" (Item 3). It prohibited contents that were illegal, detrimental to national dignity, counterrevolutionary, obscene, superstitious, absurd, deceptive, derogative about competitors, or inclusive of the national flag, emblem, or anthem (Item 8). It further prevented monopoly, unfair competition, and paid news (Item 4 and Item 9). While the twenty-two-item policy was crucial, it was also brief, vague, and general, often leading to different interpretations and implementations. China expanded the 1987 regulation and passed the Advertising Law, which took effect in 1995.

China's advertising regulations are stringent and compartmentalized; they operate on a dual-track system: the Party system and the state system. The Central Propaganda Department (CPD) and its nationwide branches represent the Party system. CPD monitors advertising content and can stop problematic advertisements at any time by issuing formal or informal notices or directives. The state system consists of three government branches: the administrative, the legislative, and the judicial. While China has a powerful administrative branch, the legislative and judicial branches are relatively weak. Traditionally, the National Congress makes advertising laws, the State Council passes administrative regulations, and various government ministries and bureaus under the State Council make policies that interpret and implement national laws and rules. Various government agencies have also created rules and circulars dealing with specific situations or product categories such as drugs, medical services, medical equipment, tobacco, alcohol, food, cosmetics, and agricultural products. However, there is no clear line between the Party and the state, given that the Chinese Communist Party (CCP) has been the only ruling party for more than six decades.

The government agency the State Administration of Industry and Commerce (SAIC) is responsible for advertising administration. It has branches in every province, county, and township in China. Unlike the National Advertising Review Board in the United States, a self-regulating entity, SAIC has legal powers granted by the state. The scope of SAIC's work includes drafting regulations and implementation methods, monitoring advertising practices, issuing advertising permits, and punishing operators for false advertisements, as well as guiding trade organizations and related institutions (Gao, 2007).

SAIC's branches provide a supportive role for the national office by coordinating campaigns to ensure compliance. Major municipal branches also spearhead actions. For example, the Bureau of Industry and Commerce in Beijing banned advertisers in 2007 from using words such as "luxurious," "extravagant," or "top-level enjoyment" because the agency considered these words "untruthful" and "vulgar," which promoted "fickle and extravagant social mores" (Sohu, 2007, May 19). In March 2011, Beijing issued another policy prohibiting outdoor advertisements from including words such as "supreme," "royal," "luxury," or "high class" to curb "hedonism" or "the worship of foreign-made products." Violators face a fine of up to $4,600 USD (Voice of America, 2011, March 21).

In addition to SAIC, other agencies regulate advertising depending on the medium and the nature of products. For example, the State Administration of Radio, Film, and TV (SARFT) regulate TV and radio commercials, the General Administration of Press and

Publication (GAPP) oversaw print advertising, and the Ministry of Industry and Technology Information controls Internet advertising. Outdoor advertising is regulated by SAIC and other government agencies overseeing a city's appearance. In 2013, SARFT consolidated GAPP into the State Administration of Press, Publications, Radio, Film and Television, which now regulates both print and broadcast advertising. China's Food and Drug Administration controls advertising of health products, food, cosmetics, beauty services, medical products/services, and agricultural chemicals. China's State Language Affairs Commission also supervises the use of standard written characters and proper pronunciations in media programs and can file complaints if advertisements contain nonstandard use of written and oral Chinese. Since 2005, a system of collaborative action has been established that involves SAIC and ten other central-level government agencies (G. Zhang, 2009).[78] A specific campaign can also engage other relevant government agencies.

Not every advertisement has to be approved by Chinese authorities prior to placement. On the contrary, only advertisements in special categories such as health products, food, medicine, medical equipment/services, cosmetics, beauty services, and agricultural chemicals must be pre-approved. Other types of advertisements mainly undergo self-regulation through three steps. First, advertisers and agencies apply self-censorship. These enterprises are legally required to have certified personnel, who must have passed exams administered by SAIC and its branches, to be in charge of censorship ("SAIC Advertising Censorship Personnel Management Methods," 1996). A censor reviews an operator's licenses and qualifications, advertising contents, formats, and an advertisement's overall effect to make sure it contains no untruthful, illegal, or misleading information.

Second, large advertisers and their agencies often voluntarily consult with the China Advertising Association (CAA), a semi-official organization under SAIC's leadership. The CAA's consultations are paid services. However, CAA's approval does not carry any legal power, despite its skill at grasping what SAIC is likely to suppress. Ultimately, only SAIC has power to determine the legality of an advertisement. While SAIC is required to follow the laws and regulations, it may use inconsistent criteria depending on an advertiser's and an agency's relationship with the SAIC leaders. The standards used by one local SAIC branch may be different from other branches or the national office. Furthermore, small businesses with limited resources often choose to not work with CAA and thus are more likely to place problematic advertisements than large advertisers (Tong, 2012). Lastly, Chinese media are also required to censor advertising. They are required to hire certified in-house censors. Again, inconsistent criteria are used: approval by one media organization does not mean approval by others; and approval by regional-level media does not guarantee national media's approval or vice versa. Even an advertisement that has passed all hurdles can run into trouble. For example, Pond aired a commercial on CCTV that features actress Tang Wei—who starred in the film *Lust, Caution*—touting the brand's benefits in 2008 before the Beijing Olympics. However, it was withdrawn within a week after it was aired because SARFT had already banned the actress from appearing on Chinese TV and films (Fitzsimmons, 2008, May 16).

In addition to constantly issuing new regulations, China has also started to license advertising professionals. In 2007, the Ministry of Personnel (now the Ministry of Human Resources and Social Security) and SAIC issued a joint degree, specifying criteria to evaluate and grant certificates for the titles of "assistant advertising expert," "advertising expert," and "senior advertising expert" through annual exams. The first qualifying exam was held in 2011 and overseen by CAA; the subjects included advertising laws, regulations, practices, copywriting, design, and planning. This makes China the only country that grants government certifications to advertising professionals.

ABSOLUTE TRUTH, FRAUDULENT AND ILLEGAL ADVERTISING, AND MORAL CODES

Chinese laws and regulations stipulate that an advertisement must be truthful and moral, focusing particularly on preventing misleading and fraudulent advertising. Initially, the authorities insisted on absolute scientific truth. Artistic exaggeration was equated with untruthfulness. For example, in the early 1980s Japanese automobile company Toyota launched an influential campaign based on the Chinese proverb that things tend to sort out eventually. The proverb states, "Whenever you drive your car into the mountains, there is always a road out." In addition to using the proverb, Toyota added, "wherever there is a road, there is Toyota." The ads appeared on billboards, in newspapers, and on television. However, the authorities halted the campaign because, as one official reasoned, Toyota automobiles did not appear on every road in China nor did all other countries necessarily have Toyota on the road (Tong, 2012, p. 209). Another example concerns a Shanghai facial soap, which promoted its product function in 1989 by employing the slogan: "this year [you are] twenty, [and] next year [you will be] eighteen." SAIC banned the commercial since people cannot reverse their biological age.

With increasing administrative experience, the authorities have become more tolerant toward artistic exaggeration. However, the compartmentalized regulatory regime and the rapidly developing market have been accompanied by an increasing number of consumer complaints about misleading practices and the consequent interventions from authorities since the 1990s. When the Advertising Law became effective in 1995, SAIC started to collect data about illegal advertisements and identified 26,615 as in violation of the law in that year. In 2007, the number rose to 56,627, including 16,384 advertisements making false claims. Although advertisements for food, medicine, medical treatment, cosmetic products, and beauty service have to be pre-approved, they are also among the top product categories that are illegally advertised, suggesting the ineffectiveness of China's regulatory regime. While the China Consumer Association, a semi-official agency for consumer protections, received about 7,000 consumer complaints about advertising in 1986, the number rose to more than 656,000 in 2007, a more than ninety-fold increase in twenty-one years (Fan, 2009). By 2009, the association and its branches had handled 11.96 million cases and retrieved approximately $1.6 billion USD losses for consumers.[79] These illegal advertisements are mostly placed on outdoor billboards; print media and television commercials account for most of the rest.

The pace of change in China's market necessitates passing new rules and amending old ones. The growing importance of broadcast advertising, for example, led SARFT to issue a few influential decrees to regulate TV, film, and radio ads.[80] Growing pharmaceutical and health industries are top advertising spenders and are also accused of placing a large number of illegal ads. The chaotic market has prompted the authorities to implement increasingly stringent laws. Now, advertising of pharmaceutical and health products can no longer include testimonies or images of doctors, experts, and patients. Any claim about product effects must be substantiated by scientific evidence. Recently, celebrity advertising has also been more strictly supervised. Violations can result in media exposure, warnings, fines, business suspensions, or license revocations.

Furthermore, an advertisement cannot include images of the national flag/emblem, lyrics or the tune of the national anthem, or the names or images of state organs, the military, and their functionaries (even dead Chinese officials). Nor can an advertiser use comparative advertising or superlative words such as "state-level," "the highest grade," or "the best." Furthermore, an advertisement cannot include pornographic, superstitious, terroristic, violent, or repulsive information, or discriminatory messages about ethnicity, race, religion, and gender. New terms such as "specially supplied," "specialized use," "specially produced," and "internally used" have been recently added to an expanding list of forbidden terms that fuse laws, ethics, and moral codes.[81]

In addition, moral codes are built into advertising regulations. The values of Confucianism and socialism influence ad rules, and advertising's expected role is to support "cultural and ideological progress" (Tong, 2012, p. 204). Moral codes aim to promote collective interests and regulate social relations and human behaviors, but they are often vaguely stated, and are thus flexible and changing. Although there are tensions among capitalism, socialism, and Confucianism, there is a general understanding that collective interests supersede personal interests. Still, individualism is advocated within socially acceptable parameters (Wang, 2008).

So far, I have discussed how advertising is controlled by institutional factors. Because of China's economic decentralization, however, leaders of local government agencies have huge power over local activities. Personal preferences of local government authorities can shape regulations. Advertising rules can change depending on who is in power. For example, Bo Xilai, former governor of Chongqing Municipality, launched a multi-year "red campaign" to promote CCP's revolutionary legacy, puritanism, and collectivism. Accordingly, the Bureau of Industry and Commerce in Chongqing issued a policy in 2011 forbidding real-estate advertisements from using adjectives such as "unique" and "irreplaceable." In March 2011 the Chongqing satellite TV channel announced that it would carry no more commercial advertising in the future, as part of a strategy to become China's "No.1 red channel," in order to rectify excessive entertainment culture and consumerism. When Bo lost power a year later, the TV station quietly resumed commercial advertising. Many other policies implemented when Bo was in office were also overturned. The example suggests advertising's uneasy relationship with China's official ideology, leading to the scapegoating of advertising as a source of social and political problems.

PROBLEMS WITH CHINA'S REGULATORY REGIME

Chinese advertising regulations are problematic in several ways. First, the laws and regulations are often too vague and general, fusing law and ethics. The Advertising Law, for example, states that an advertisement must "comply with the requirements of building the socialist spiritual civilization," "safeguard the dignity and interests of the state," and avoid "violating sound social morals," but there are no guidelines about the meanings of these strictures or what implementation methods might be needed. This leaves ample room for local authorities to interpret and implement laws, creating inconsistency across regions that have different moral codes and cultures (Gao, 2007; 2008).

Second, Chinese media, dependent as they are on advertising as a main source of income, do not necessarily share the interests of state regulators. Instead, they are willing to work with advertisers to maximize profits as long as they fulfill minimal political requirements. Small local media outlets with little leverage are especially subject to market pressures and often have to take any available contracts. In addition, commercial programming and advertising contents are less censored and less likely to be suppressed than coverage of sensitive political and social issues. In a post-WTO era, China has pushed media to become more financially independent.[82] The pressure from both the state and the market means that maximizing profits is crucial for media survival.

Third, local officials often half-heartedly implement top-down advertising controls, because of protectionism and developmentalism. Local officials have reportedly intervened to prevent local SAIC branches from punishing violators. Because local governments rely on tax money from the local media and advertisers, they share mutual interests with them.

Fourth, China is one of the world's most corrupt nations, and the corruption is getting worse (Transparency International, 2014).[83]

Chinese advertising is characterized by rampant corruption: paid news, advertorials, and other kinds of paid contents, which are symptomatic of widespread corruption in Chinese media and the economy (S. Zhang, 2009; Zhao, 1998). For example, a company can pay CCTV news programs to feature its top executive for $4,000 USD a minute; *Workers Daily* reportedly charges $1 USD per Chinese character for a flattering article; and many broadcasters offer "rate cards listing news-for-sale prices" (Barboza, 2012, April 3). The Beijing office of Ogilvy & Mather openly acknowledged that it had paid for news contents. Paid news is especially common for luxury products. Contrary to the traditional "firewall" in the United States that separates the news and advertising departments, in China these two divisions generally collaborate with each other. Leading Chinese journalist Hu Shuli has called for media to establish such a wall between news and advertising (Hu, 2013, Jan. 1). Not only do private enterprises engage in paid news, but local governments also pay national media to promote economy, tourism, and achievements. Paid governmental news often concentrates in March, before the annual congress meetings, as a way to promote local officials' achievements (interview with Yao Lin from Huicong Research, July 21, 2005).

Two recent scandals suggest that media corruption has reached a deeper level and a broader scope. In 2014, Guo Zhenxi, who formerly directed CCTV's Advertising Department and the Finance and Economy channel, was arrested for blackmailing corporations, raking in an approximate 2 billion yuan (approximately $330 million USD) over eight years (people.cn, 2014, June 17). He allegedly used two mechanisms: he either threatened to use CCTV to expose a company's problems and give the company bad publicity or promised to give a company positive publicity through news and feature stories. Guo leveraged CCTV's resources and unique status as the only national TV network and CCP's most powerful mouthpiece to gain profits. A few months later, the 21 Century Media Group was reported to have similarly blackmailed corporations. The firm coerced more than 200 companies to pay for good coverage or to suppress bad coverage in the group-owned media outlets (Tech.163.com, 2014, Sep. 29). Consequently, the president and several leaders were arrested and more than thirty people were investigated. Widespread media corruption is closely related to systemic corruption in Chinese politics and the economy. As a consequence, China's disciplinary authorities have recently vowed to suppress media corruption and hidden rules, promote clean governance by establishing formal policies for media workers, and involve non-state players in drafting self-regulation rules (Sun, 2015, Jan. 30). This is unlikely to curb media corruption, given the pressure that media experience from the state and the market.

Lastly, the implementation of regulations varies depending on geography and business size. For example, remote areas and small businesses are often subject to less governmental control than large businesses in large cities. Chinese authorities constantly change regulations as well, making it difficult for operators to keep up with the requirements.

In the past decade, the Advertising Law was criticized as outdated. In February 2014, the State Council issued a revised draft and invited the public to submit comments and suggestions. The Standing Committee of the People's National Congress passed a revised version of the Advertising Law on April 24, 2015, which has become effective since September 1, 2015. The new Advertising Law adds more rules over advertising placed online and via new media, and further tightens control over deceptive advertising, celebrity advertising, tobacco advertising, as well as advertising for medicines and medical apparatus and advertising targeting or using minors. It further increases fines for deceptive and illegal advertising practices.

An understanding of the regulatory environment provides context for looking at controversial advertising: ads that highlight conflicting views about the country's sociopolitical and cultural transformations as well as the tensions between economy and politics, and capitalism and socialism.

ADVERTISING AS A CONTROVERSIAL FORM

I use the term "controversial advertising" to refer to both offensive and non-offensive ads that stir discussion. While controversial ads are not necessarily offensive, offensive ads are often controversial. Controversial advertising in China is shaped by political and commercial logics. In the late 1970s and 1980s, advertising in itself was controversial, because it was incongruous with socialism. With gradual acceptance of advertising as a medium, controversies now result mostly from the nature of the product or service being sold, or the execution of the ad, or both.

When advertising was resumed in 1978, advertising professionals faced a huge challenge in addressing socialist citizens as consumers. Because China had deeply politicized social and cultural lives in previous decades, there was a strong desire for depoliticization (H. Wang, 2003). Reform-minded officials treated advertising simultaneously as an economic and a political instrument for reforms in line with emerging pragmatism. This budding pragmatism conflicted with previous interpretations of socialism and class struggle. In order to reconcile these tensions—especially those between the centralized planning system and the decentralized market—the Party-state proposed confusing and contradictory policy concepts in the 1980s.[84]

Any new practices, however, are likely to encounter resistance and criticism. For example, celebrity advertising first appeared in 1985 when the renowned stage-play actor Li Moran appeared in a commercial for the San Jiu Pharmaceutical Company. Li received overwhelming criticism because acting in the commercial was viewed as debasing his reputation. Now, however, celebrity advertising is pervasive, and celebrity endorsers promote values ranging from quality and effectiveness, success and status, beauty and youth, to enjoyment and leisure in China (Sun, 2013; Wang & Chen, 2007).

Foreign advertising was especially controversial because various political movements had attacked Western imperialism, capitalism, and commercialism for decades. Even in the 1980s, the government continued to condemn capitalist lifestyles through campaigns such as the Anti-Spiritual-Pollution Campaign and a series of Anti-Liberalization Campaigns. Foreign advertisements and billboards were criticized for spreading capitalism and foreign lifestyles. For example, when CCTV aired the first foreign commercial (for Coca-Cola) in 1980 in an imported program—arranged through CCTV's package plan to obtain US programming by paying with "free" advertising time—it attracted overwhelming criticism in China. Translated directly from the US version, the commercial depicts a mother and a child happily drinking Coca-Cola outdoors. Conservatives criticized the station for spreading a capitalist lifestyle and marketing a product inaccessible to ordinary Chinese. The authorities ordered CCTV advertising director Wang Nansheng to write a self-criticism report, a common practice in the Mao era. The station's subsequent airing of a Levi's commercial also encountered similar criticism. Both advertisements were banned.

On December 27, 1979, Beijing Advertising Corporation (BAC) set up a 3-month window display for the Japanese brand National (now Panasonic) in Beijing's Wangfujing commercial district. The display included a washing machine, stereo sound equipment, a TV set, and a Western mannequin wearing a red skirt, all of which aimed to portray a typical middle-class family. The display attracted large crowds, but the authorities were concerned that it advertised "the lifestyle in capitalist societies." People's Daily strongly criticized the display. Facing overwhelming condemnation, BAC's director, Cheng Chun, submitted a self-critique and explanation to Beijing's mayor. The critique was passed to a central government official and eventually to the Standing

Committee of China's top leadership, the Politburo (interview with Cheng Chun, July 19, 2005). A few Politburo members eventually endorsed the display. After this incident, however, Beijing Municipality issued a circular forbidding Chinese agencies from signing future window display contracts with foreigners.

Japanese advertising was especially controversial in the 1980s for two reasons: first, it had a dominant presence in the Chinese market; second, it was often associated with Japan's past military invasions. Sanyo, Rico, and Sony erected large billboards in Beijing's landmark locations: Xidan, Liubukou, Wangfujing, and Dongdan. There were complaints that Chang-An Avenue, the main street that cuts through the heart of Beijing, had turned into "a Japanese boulevard."[85] Consequently, Beijing issued a notice in 1985 limiting outdoor advertising, especially foreign advertising, along Chang-An Avenue, at Beijing Railway Station, and at Beijing Airport. Furthermore, the Sony billboards and many other foreign billboards erected previously were dismantled in 1986 when Beijing cleaned up the outdoor advertising environment.

In response, when foreign advertisers first entered China, many stressed friendship with China and Chinese people, and emphasized their support for the country's modernization and its socialist economy. Lyric Hughes, founder of a Chicago-based firm that sold time and space for Chinese advertising, advised American advertisers to "talk about friendship" and show sincerity "about helping China modernize" in their ads (Landis, 1985, Nov. 4). Other examples include Sony, Seiko, and Titus Watch: Sony declared it wished to provide "excellent electronic technologies to develop Sino-Japanese friendship"; Seiko claimed to "provide precise timing to all social areas," linking the product to China's modernization; and Titus Watch asserted their goal was to "serve the people [and] to keep time for the public."

Shanghai, now loaded with foreign advertisements, also ran into a major controversy in 1985. In that year, Shanghai Advertising

Decoration Company placed two large Toshiba billboards at the top of the Shanghai International Hotel, the tallest building in Shanghai then. However, the billboards greatly worried college students and old cadres, who viewed them as symbolizing a Japanese economic invasion, which they further linked to Japanese military invasions in the past. Some even threatened to bomb them and this threat forced the Shanghai municipal government to request that the advertising agency place a Chinese billboard at the top of the hotel to neutralize the political effect. The measure gradually cooled down the protesters.[86]

These examples show how controversial advertising resulted from China's problematic foreign relations and contradictory economic policy and official ideology. Decades of attacks on capitalism had sensitized Chinese citizens to politics and ideology. Foreign advertising especially reflected inherent contradictions in policies and the legacy of the country's class struggle. Unsurprisingly, Chinese advertising professionals working with foreigners bore tremendous psychological pressure and were often accused of "walking the capitalist road."

The distinctive challenge faced by Japanese advertising was also due to Japan's invasions in China during World War II. Collective memory of Japanese atrocities was kept alive through the constant circulation of media products, textbooks, and personal accounts. Chinese citizens' responses to these advertisements were also shaped by a general belief that they had the right to determine the use of public space. These examples show how controversies were predominantly shaped by the constructed global and local, state and media, and advertiser and consumer relations in that era.

CONTROVERSIAL ADVERTISING SINCE THE 1990s

Since 1992, advertising has lost some of its provocative power in China because of further economic liberalization and fading ideological concerns over capitalism versus socialism. Instead, contentions focus mainly on specific products or advertising campaigns.

Researchers separate controversial advertising into two camps: one concerns controversial or offensive products or services that anger, offend, or embarrass people; the second concerns controversial or offensive executions, that is, whether promotional materials contain offensive elements (Barnes & Dotson, 1990; Prendergast, Cheung & West, 2008; Waller, 2005). Controversial advertising normally contains "unmentionables." Wilson and West (1981) define unmentionables as "products, services or vices, or concepts that for reasons of delicacy, decency, morality, or even fear tend to elicit reactions of distaste, disgust, offence, or outrage when mentioned or when openly presented" (p. 92). These "unmentionables" do not necessarily offend all populations, but *some* significant segments (Katsanis, 1994).

Different cultures have different views about what is offensive. For instance, the three most offensive products and services in the United States include women's hygiene products, women's underwear, and hemorrhoid treatments (Aaker & Bruzzone, 1985). The three most offensive matters in Australia are racism, religious denominations, and feminine-hygiene products (Waller, 1999). Prendergast, Cheung, and West (2008) identify thirteen offensive products and services in China, including alcoholic drinks, condoms, dating services, female contraceptives, feminine hygiene products, female undergarments, funeral services, hair-replacement products, male undergarments, pharmaceuticals, sexual disease prevention, AIDS prevention, and weight loss programs and products.

Huhmann and Mott-Stenerson (2008) define controversial advertising executions as "provocative images, words or situations that utilize or refer to taboo subjects...or that violate societal norms or values" (p. 294). In China, offensive executions include cultural stereotypes, unnecessary fear, indecent language, nudity, sexism, and sexual connotations as well as offensive etiquette (Prendergast, Cheung & West,

2008). The manner sometimes offends the Chinese more than the matter. The following sections identify four types of advertising controversies in China, followed by an analysis of controversial campaigns conducted for the Chinese brand Naobaijin, which are symptomatic of an ineffective regulation system, changing consumer tastes, and problematic media-advertising relations.

CONTROVERSIAL PRODUCTS AND SERVICES OR EXECUTIONS

The first type mainly concerns the nature of products and services as well as how advertisers inappropriately target minors. Chinese legislators have only established rudimentary rules for the protection of minors.[87] In 2008, an advertisement of a women's sanitary product appeared in the CCTV's Children Programming channel and received overwhelming criticism. The advertisers were criticized for tastelessly exposing the product to minors. In 2010, a hospital in Wuhan placed an advertisement in a local newspaper, featuring children's favorite cartoon characters in order to target teenage girls and promote abortion as a pleasant and easy experience. The advertiser and the media were criticized for encouraging teenagers, especially teenage girls—a group whose use of abortion was becoming more common in China— to engage in sexual intercourse. The ads were also criticized for downplaying the trauma and harm done to a girl's body.

The second type concerns an advertisement's execution and improper use of appeals to sex. Sexual advertising strategies have increased in China (Croll, 1995; Yan, 2004; Hong, 2005; Zhang, 2006). Sexual messaging is used "to attract attention…to appeal to audiences that approve of its use, and to demonstrate the 'outcomes' of buying and using the brand" (Reichert & Carpenter, 2004, p. 824). Hong (2005) finds that advertisements placed in two international fashion magazines (*Shishang* and *Cosmopolitan*) in China have increased the use of revealing models over time, although the degree of nudity is still mild compared with the foreign editions of these magazines.

Although increasing sexual culture in mediated space can cause discomfort among conservatives, sex appeal in an advertisement is not necessarily controversial. Instead, controversy mostly stems from how sex appeal is represented. For example, Chinese media generally welcome mediated messages promoting traditional femininity and women as dependent and submissive Oriental beauties (Li, 2011). Stereotypical portrayals of women as elegant, gracious, lovely, and beautiful have rarely caused controversy. While Chinese media and officials commonly attribute the use of sex appeal to Western influence, foreign advertisers' execution of sex in advertising in China has rarely been controversial largely because they are more skilled in using this tactic in ways that suit the context. On the contrary, it is Chinese advertisers whose use of crass sex appeal often becomes controversial. The following two examples illustrate how Chinese advertisers tastelessly sell sex.

A common strategy is to directly associate a product with a woman's body, even if the product has no natural connection with women. Drinks, beer, medicinal liquor, drugs, and related products often use such a strategy. For example, a Hanai-based coconut juice commercial features a scantily dressed Caucasian woman, showing cleavage, and holding a can of coconut juice while saying "white, tender, and attractive curved shape." Another commercial for the same product placed in 2010 was even more blatant, featuring the same model climbing up a coconut tree, shaking her large breasts, and repeating the same tagline. The commercials were considered vulgar because they objectified women's bodies through the male gaze. Although only men and women who cater to the male gaze are likely to accept the message, interestingly, the product sells to men, women, and children, which reflects that Chinese advertisers often act on intuition and do not do copy testing before placements.

A second example deals with a TV commercial for a Chinese detergent. It portrays a housewife asking her husband whether he has used the detergent to *pao* (meaning "to soak" as well as "to pursue women"), *piao* (meaning "to rinse" as well as "to prostitute"), and *gan* (meaning "to dry" as well as "to have intercourse"). The commercial uses word play, a common advertising strategy in China. Public complaints prompted the authorities to ban the commercial.

The preceding examples used crude appeals to sex and were considered vulgar and distasteful. The misuse of sexual content has a lot to do with how Chinese marketers understand marketing success. For many, brand recognition is often the one and only criterion to measure branding success. Advertisers tend to come up with a concept based on instinct rather than careful research, as discussed in chapters three and four. Many do not perform copy testing before placing advertisements, nor do they have adequate in-house reviewers. Some intentionally place controversial advertisements to attract attention, good or bad. Furthermore, Western models are generally more sexualized than Chinese models, and female models are more sexualized than male models (Huang & Lowry, 2012). While sex appeal may increase a brand's salience, it can negatively affect its reputation among potential consumers (Cui & Yang, 2009). Different generations of Chinese consumers have different attitudes toward offensive advertising executions: the less educated who live predominantly rural lifestyles and adhere to traditional values, as well as the highly educated, global-minded, and media-savvy consumers, are more likely to be offended by sex-related ads than other generational cohorts (Fam, Waller, & Yang, 2009). Thus, advertisers selling to highly educated and globally minded consumers, as well as to rural residents, should be more cautious when using sex-based strategies.

The third category of controversies concerns offensive matters as well as unacceptable executions. For example, a commercial for a women's hygiene product, Fuyanjie (meaning "cleansing women's vaginitis"), created by adman Ye Maozhong, who is analyzed in chapter three, features a celebrity couple: Fu Disheng and Fu Jing. The ad claims that the product has the capacity to kill germs and make one feel fresh, cool, clean, and "more healthy." The commercial sells an unmentionable product and alludes to genitals and sexual intercourse, a taboo in Chinese culture.

In 2008, a competing product called Jieeryin (literally meaning "vagina cleaning liquid") also became controversial. The commercial featured Cecilia Cheung, a Hong Kong actress and Canton pop singer whose reputation was severely damaged after her involvement in a widely publicized celebrity sex photo scandal. Despite being a victim, Cheung was blamed, due to China's patriarchal culture. While other brands cancelled contracts with Cheung and the Beijing Olympic Committee banned all implicated stars, Jieeryin aired its commercial featuring Cheung on CCTV and major provincial and satellite TV stations one month after the outbreak of the scandal. In particular, Chinese Internet users criticized the advertiser for failing to show respect for prevailing social norms. The advertiser was also criticized for using a celebrity as a drug endorser, which was banned by the Bureau of Drugs Supervision in 2007. Interestingly, the commercial was broadcast hundreds of times before it was withdrawn (Li, 2008, March 16), which enabled the advertiser to capitalize on Cheung's controversial publicity. This suggests that rules always differ from implementations.

Finally, an advertisement can become controversial simply because consumers have changed their tastes. For example, during the Chinese Spring Festival of 2008, wool producer Heng Yuan Xiang debuted a sixty-second spot touting its sponsorship of the Beijing Olympics. The commercial features a girl's voice calling out each of the twelve zodiac animals three times, interspersed with the company's name, announced by an adult. The spot runs like "Rat, rat, rat! Heng Yuan Xiang, the official sponsor of the Olympic Games! Ox, ox, ox! Heng Yuan Xiang, the official sponsor of the Olympic Games! Tiger, tiger, tiger!..."[88] The advertiser used a strategy similar to one used in its commercial for the Year of the Goat in 1993. While its 1993 commercial was successful in boosting brand recognition and sales, the 2008 spot was described by Chinese viewers as "intolerable" and "the worst spot." Internet users even produced many online parodies. The commercial was generally viewed as lacking imagination and creativity and belittling consumers. The timing and the advertiser's Olympic sponsorship also contributed to the scrutiny. As an Olympic sponsor, the brand was expected to air creative ads and win glory for China. However, it was considered to have squandered the opportunity and failed to meet the expectation. The commercial was withdrawn a week later. Responding to criticism, the company's general manager remarked, "We would rather be criticized than forgotten" (Wu, 2008, Feb. 15), suggesting that publicity was more important than a good impression. These examples show that a combination of policies and culture produces advertising contentions.

NAOBAIJIN

Naobaijin (literally meaning "brain platinum"), a medicinal product whose main ingredient is melatonin, is a classic example of controversial advertising, resulting from an ineffective regulatory system, illegal practices, and changing consumer tastes. Its commercials have been consistently ranked among the most offensive in China. The case also symbolizes how opportunistic marketing strategies enable a brand's exponential growth in a short time but potentially damage the brand's long-term reputation and prospects.

Founded in the mid-1990s by legendary Chinese entrepreneur Shi Yuzhu, Naobaijin became the backbone product of his company after the founder experienced major financial troubles. Newspapers and TV stations published paid news reports and advertorials to tout the brand's misleading claims about its ability to solve sleeping problems and digestive issues, lower blood pressure, prevent cancer, increase sexual pleasure, and defer menopause. Exploiting people's fear of aging, Naobaijin published numerous pseudo-scientific reports and commentaries claiming that the product could make consumers younger. For example, the company claimed that 50 million Americans, and world leaders such as Bill Clinton and Pope John Paul II, were consumers of Naobaijin. The message was misleading not only because Chinese consumers had no way to verify the information but also because it intentionally confused Naobaijin as a brand name with melatonin as a generic name. Advertised as a huge breakthrough in life science, the brand boasted that melatonin was essential for the formation of brain cells called "naobaijin ti" (brain platinum form), cells responsible for one's health and intelligence. To consumers with little knowledge of life science, such information proved misleading. Parents reportedly purchased the brand for schoolchildren hoping to increase their grades and adults purchased the product to show filial piety to grandparents, parents, and in-laws.

Despite the Advertising Law, in effect since 1995, prohibiting unproven scientific claims, Naobaijin continued to illegally advertise until 2000. While Naobaijin's messages must be pre-approved, local authorities did not strictly implement the laws. Furthermore, the brand reportedly changed its pre-approved advertising messages from time to time (Xinhua, 2008, Aug. 1). The fact that it mainly sold in small cities and rural places also means that its advertising messages faced less regulation.

Because of increasing complaints about health products, medicine, cosmetics, food, and related product categories, Chinese authorities have intensified control over advertising in these areas. Facing increasing scrutiny, the brand shifted its product position to gift-giving in 2000. Different versions of Naobaijin commercials feature an animated elderly couple dressed in costumes of different kinds: ballet dress, a

Hawaiian hula skirt, a Turkish turban, and a cowboy outfit.[89] The couple dance and repeatedly sing, "During this year's holidays, we won't accept any other gift except Naobaijin." The slogan refers to "this year's holidays" rather than specific holidays because the same commercial is aired during the Moon Festival in August and the Spring Festival, both based on the lunar calendar.

Indeed, each year, the brand's promotions center on two traditional Chinese holidays: the Spring Festival and the Moon Festival. The company advertises intensely on CCTV and local TV stations ten days before and after the Spring Festival. It purchased tremendous advertising volume during the ten days prior to the Moon Festival. Believing that advertising volume was the most important, Shi Yuzhu admitted that he spent lavishly during these periods on repeated ads until consumers felt "annoyed" (Shi, 2004, Oct. 27). During these periods, the company also placed huge outdoor billboards, bus body advertising, mural advertising, and banners to integrate the marketing campaign. Many regard the bombarding strategy as unsophisticated and disrespectful toward consumers.

During the Beijing Olympics, SARFT criticized the company's gift-giving message as vulgar and corrupt (Zhang & Li, 2008, Aug. 15). It pointed out that adults may bribe officials and students may bribe their teachers with the product. The company removed gift-giving and gift-sending contents from the commercials. However, after the Olympics, the company resumed the gift-sending message in a different way. Its 2010 version features the elderly couple dancing in Michael Jackson's moonwalk style and urging consumers to buy the product as a gift for their parents and grandparents.

In addition to marketing campaigns, the company also sought endorsement from influential state and nonstate players. For example, SAIC once named the product "China's Famous Trademark." The founder Shi Yuzhu has received many awards from different government agencies and nonstate players, including the titles of "China's

Famous Person for Economic Reforms," "CCTV's Person of the Year for Economic Development," one of the "Top Ten Persons Influencing Chinese Economy," and many other awards. A dubious experiment conducted in the 1990s by researchers from the People's Liberation Army General Hospital, the Air Force General Hospital, the Medical School of Peking University, Tongren Hospital, and three other prestigious institutions that endorsed the product's ability to improve sleep problems, decrease risks for enteric diseases, and other benefits continues to circulate on the Internet (finance.qq.com, 2010, April 1).

Despite criticism and questions, Naobaijin's marketing campaigns proved effective. It grew rapidly in the Chinese market. The growth of the brand also benefited from little competition in the 1990s as it was marketed as a "health product," a newly created category. Its sales revenue reached 1.2 billion yuan in less than three years (Chen & Price, 2005). The brand was reportedly the best selling health product in the ten years from 2001 to 2010 (ce.cn, 2011, March 24). The product's market share allegedly reached 9.32 percent by 2010 (finance.qq.com, 2010, April 1). The brand generated 10-billion-yuan revenue between 1998 and 2008 (Tang, 2011, Feb. 28).

The case of Naobaijin symbolizes China's chaotic market, an ineffective regulatory regime, unethical advertising practices, and consumers' sense of insecurity associated with pervasive corruption in China. A general problem in the regulatory regime is that top-down policies are often compromised by local countermeasures. In addition, Chinese authorities often change regulations and implement them inconsistently, making it challenging for operators to follow rules.

Naobaijin commercials are controversial for a number of reasons. First, with a media system controlled by the Party-state and influenced by the market, consumers have little access to unbiased information. The brand's early pseudo-scientific reports, paid news, and advertorials continue to circulate online. Further, Chinese authorities are inconsistent in implementing laws. For example, Naobaijin commercials were banned and the company was required to pay a fine by the Shanghai authorities in February 2001. The company was fined again by the Hangzhou authorities in February 2005, the Taizhou authorities of Zhejiang Province in January 2006, and the Bureau of Drugs Supervisions in Henan, Zhejiang, and Ningxia provinces in 2008. Despite the numerous fines, their commercials continued to appear on CCTV and other provincial and cable TV stations (Cheng, Hao & Yang, 2008, March 13).

Second, the brand's bombarding strategy bores consumers. The airing of the same commercial, with some variations, is often associated with the brand's lack of creativity. The use of lowbrow cultural symbols, bright colors, and animated characters was criticized for treating consumers as unintelligent, naive, and childish. The brand's inattention to creativity was also reflected in what they chose to spend money on. Initially, the company did not hire an advertising agency. Instead, the founder Shi Yuzhu created the advertising concept and oversaw the commercial production. In contrast with its huge budget for media buying, the company spent little on creative production. In its early years, the ad design and production costs were estimated to be about 30,000 yuan (approximately $3,700 USD), while the company spent 140 million yuan (approximately $18 million USD) on airtime at satellite TV stations in 2001 alone (Zhang & Li, 2008, Aug. 15). Advertising professionals, especially those working in multinational firms, often criticized Naobaijin commercials as naive, narrow-minded, uncouth, uncreative, and boring. Josh Li, former general manager of Grey Beijing, stated that Naobaijin's "overwhelming exposure has eliminated the need for a good marketing strategy or creative execution" (Liu, 2003, June 13).

The brand was also criticized for irrational and exploitative spending, which symbolizes a generally shortsighted marketing strategy for health products. Health product brands generally cannot survive for more than five years in China (Chen & Price 2005). Similarly,

Naobaijin was criticized for using short-term strategies to maximize profits. The brand was also criticized for exploiting China's *severe acute respiratory syndrome (SARS)* crisis in 2003. During the crisis, the company dramatically increased its advertising volume and its advertisements claimed that the product could improve one's immune system (Liu, 2003, June 13).

The Naobaijin controversy also reflects a general problem for advertisers in China, a country of vast size and different tastes and norms. While urban consumers in large cities are more experienced and sophisticated, rural residents prefer more straightforward messages. Precisely because the brand chose CCTV as its main channel to reach national consumers, the commercials also simultaneously reached urban consumers. While Naobaijin sold poorly in first-tier cities, it had a large market share in second-tier cities in central and eastern China, small towns, and rural markets (Zhang & Li, 2008, Aug. 15). This analysis of Naobaijin's ad strategies reflects complex interactions between the state and the market, politics and commerce, and the urban and rural divide.

CONTROVERSIAL FOREIGN ADVERTISING

Foreign advertisers have also aired controversial ads. Controversy here rests on the dynamics of local and global forces, and cultural and technological factors. I first compare and contrast Chinese responses to banned advertisements of two Japanese brands (Toyota and Nippon) and those of two American brands (Nike and McDonald's). The analysis is then contrasted with two controversial commercials for Kentucky Fried Chicken (KFC) that were not banned. The investigation here advances my argument made elsewhere about the challenges Japanese brands encounter in the Chinese market (Li, 2009).

In 2003, Toyota launched a contentious campaign in China in partnership with its advertising agency Saatchi & Saatchi. One advertisement features a stone lion saluting and another lion kneeling down to a Toyota Prado using the slogan "You cannot but respect Prado" in written Chinese. Another advertisement features a Toyota Land Cruiser towing a green car, which was interpreted as symbolizing the Chinese military, in a sparsely populated area in Tibet, implying Toyota's superiority over the green car.

A year later, Nippon Paint also published a controversial advertisement, created by its agency Leo Burnett, in the Chinese magazine *International Advertising*, aiming to show the company's creativity in using Chinese cultural symbols to highlight their product's features. The advertisement features two dragons winding around two pillars in a Chinese pavilion. While one dragon is stuck to the pillar, the other dragon is falling off, apparently because of the glossy Nippon paint. All three advertisements attracted overwhelming criticism and the Chinese authorities ordered them to be withdrawn.

In November 2004, CCTV and several provincial stations in China aired a Nike spot. Stylized to look like a video game, the commercial features the NBA's LeBron James defeating flying angels in traditional Chinese attire, a white-haired Kung Fu master, and a pair of dragons.[90] The commercial was controversial as it was accused of showing disrespect toward Chinese cultural icons. In addition, the juxtaposition of an image of US dollar bills with these symbols was considered inappropriate. Nike initially refused to withdraw the advertisement, but continuing criticism from Internet users pushed the SARFT to issue a ban. Nike eventually withdrew the commercial and apologized for "having insulted the feelings of the Chinese."

A thirty-second McDonald's commercial, aired in 2005, also raised controversy in China. The last five seconds of the TV commercial portrays a Chinese consumer kneeling before a macho man at a video store and begging for the extension of a promotional deal. A voice states, "Fortunately McDonald's has relieved my pain in having lost the great opportunity. It offers me discounts every day." After the commercial was aired, consumers in Xi'an, Chengdu and Zhengzhou expressed their discontent to the authorities. Chinese Internet users also accused the commercial of damaging consumers' self-respect, which prompted the company to withdraw the commercial.

The controversies here show several patterns. First, the advertisers and agencies were all accused of misusing Chinese cultural symbols (such as the lion and the dragon), and thereby "hurting the Chinese people's feelings." Second, Chinese Internet users played an active role in setting the agenda and shaping the discussions. Traditional media then followed up with coverage, which drew more attention to the controversy. This reflects a new trend in the Chinese media industry: the Internet has now become a source of news for newspapers and TV stations (Shirk, 2010). With more than 600 million Internet users, the Internet is now a powerful force in shaping public opinions and discourses. Social media such as Weibo and Weixin (WeChat) are particularly influential in structuring the ways Chinese consumers access information, share ideas, and produce and consume content.

Third, some Chinese advertising professionals used the controversial advertisements to promote Chinese agencies and nationalism at large. According to them, only Chinese advertising professionals possess local knowledge and would genuinely support Chinese culture. For example, Ai Cheng, a prominent adman and founder of a Chinese advertising agency, stated at an online advertising forum,[91]

> I will say that Chinese elements, the Chinese dragon and lion will not bow their heads. I think the Chinese Internet friends know what I mean. Nike China will be beaten, Nippon will fall down, but I will tell you, the Internet friends, that Chinese people will not bow their heads nor will Chinese advertising professionals bow their heads.

He sided with nationalistic discourses by calling those Internet users who expressed nationalistic sentiments his friends. By expressing his thought that Nike and Nippon would be eventually beaten he implied his ambition and his determination to win on behalf of the Chinese people. In this way, he catered to cultural and economic nationalism. As a Chinese advertising professional who owned an advertising agency, he used nationalism to get support for Chinese agencies at large. Considering that Chinese creatives created these controversial advertisements and that most of employees in foreign agencies are Chinese, he further de-legitimized these Chinese in order to support the Chinese working for Chinese agencies. He stated:

> Many Chinese with black hair and yellow skin, who eat rice and steamed buns, have done many stupid things due to worship for foreign things. I know the Nike ad was created by Chinese. I also know that the Nippon ad that downs the dragon was also created by Chinese. I also know that the ad that portrays the lions lowering their heads to Toyota cars was created by Chinese. I think these people are very stupid. They forget their mothers. They forget their fathers and forget Chinese culture.... Had Japanese and Americans created these ads, we would have no reason to criticize them, as that would at most mean they were insufficiently globalized to understand Chinese culture. Exactly because these ads were created by Chinese, I think these people do not understand the meanings of nationalism or globalization.

Ai's remarks were consistent with China's rising tide of nationalism (Lin & Galikowski, 1999). Many Chinese have been accused of being traitors and having lost their backbones so that they could not stand up against foreign aggression. Nationalism since the 1990s became both a cultural and a business strategy, precisely because Chinese advertisers and advertising professionals felt that transnational corporations had more power in controlling advertising discourses. Further, Chinese media were accused of being greedy and failing to identify the problems before the advertisements were published. As discussed before, Chinese media, CCTV included, are more likely to work with advertisers to maximize profits rather than function as strict censors because of their shared interests.

This does not necessarily mean that all Chinese advertising professionals sided with nationalism. On the contrary, many criticized nationalistic sentiments as well. For example, a founder and executive creative director of a Chinese agency remarked, "While these ads are inappropriate, Chinese are too easily offended by things that are perfectly normal.... Chinese people are too inferior and too intolerant. We have killed dragons many times" (interview with forty-two-year-old Chinese man who was executive creative director, general manager, and founder of a Chinese firm, June 12, 2005). His remarks critiqued Chinese nationalists for lack of confidence and double standards: while Chinese can criticize Chinese cultural symbols as a way of self-reflexivity, foreign criticisms are often associated with conspiracy.

Last, Chinese consumers had different responses toward controversial ads placed by Japanese companies and American companies, which reflected the experiences of these entities in the Chinese market. When Chinese Internet users discussed the Toyota and Nippon ads, they extended criticism to Japanese products and Japan in general. However, their criticism of Nike and McDonald's were limited to the two advertisers. While the Toyota and Nippon ads were rhetorically associated with Japan's invasions of China because memory of Japanese military atrocities was and still is alive, discussions about the two American brands rarely criticized American imperialism. Instead, many Chinese users supported the creativity of Nike and criticized Chinese viewers as being oversensitive.

The different responses reflect that China has different relations with the two countries: while the US-China relationship can be characterized as a love-hate relationship, China has expressed a prevalent hatred toward Japan (Gries, 2004; Li, 2009). Thus, Japanese companies

tend to be more cautious when marketing products in China. On sensitive dates that were associated with Japanese military aggression, such
as September 18 and December 9, Japanese advertisers were especially
cautious not to provoke Chinese consumers. Some even choose not to
advertise on those days. On the other hand, American companies have
more room and freedom to show their creativity and have to worry less
about offending Chinese consumers. Indeed, Chinese consumers are
more likely to openly support American products in comparison with
Japanese products.

In all four examples, the authorities intervened and ordered the
advertisements to be removed, because they were perceived as hurting
the dignity of China and Chinese people. Not all controversial foreign
advertisements lead to official bans. The following two commercials for
American fast-food brand KFC, while controversial among some consumers, also received strong support. In 2006, a KFC commercial
portrayed three high-school friends studying together for China's
annual college entrance exam, arguably the most important exam in
the country. While a boy and a girl are devoted to their schoolwork,
another boy is shown having fun, roller-skating and goofing around,
and constantly eating KFC food. Yet only the playful boy and the girl
receive college admissions from Beijing. In the end, the two friends
encourage the hard-working boy, promising to wait for him in Beijing.[92]
The commercial aims to celebrate friendship and associate KFC with
a young demographic. However, it was criticized for discouraging students from studying hard. A post appearing on Tianya, China's largest
online community, first criticized KFC for awarding success to the child
who didn't work for it. The post received more than 60,000 views within
days. Some, particularly parents, were concerned that the advertisement
would mislead high-school students. KFC voluntarily pulled the commercial in a week and resumed the campaign with a modified version,
which showed all three kids being admitted by colleges in Beijing.

Two months later, another KFC TV commercial was under fire. The commercial refers to the popular kung fu film *The Seven Swordsmen*, which portrays Taoist masters from the Heavenly Mountain area fighting against foreign invaders in the seventeenth century. In the advertisement, a Taoist master orders his followers to get out of Tianshan Mountain and put down an insurrection. While one follower does not fear death, he expresses his fear of not being able to eat cumin products in central China. And they are relieved to find that KFC offers roasted chicken peppered with cumin. Following an authoritative male voice-over announcing the KFC cumin chicken wings, three Taoist followers are shown enjoying the product, with one follower smilingly stating, "Wow, the master even knows about this."[93]

While this commercial was popular with younger audiences, older audiences were offended, arguing that KFC trivializes and disrespects Taoism. They argued that Taoist followers are vegetarians; eating meat is inappropriate. They stated that the commercial trivializes Taoist masters, who should show concern for social justice instead of roasted chicken products (Hu, 2006). Seven influential media outlets, such as the *Financial Times* and the *Xinhua News Agency*, published articles criticizing KFC for corrupting Chinese culture. However, the commercial was not banned, largely because the complaints against it rarely accused it of "having hurt the Chinese people's feelings." Instead, young consumers liked this commercial and some were reportedly attracted to buy food at KFC because of the campaign. Further, Taoism, a religious sect in China, does not have as wide an audience as cultural symbols such as the dragon and the lion. Also, as an American brand KFC does not shoulder the same burden as a Japanese brand. If a Japanese brand used the same strategy, the reactions might have been different.

China's relationship with a product's country of origin influences how controversies unfold. At the same time, Chinese citizen-consumers have long shown frustration toward China's regulatory regime as well as the unequal treatment they receive from foreign advertisers. Chinese consumers have used outlandish strategies to publicly shame foreign products, some having attracted media attention.[94]

THE BLURRING OF GEOGRAPHICAL BOUNDARIES

New communication technologies have blurred geographical boundaries and made advertisements targeting one geographical space controversial among non-target consumers in another space. Given that celebrity endorsement is a commonly used tactic in China, many such advertisements either use celebrity look-alikes or illegal images of celebrities. A related issue is that foreign advertisers using Chinese icons targeting consumers in their home markets can also cause complaints.

In 2010, Chinese lingerie firm Jealousy International Garments publicized an advertisement that depicts a Princess Diana lookalike posing in a blue bra, a tiara, necklace and knickers on the thirteenth anniversary of Diana's death. The lingerie-clad princess is holding a cello and a bow as she smiles upon a child. The slogan reads, "Feel the Romance of British Royalty, Diana Underwear." On the company's website, the underwear producer described its brand using words such as "free your mind, free your style." It also portrayed the brand's taste as "French Romantic," mixing Frenchness and Englishness. The advertisement appeared on billboards, in shop displays, and at airports. An English reporter first noticed the advertisement at the Shenzhen Airport. Several English newspapers then covered this issue. Many English online users described this advert as "outrageous," "shameless exploitation," and "low taste." Chinese newspapers and websites translated English reports and gave follow-up coverage. Many Chinese readers considered it inappropriate to exploit Princess Diana's image. Coincidentally, this underwear brand was also registered in 1997, the same year Princess Diana died in a car crash. Since then, the manufacturer has marketed this brand as one of China's top brands.

The example symbolizes a trend in China to use foreign celebrities illegally or unknowingly. Advertisers, especially small ones, utilize either lookalikes or the images of real celebrities to promote products. Politicians such as Bill Clinton and Barack Obama, businesspersons such as Bill Gates and Warren Buffett, sports stars such as David Beckham, entertainment celebrities such as Kelly Brooks and Mena Suvari are featured in advertisements for products ranging from real estate projects, smartphones, anti-impotence drugs, condoms, and other goods.[95] Even deceased celebrities can be victims. In March 2011, the late John Leighton Stuart, first president of Yenching University and former US ambassador to China in the Republican era, was used as a spokesperson for a housing block called "Consulate Mansion" in Hangzhou ("Situ Leideng," 2011, March 30). These examples not only harm the interests of foreign celebrities but also create a particular kind of imagination about Western symbols, which in turn places Chinese culture in a secondary place. Faster information flows between China and foreign countries increases the likelihood that such practices will be exposed.

While the above examples analyze how Chinese advertisers use foreign icons illegally, the following example shows how a foreign advertiser used Chinese symbols inappropriately, which potentially affects its China business. In 2008, a Citroen dealership in Spain published an advertisement in the Spanish newspaper *El País*, featuring the image of Mao Zedong with a twisted mouth, in order to advertise its annual sales championship. The tagline read, "Without doubt, we are the king. To Citroen the revolution is far from over. We will utilize our technical advantages in 2008."[96]

Chinese immigrants in Spain first noticed this advertisement and started online protests. The Chinese tabloid *Global Times* and Chinese

Internet sites gave follow-up reports. Tens of thousands of Chinese Internet users left comments on the Chinese portal Netease, expressing their outrage at the cynical use of the deceased Chinese leader (Wang, 2008, Jan. 14). Citroen's headquarters issued a written apology in the *Global Times*, obviously afraid that the controversy could affect its Chinese market, and the advertisement was immediately removed (Zhang, Wang, Li, & Liu, 2008, Jan. 14).

As digital technologies are blurring geographic boundaries, advertisements targeting one geographic location may become controversial in another. As travelers and immigrants increase around the world, inappropriate advertising messages and strategies can be quickly translated into another language, thus enabling controversies to migrate to other places. This issue poses a special challenge for global advertisers, since different localities have different views about what is considered offensive and controversial. Coordinated global strategies can offset such challenges to some extent, which suggests that using global advertising agencies can be a good idea in this case.

CONCLUSION

Advertising controversies are governed by intertwining logics of politics, commercialism, and culture. They are functions of ineffective regulations, opportunistic business culture, corrupt media practices, and changing consumer tastes, as well as conservative culture. Evolving local-global interactions, advertiser-consumer relations, and state-media relations all contribute to the rise of (deliberately or unwittingly) controversial ads. Geographical boundaries are becoming more difficult to define. Rapid flows of information across national boundaries can cause controversy to blow up among unintended audiences. Some of these bumptious infractions of taste are unintended, but others are deliberate attention-getting strategies.

Controversial advertising also results from the Chinese ad sector's particular situation: creative advertisements coexist with unsophisticated ones, and jaded consumers in large urban areas coexist (in the reach of advertising media) with unsophisticated folks in rural markets. This shows that Chinese advertisers' singular strategy centered on CCTV, aiming to reach both urban and rural markets, is often ineffective. Considering the enormous waste of advertising money, shrewder Chinese advertisers have gradually changed their strategies. As will be discussed in chapter seven, Chinese advertisers have gradually shifted from mass marketing to precise targeting by effectively using social media and other new practices.

From Mass Marketing to Participatory Advertising in the Digital Age

Advertisers in the developing universe of Chinese markets are shifting from mass marketing to more precise targeting in the digital age. This chapter focuses on three trend-setting practices, including CCTV's media auction, Unilever's branded entertainment, and Xiaomi's participatory marketing. These changes reflect how technologies shape the dynamics among advertisers, media, and consumers, and the increasing role of audiences in co-creating a brand's future.

CCTV'S COMMERCIALIZATION AND MEDIA AUCTION

Chinese media are both propaganda machines and instruments for profit, aiming to satisfy the bottom line of political demand while prioritizing the financial objective (Zhao, 1998, 2008; Wang, 2008; Zhu, 2012). They serve three different but overlapping constituencies: the party-state, the market, and the public.

CCTV was founded in 1958. It was originally called Beijing TV and was changed to CCTV in 1978. As China's only state-level TV broadcaster, CCTV now has a national penetration rate of 96 percent and reaches an audience of 1.2 billion.[97] CCTV's authoritative position—as the party-state's most important mouthpiece and the only TV station tied to the central government—is associated with political privilege, favorable policy, and advertising domination (Hong, Lu, & Zou, 2009; Zhu, 2012). Only CCTV is allowed to provide national coverage in the TV market. Other provincial and local stations can reach audiences only within their geographical jurisdiction. Even though each provincial TV station now operates a satellite channel, local protectionist policies, cumbersome administrative process, and time-consuming negotiation with individual local cable carriers for landing rights make it difficult for them to achieve national coverage. CCTV has also a natural authority. Its news programs, in particular, are viewed as representing the voice of the central government. Government policy requires all provincial stations to carry CCTV's thirty-minute *National Network News* program—as well as the commercials that come with the broadcast (Wang, 2008). Further, as a subordinate enterprise directly under China's TV regulator (the State Administration of Radio, Film and Television, or SARFT), CCTV receives favorable treatment that advances its monopoly and economic status (Zhu, 2012). Because the station's leadership and management overlap with those of SARFT, CCTV's deep involvement in policy making allows it to advance its own benefits. The CCTV empire now includes twenty-four public channels (including five foreign-language channels), forty-six digital pay channels, and a 3D experimental channel.

Politics and economy are two major drivers shaping CCTV's growth. Ying Zhu (2012) analyzes CCTV's changing journalistic practices and restructuring, and provides insight about how media professionals attempt to balance propaganda, profit, and professionalism. Zhu argues that CCTV is a model of state capitalism benefiting from China's interventionist economic and media policies. Jing Wang (2008) also argues that CCTV, as a conglomerate and the government's mouthpiece, dominates the Chinese advertising market. My analysis of the CCTV media auction coupled with its commercialization complements Zhu's and Wang's research.

CCTV MEDIA AUCTION

CCTV began auctioning its airtime in 1994 because its limited prime-time advertising slots could not satisfy demand. At that time, advertisers relied on personal relationships—often manifested in the form of paper slips and administrative orders endorsed by higher-ranking officials—to gain a CCTV spot. In 1994 CCTV had only one minute of advertising time after the *National Network News*; the advertising director Tan Xisong received twenty-six requests for this minute. Given that CCTV could only satisfy twelve clients with a five-second commercial at most, the station tried out a media auction, pre-selling airtime to the highest bidder (called "the bidding king").[98] The Shandong-based liquor brand Kongfu Yanjiu (meaning "Confucius Banquet Wine") became the first bidding king, paying 30.79 million yuan (about $3.8 million USD) for an entire year. Its commercial slogan "Drink Confucius Banquet Wine, Produce Unparalleled Essays" quickly made the little-known liquor brand a household name. The initial success prompted CCTV to expand the auction to an annual event, which usually occurs on November 18 (the pronunciation of the month and date in Chinese sounds similar to "getting rich"). Proclaimed to be the "barometer of the Chinese economy," CCTV's annual auction has attracted the attention of advertisers, media, ad agencies, and the general public. CCTV's pre-sale revenue now constitutes more than half of its total annual advertising revenue (Ding, 2005).

The increasing importance of the CCTV auction and the advertising it disseminates is also accompanied by the station's changing attitude toward advertising clients: from a condescending acceptance to an active co-pursuit of financial interests. It now produces and airs more advertising-friendly content (such as entertainment and infomercials), thus blurring the line between regular programming and advertising. CCTV has also been criticized for protecting its clients from negative coverage while exposing non-clients through its annual March 15 Evening Party program (Xiao, 2013, March 17). This annual public service program, produced by the Financial and Economic channel, has been accused of taking bribes and blackmailing advertisers. Launched in 1991, the program aims to expose enterprises' misleading and illegal practices and to celebrate socially responsible conduct. While CCTV denied the charges, Guo Zhenxi, former advertising director and director of the Financial and Economic channel, was arrested in 2014 for blackmailing (people.cn, 2014, June 17).

CCTV monopolizes the Chinese advertising market (Wang, 2008; Zhu, 2012). Its advertising revenues have increased dramatically since 1991, when television became the most important advertising medium. The station consistently takes up one-third of the TV advertising market while the combination of China's thirty-one provincial TV stations constitutes only 40 percent of the market (Zhu, 2012). While CCTV's advertising revenue in 1992 was only 100 million yuan (about $17 million USD) (Yang, 2008, March 13), it reached 27 billion yuan (about $4.3 billion USD) in 2012 (Ji, 2013, March 12). Also, its exclusive rights to national and international news and sports events, such as the Olympics, the World Cup, and the National Basketball Association games, further reinforce its privileged position.

CCTV's auction is a typical example of media commercialization. Over the years, the station has been constantly restructuring and refining the auction practices to meet the advertisers' needs. The auction has shifted from a singular event to a central mechanism through which CCTV organizes programming and marketing supported by ratings, scheduling, and other strategies (Ding, 2005). CCTV's key objective is to standardize the auction and be more responsive to advertisers' demands. It thus specifies meticulous details of the auction processes, the allocation of media resources, and implementation. While only prime-time media resources were initially auctioned and enterprises had to purchase advertising time for an entire year, the pre-sale package deals now include a wide range of resources, and the auctioned length varies: a year, half a year, quarterly, and bi-monthly. Airtime during specific events and in seasonal programs is also auctioned, such as the highly popular *New Year Evening Gala* and the documentary *A Bite of China*. At its 2014 auction, CCTV for the first time offered combo deals combining popular TV programs with online, interactive, and mobile outlets, thus maximizing the programs' economic value (Ding, 2015). While earlier auctions occurred only on the spot, offsite contracts are now included. Over the years, CCTV has changed the length of spots to ensure that medium-sized companies with less money can still participate in the auction. Consequently, CCTV offered spots of 5, 7.5, 10, 15, 20, 25, 30, and 60 seconds in various time slots. Now, its advertising times centered on three news programs—*National Network News (Xinwen Liaobo), Evening News (Wanjian Xinwen),* and *Morning News (Zhaowen Tianxia)*—only auction five-second and ten-second spots. Winners are given "free" advertising times in less competitive TV programs and on the CCTV website.

CCTV's advertising is supported by extensive promotional efforts and state policies. The *National Network News* program has consistently achieved high ratings, and the slots before and after the program are among the most expensive, precisely because other TV stations must carry CCTV's news program. In the first six months of 2014, the ratings for the program reached 11.06 percent of audience (7.2 billion views a month), four times higher than the second best-rated news program in China (Yule.sohu.com, 2014, Oct. 17). At the 2013 media auction pre-selling media for 2014, for example, the total presale of ten-second spots immediately after the *National Network News* went for 3.5 billion yuan (approximately $600 million USD) and the presale of ten- and five-second spots reached 4.1 billion yuan ("Yangshi guanggao," 2013, Nov. 19). CCTV news continues to achieve high ratings, followed by CCTV-1 (the Comprehensive channel), CCTV-4 (the Chinese Language and Culture International channel), CCTV-5 (the Sports channel), CCTV-7 (the Military and Agriculture channel), CCTV-3 (the Variety Show channel), and CCTV-2 (the Financial and Economic channel) as of June 2015. Other top programs at CCTV include *Focus, Today's Focus, Avenue of Stars,* and *Lecture Room.*[99]

The CCTV auction was based on media scarcity. Earlier advertisers on CCTV could achieve dramatic brand recognition and enhance sales. Consequently, small enterprises risked every advertising dollar to gain a CCTV spot. Because of the failure of many earlier bidding kings, however, there was a backlash, and CCTV became more committed to supporting advertisers' long-term growth (Wang, 2008). Because of the high prices of CCTV spots, the auction now becomes a grand banquet for the powerful. While medium-sized companies may participate as challengers (Huang, 2005), small enterprises are generally screened out. Table 7.1 includes information about CCTV's bidding from 1995 to 2014.[100] The following sections discuss major characteristics of CCTV bidding kings.

Table 7.1 CCTV Bidding Kings in 1995–2013 (million yuan)

Year	Company	Bidding amount	Total presale
1995	Kongfu Yan Wine	31	N/A
1996	Qinchi Wine	67	N/A
1997	Qinchi Wine	320	N/A
1998	Aiduo VCD	210	N/A
1999	Bubugao VCD	159	N/A
2000	Bubugao VCD	126	N/A
2001	Wahaha (soft drink)	22.11	N/A
2002	Wahaha (soft drink)	20.15	2,626
2003	Panda Cellphone	108.89	3,315
2004	Mengniu Milk	310	4,412
2005	P&G (consumer product)	380	5,248
2006	P&G (consumer product)	394	5,869
2007	P&G (consumer product)	420	6,796
2008	Yili Milk	378	8,028
2009	Naaisi (consumer product)	305	9,256
2010	Meng Niu Milk	203.9	10,966
2011	Meng Niu Milk	230.5	12,668
2012	Mao Tai Wine	443	14,200
2013	Jian Nan Chun Wine	609	15,881
2014	Lulu (soft drink)	over 500 (es.)	N/A

All bidding kings sell fast-moving consumer products, ranging from wine, milk, drinks, technological goods, and other products for daily use. CCTV's capacity to reach a national audience is its major attraction. Even though in large cities such as Shanghai, Guangzhou, and Shenzhen, provincial and city TV stations are its strong challengers, CCTV still has a huge attraction in inland areas. Having a CCTV spot may be more cost-efficient than placing commercials in multiple provincial or city stations. Early bidders were irrational in their intense desire for a CCTV spot, because the title of "bidding king" was so prestigious (Ding, 2005). CCTV's endorsement also helped boost wholesalers' and retailers' confidence. However, the bidders' irrational spending often led to financial disasters, and several bidding kings later encountered tremendous financial difficulties (XinhuaNet, 2012, Nov. 20). For example, even though the 1995 bidding king Kongfu Yanjiu (Confucian House Banquet Wine) became one of the top three liquor brands after CCTV aired its prime-time commercial, it experienced difficulties later and the company was sold merely for 80 million yuan (about $10 million USD) in 2004. Qinchi Wine, a small state-run company in Shandong, is an even more obvious example of irrationality. At the 1995 auction, Qinchi became the bidding king, offering 66.66 million yuan ($7.5 million USD), which was seven times its entire investment, and the final bid was about forty times CCTV's suggested starting bid, which was 1.7 million yuan. In 1996, the company offered 320 million yuan and once again gained the title of bidding king. However, the offer drastically exceeded the advertiser's ability to pay. The county government, where Qinchi was based, had to pay Qinchi's advertising expenditure using taxpayers' money. The company almost went bankrupt and faded from public attention a few years later.[101] Other bidding kings such as Aiduo VCD and Panda Cellphone also enhanced sales and name recognition only in the short term; their poor decisions led to long-term financial difficulties. These earlier failures were cautionary for Chinese companies. For example, soft-drink company Wahaha became the bidding king in 2002, offering only 20 million yuan ($2.4 million USD), much less than the amount paid by previous bidding kings. Considering the currency inflation in China in the last two decades, the amount offed by Wahaha was even less. The varying amounts of bidding kings' winning bids also reflected the fact that Chinese companies' decisionmaking was based on experience and instinct instead of systematic data. While gaining a CCTV spot might temporarily boost a company's performance, the value of the exposure has rapidly declined, as jaded consumers are now bombarded by ads. Facing a backlash since the turn of the twenty-first century, CCTV has become more aggressive in forming strategic collaborative relationships with advertisers.

Only large advertisers with financial strength now participate in CCTV auctions. Increasing advertising rates and other requirements screen out small companies. In order to attend the annual auction, a company has to pay a large deposit. In 2014, this deposit was 1.6 million yuan, with 1 million from the enterprise and 600,000 from its ad agency ("Zhongyang dianshi tai 2015," 2014). Only existing clients in good standing and advertisers who spent more than 50 million yuan on CCTV in 2014 could get the fees waived.

Also, the media auction is a unique practice in the Chinese market (Wang, 2008). Initially, multinational corporations did not know how to deal with it, since there was no systematic measurement data about its effectiveness. As China has gradually established media metrics, and CCTV is more aggressive in marketing its resources, multinational corporations have become big players. For example, Proctor and Gamble (P&G) first participated in 2003 and bid for more than 100 million yuan CCTV media resources that year (Chen, 2005). P&G became the bidding king in three consecutive years from 2005 to 2007, which corresponded to the company's effort to market products to small-town and rural markets in China. The involvement of multinational corporations improves the professional image of the CCTV auction and has further pushed CCTV to focus on media metrics and program ratings.

CCTV'S PROMOTIONS AND MEDIA RATINGS

Rating has now become a media currency for CCTV. Guo Zhenxi, who became CCTV's advertising director in 2001, played a key role in making the station more proactive in pursuing advertising money and establishing closer collaborations with advertisers. He not only aggressively promoted CCTV media resources through various channels, but also approached multinational corporations and encouraged their participation in CCTV's auctions (Guo, 2005). Rather than promoting single prime-time spots, he capitalized on CCTV brand and influence. During his time, CCTV was more aggressive in promoting its "strong brand" through conferences, seminars, trade journals, and other venues. For example, in order to promote CCTV's strategic advertising resources, in 2005 Guo published two edited books: *Pinpai Shixiao Chuanbo* (*Brand Effectiveness Communication*) and *Yingxiangli Yingxiao* (*Influence Marketing*, co-edited with leading advertising scholar Ding Junjie). *Pinpai Shixiao Chuanbo* (Guo, 2005) includes many case studies about how CCTV promoted brands' sales and recognition, with endorsements from well-known ad professionals, advertisers, and academics. *Yingxiangli Yingxiao* (Guo & Ding, 2005) celebrates Guo's "new idea" of influence marketing and promotes Quo as a scholar. CCTV has also recruited large advertisers, ad professionals, and academics as its board members and successfully created a circle that supports mutual interests.

In addition, CCTV has created annual slogans for its yearly auction. Its 2005 slogan was "Believing in the Brand's Power." The 2007 slogan was "I Am Part of 2008 China." The 2008 slogan was "New Vantage Point, New Starting Point," and the 2014 slogan was "[One] Knows the World through One Station; Landing on the One Station Is

Known by the World." These slogans highlight and celebrate CCTV's unique position and significance.

Together with the external branding effort, CCTV also carried out policies for internal transformation. CCTV began implementing a system called "the last rated program out" in 2002. If a program received two sequential warnings, either the producer would be fired or the program would be cancelled. Although CCTV claimed to use a more comprehensive evaluation mechanism for programs starting in 2011, including a program's leadership power, influence, communicative power, and professionalism, ratings still carry more than half of the weight in determining a programming's importance (Chinanews.com, 2011, Aug. 12). While journalists had room to pursue quality programming in the past, the station has been mostly driven by ratings since 1999 (Zhu, 2012). Now journalists and media producers face an increasing pressure to achieve higher ratings and are forced to forgo professionalism for profits. Facing audience fragmentation and challenges from new media, CCTV has recently promoted further integration between advertising and programming, and advertising personnel are now more involved in content production (Ding, 2015).

In addition, CCTV has pushed channel branding since 2005, further elevating ratings as a central mechanism that organizes TV contents. CCTV-controlled Yangshi Suofurui, with its shortened English name CSM, is now the dominant media research firm in China. CSM data are used to guide advertisers' media placements. While there is constant criticism that CSM data privilege CCTV, clients have no other choices. Media measurement creates more transparent standards for media buying, but it has also become a hegemonic regime dictating a TV station's programming and daily practices. For example, Liu Yannan's (2010, April 7) four-wave survey among Chinese TV practitioners in 1999–2008 finds that ratings was the single most important criterion determining TV programming, despite their claims of using "comprehensive criteria."

Recently, ratings have been increasingly scrutinized because of questionable techniques, the lack of a third-party monitor, unfair competition, and data inaccuracy. Forged data and corruption are two major issues. In August 2012, Wang Jianfeng, President of China Fengde Movie and TV Company, published multiple posts on *Sina Weibo* claiming that Xinjiang TV Station asked him to pay to elevate his show's ratings. His posts caused immediate repercussions. Newspapers such as *China Youth Daily*, *Wenhui Daily*, *Xinmin Evening*, *Beijing Youth Daily*, and *Nanfang Metropolitan News* reported the issue, and websites including *Sohu*, *Sina*, and *Tencent* provided further coverage. The revelation triggered a wave of criticism over CSM data, which were accused of being manipulative, corrupt, and serving CCTV's interests.[102] Well-known former CCTV anchor Cui Yongyuan has been widely quoted as criticizing ratings as "the origin of all evils." In response, there has been discussion about measuring a user's media ecology and holistic environment. The Chinese Public Security Bureau recently uncovered a few criminal cases concerning the falsification of ratings. In 2015, the State Administration of Press, Publications, Radio, Film, and Television punished several radio and TV stations and related entities that were involved in the falsification of ratings. It further summoned the leaders of CCTV and eight provincial TV stations (Beijing, Shangdong, Hunan, Shanghai, Tianjian, Anhui, Jiangsu and Zhenjiang) to sign a self-regulating agreement, aiming to govern the purchase and broadcasting of TV dramas and resist TV stations' tendency to value nothing but ratings. Starting in 2016, the regulating agency is expected to have a tighter control over false data in media metrics (Li, 2016, Jan. 6).

CCTV'S CHALLENGES

CCTV's hegemonic position has been challenged by provincial satellite TV channels and more than thirty foreign media companies. From

1989 to 1999, each of China's thirty-one provincial TV stations launched a satellite channel and signed landing agreements with provincial and city cable TV networks (Xiong, 2005). Later, Shenzhen TV, Xiamen TV, and Yanbian TV also established satellite channels. Attempting to differentiate from the competitors, some of the satellite TV channels have successfully established a distinctive brand. For example, Hainan Satellite TV is known for the travel and tourism programs. Anhui Satellite TV is a major broadcaster of TV dramas, which is the most watched genre and a cash cow since the 1990s (Guangergaozhi, 2004; Wang, 2008). In China, TV drama constitutes 30 percent of the total TV viewing market (Tan, 2012, Aug. 24). Jiansu Satellite TV is famous for reality TV shows. Hunan Satellite TV (HSTV) is known for entertainment and youth culture. Starting with its flagship program *Happy Camp*, a variety show debuting in July 1997, and its subsequent dating program *The Promise of Rose* (running from July 16, 1998 to Aug. 25, 2005), HSTV has attracted increasing audiences and ad revenues. Its reality TV shows have in particular branded HSTV since it first aired the influential idol show *Super Girl*. Now, shows dealing with dating, live performance, career development, survival, travel, and parent-child interactions are regularly aired at HSTV.

Recently, Chinese broadcasters are increasingly interested in purchasing global TV formats. Successful programs include *Ugly Wudi* (based on *Ugly Betty*), *If You Are the One* (based on the UK program *Take Me Out*), *China's Got Talent* (based on the *Got Talent* format), *Daddy, Where Are We Going?* (licensed from South Korea), *Voice of China* (based on *The Voice of Holland*), and *Chinese Dream Show* (licensed from BBC). Major advertisers often become "named sponsors" of these shows. For example, Unilever was behind *Ugly Wudi*, Head & Shoulders sponsored *China's Got Talent*. 99 Cold Cure supported the first season of *Daddy, Where Are We Going*, and Yili Milk sponsored the second season. Jiaduobao sponsored *Voice of China* and Yadi Electric Motorcycle sponsored the *Chinese Dream Show*.

Facing inhibiting advertising rates and media saturation, advertisers have steadily reallocated money to new platforms such as online video sites, search engines, and social media, pushing the Internet into becoming the largest advertising medium. In 2013 China's largest search engine, Baidu, replaced CCTV and became the largest advertising medium (Ji, 2013, March 12). In 2014, Internet advertising surpassed TV and it is now the largest advertising sector (iResearch, 2015). Consequently, traditional broadcasters have to restructure and collaborate with new players. Branded entertainment is an example of such collaboration in the new media environment.

BRANDED ENTERTAINMENT

Expensive media rates, consumers' evasion of advertising, and China's control over TV commercials have driven advertisers, broadcasters, and content producers to content-led solutions.[103] Product placement is a widely accepted practice in Chinese TV, film and video productions. The film and movie directors Feng Xiaogang and Zhao Baogang played a central role in popularizing this in television and film. The TV drama *Stories of the Editorial Board* (1991, directed by Zhao, with Feng as a scriptwriter) incorporated China's first product placement (Niu & Bai, 2013, Oct. 10). Zhao's TV drama series, such as *My Youthfulness* (2009), *Marriage Battle* (2010), *The Beijing Youth* (2011), and *Secret Society of Men* (2011), were criticized as being long commercials. While initially ambivalent, Feng gradually embraced product placement. His films, including *Cellphone* (2003), *A World Without Thieves* (2004), *If You Are the One II* (2010), and *Personal Tailor* (2013), were filled with commercial messages.

Most recently, Chinese ad professionals have shown an increasing interest in branded entertainment. Although "product placement" is sometimes used interchangeably with "branded entertainment," the latter suggests a closer integration between content and advertising through a deeper collaboration between producers and advertisers and their agencies. As a non-intrusive way to engage consumers, quality branded entertainment requires effective storytelling and fan participation.

Branded entertainment first appeared in China in 1993 when home appliance producer Haier created a children's cartoon called *Haier Brothers*. The show features Haier's two newly created mascots and twin brothers (one Chinese and the other European) to represent its collaboration with its German partner. Created by the Old Man of Wisdom, the twin brothers travel from their home in the Pacific Ocean to North America, the South Pole, Australia, Africa, and Europe, and finally back to their birthplace. On the road, the brothers resolve different kinds of challenges, help other people, and make friends using their wisdom and scientific knowledge. A total of 212 episodes were aired from 1993 to 2001. The show won major awards and was popular among children. Critics argue that the show, promoting Haier's global identity, adventure, and wisdom, contributed to the brand's success in the Chinese market.

Most recently, branded contents are distributed through TV broadcasters, video sites such as YouTube, Youku Toudou, and Iqiyi, and advertisers' websites, as well as mobile phones. Often called microfilms, short online branded segments range from thirty seconds to a few minutes. They predominantly use humor and entertainment to engage users. Successful videos depend on viral communication, word of mouth, and sharing. In 2010, often called "the Year of Micro-film" in China, advertisers sponsored many online short clips and professional filmmakers produced a number of them, such as *Old Boys* (featuring Chevrolet, directed by Xiao Yang), *Journal of Game Watching* (featuring Canon, directed by Jiang Wen), *The One* (called *Yi Chu Ji Fa* in Chinese, featuring Cadillac driving in Hong Kong and Shanghai, directed by graduates of the Beijing Film Academy, played by Hong Kong American actor Daniel Wu), and *Highway Number 66* (featuring Cadillac as a symbol of freedom, played by Karen Mok). Global brands such as P&G and Unilever are especially skilled in sponsoring branded contents in China. In 2009, for example, P&G invested in an online film series called *An and An Xun*, promoting a wide range of P&G products by telling romantic stories among professionals in the fashion and advertising industries.

Ugly Wudi and *Unbeatable*, both sponsored by Unilever, are typical big-productions and branded entertainments sponsored by global brands. Aired on HSTV and licensed from the Mexican TV network Televisa's *La Fea Más Bella*, *Ugly Wudi* (meaning "ugly invincible," called *Wudi* hereafter) was modeled on *Ugly Betty*. Originally based on the Colombian soap opera *Yo Soy Betty*, *Wudi* was produced by HSTV-invested Nesound International Media. It features career life, youth culture, romance, and workplace competition. *Wudi* was popular: around 240 million consumers watched Season I and the market share of the last episode of Season I reached 9.3 percent, the highest rating for HSTV in four years (Yan, 2008, Dec. 24). The average audience share of Season I was 8 to 9 percent (Zhang & Fung, 2011). Altogether, four seasons were aired from 2008 to 2010. The show enhanced Unilever product Dove's brand recognition. Unaided awareness of Dove products at the end of the first season reportedly rose 44 percent and more than tripled among viewers (Fowler, 2008, Dec. 29). The internal shipment numbers for Dove Shower Cream increased 21 percent in comparison with the same month of the previous year.

Despite *Wudi*'s success, the show was criticized for being too aggressive and too commercialized, with roughly one ad in every minute on average ("Hunan Weishi Zihui Pinpai," 2008). It was criticized for placing blunt and crude ad messages for four Unilever brands (Dove, Clear, Lipton Tea, and China Toothpaste) as well as brands of other companies.[104] While *Wudi* focuses more on Dove in later seasons, the choice of four brands was viewed as having diverted consumer attention. What is more, Dove's campaign of "real beauty" in general was only partially successful in China because Chinese women generally were and still are not much bothered by the models used to market beauty products. Even though Western feminists have praised Dove's progressive "Real Beauty campaign," launched in 2004, the message did not resonate well with Chinese women. According to Mike Bryce, Unilever's Asian regional brand development manager for Dove skin care, "a model on billboards is something [Chinese] women do aspire to, and feel is attainable" (Fowler, 2008, Dec. 29).

Unilever's partial success with *Wudi* prompted the company to sponsor *Unbeatable*, a show that was completely devoted to Clear, Unilever's hair care brand, which debuted in the Chinese market in March 2007. In contrast with *Wudi*, which had to obey the requirements of a foreign licenser, *Unbeatable* was a show made for Clear. Its Chinese name, Wu Xie Ke Ji (meaning "invincible" as well as "no dandruff") comes from Clear's advertising slogan in China. Consisting of thirty-six episodes and produced by Jiangsu Broadcasting Group, the first season of *Unbeatable* was one of the most successful branded content shows in China at the time. It won multiple marketing awards, including a silver medal for Marketing Innovation at China's Seventeenth International Advertising Festival in 2010, iResearch New Marketing Award, and Sohu's Most Innovative TV Series Award. Even though three seasons were aired on popular provincial satellite TV channels, this chapter only focuses on the first season (hereafter called *Unbeatable*).[105]

In contrast with *Wudi*, *Unbeatable* is more stylish, modern, and cosmopolitan. It is set in a French public relations agency in China. The show inserts product information more naturally and subtly into the show. Only Unilever's Clear is prominently featured in the storylines, thus allowing full portrayal and exploration of the brand to the consumers. Featuring stars from Mainland China, Hong Kong, and Taiwan, *Unbeatable*, with the subtitle *Numerous Beautiful Women*, tells a thrilling story of the newly minted college graduate Lu Xiaoxiao, who won the positon of executive creative director in a French public relations agency, with the help of some mysterious force. The show portrays business conspiracy, competition, betrayal, friendship, youth culture, and lifestyle. Lu and her friends experience heroic fighting with the Union, a large international finance company that attempts to control the Chinese PR world. In the end, Lu and her trustworthy friends win the battle. As a show for urbanites, it features highly educated women who are beautiful, independent, and fashion-conscious, and ambitious handsome men, thus fulfilling consumers' desire to know more about the life of white-collar professionals working in the global creative industry.

The show was premiered in August 2010 in prime time on Jiangsu, Anhui, Tianjin, Chongqing, and Liaoning satellite TV channels. The total average prime-time TV rating was 2.41 and its market share was 6.4 percent (Sohu, 2010, Oct. 15). It was also one of the most viewed shows on *Sohu*, with more than 100 million total views online. Internet searches of Clear after the show increased 6 to 10 times (Wang, 2011, Jan. 12). Within a week after the show was aired on TV and over the Internet, a survey found that 94 percent stated that they knew more about Clear than before (Sohu, 2010, Oct 15).

CO-CREATION AND CROSS PROMOTION OF MEDIA CONTENTS AND ADVERTISING CAMPAIGNS

Both shows used integrated marketing campaigns and cross promotions to organize fragmented audiences. They combined advertising and public relations, traditional and new media, online and offline events, and entertainment and informercials. Aired and shown on popular provincial satellite TV channels and on online video sites, the shows reached national and even global Chinese-speaking audiences. Different parties, including the advertisers, their advertising and media agencies, the producers, and the broadcasters, were involved in co-creational and cross-promotional activities so that their mutual benefits were served. Prior to launching the shows, these parties had already established cooperative relationships. For example, Unilever became the major sponsor of *Wudi* precisely because of the recommendation from its media agency Mindshare, who had already established a relationship with the production company Nesound. Mindshare not only proposed the idea of branded contents to Unilever, but also established a team—consisting of account personnel, content production, and digital media—to work with Unilever's ad agency Ogilvy & Mather, to evaluate and develop the contents (Ting, 2008). In the process of shooting, the appropriate exposure of the featured brands was looked after by the production team that designated specific personnel to communicate regularly with the advertisers to ensure their interests were being served (Zhang & Fung, 2011). While the figure was not disclosed, Unilever was estimated to have paid 150 million yuan (about $21 million USD) for product placement in *Wudi* (Yan, 2008, Dec. 24). What is more, all related parties (the producer, the broadcaster, and the advertiser as well as the ad and media agencies) launched concerted efforts to cross-promote *Wudi* because high ratings served their mutual interests. Indeed, Nesound's executive producer Zhou Heng stated in an interview that high ratings served the clients' interests, that having attractive storylines was an inherent part of the contract implementation, and that she aimed to satisfy the audiences, her company, and most important, the clients (Ting, 2008).

HSTV promoted *Wudi* through its own media resources, media interviews, teaser ads, and official website. Fans were engaged through blogs, online forums, special topics, interactive online games, sweepstakes, and other tactics. For example, the heroine Wudi opened a blog on *Sina* using her TV persona—an unprecedented practice in China—and constantly provided updated information about her experience and her challenges in the workplace. Fusing her genuine experience with the show, she constantly sought fans' input and recommendations for how to handle various issues. She also leaked information about the next episode. Other major characters also opened blogs, using their real names, and shared inside information from behind the scenes about the shooting to maintain fans' interest. To coordinate with their blogs, Dove's website also had a special section called "A Blog on Wudi's Feelings." In order to engage consumers, Dove provided biweekly awards to active participants: posters with Wudi's signature, Wudi dolls, Dove products, and the mousepad featured in the show. In addition, fans were encouraged to provide ideas for future scripts, character setups, the representation of Wudi and other characters, the background, props, product placement, music, and so on. HSTV allocated about a million yuan (about $160,000 USD) to award fans for their ideas and suggestions (Yan, 2008, Dec. 24). Furthermore, HSTV launched a large-scale campaign to choose the hero for the third season, producing several online episodes for the competition. In the end, the hero was determined by viewers' votes.

Unilever launched integrated advertising campaigns that corresponded with the shows. The company not only used different media, such as television, newspapers, magazines, the Internet, mobile, and out-of-home advertising, but also produced new ads. When the first season of *Unbeatable* was aired, for example, Unilever replaced its long-term commercial featuring Little S (Dee Hsu) with a commercial featuring the hero Peter Ho and heroine Karina Zhao. Not only were celebrities interviewed by TV stations as a promotional strategy but they also maintained regular online presences to interact with consumers.

The Internet, in particular, played a key role in promoting *Unbeatable*, with regular updates and new events to maintain the audience's interests. Although the show was webcast on six major video sites, Sohu was Unilever's main digital partner, which launched a comprehensive digital campaign. Prior to the airing of the show, Sohu

Entertainment channel published numerous reports and interviews with the production team and the movie stars. Not only did it help launch an official website (http://yule.sohu.com/s2010/wxkj/), it also released various promotions and media hype as online news. Sohu gave extensive coverage to the opening ceremony. Playing on the show's themes, Sohu started an online talk show discussing how to deal with workplace and career challenges targeting the post-1980s generation of college graduates. Career experts, TV stars in the show, and other celebrities were invited to advise consumers on how to deal with career challenges, workplace politics, romance, and other related issues. Sohu's *New Face* program regularly introduced new actors and actresses featured in the show. In addition, the site selected plots, images, and commentaries on a daily basis in addition to weekly reports on celebrities, fashion, and career advice. Sohu developed interactive games, and various forty-eight-hour challenges—to dump bad habits, quit a job in a smart way, and speak English exclusively—to maintain viewers' interests. The website also launched a range of interactive activities offering awards and sweepstakes, including iPads, and the opportunity to visit Clear's R&D headquarters in France. These activities highlighted Clear's brand name, and core values such as their emphrasis on adventure, risk-taking, youth culture, breakthroughs, and confidence. Sohu's marketing matrix and mix was widely celebrated as having contributed to the show's success.

CLOSE INTEGRATION BETWEEN MEDIA CONTENT AND ADVERTISING

A key characteristic of the two shows is the close integration between programming and advertising. Such an integration is made possible because branded entertainments often feature professionals in media, advertising, and PR firms and thus naturalize the incorporation of brands into the characters' daily work and life. What is more, media professionals are often viewed in China as possessing social, economic, and cultural capital, making them natural spokespersons for middle-class and upper-class fashion.

Product information is inserted using different tactics. First and most important, the shows portray the spirit and core values of products through the storylines. The leading characters personalize and embody the brand values. While advertising has been generally criticized as fetishizing products, branded entertainments take this one step further by more closely associating brand values with TV personas. For example, the heroine Wudi is portrayed as having an unappealing outward appearance but internal beauty: she is diligent, caring, kind-hearted, confident, upbeat, and has a positive attitude. These characteristics are said to represent Dove's core value of "real beauty." In *Unbeatable*, Clear's core values are embodied by leading male and female characters who are intelligent, upright, confident, ambitious, adventurous, and perfection-driven. In particular, the young college graduate Lu Xiaoxiao overcomes all types of challenges and impossible missions because she dares to be different, trusts in others, and is trustworthy. She possesses beauty and wisdom, and claims to "trust Clear for a lifetime." The janitor and her boyfriend, Zhuo Yuan, possesses intelligence, integrity, trust, perseverance, and a sense of justice. Lu's claim, "Zhuo Yuan, I trust you for a lifetime," also reinforces her trust in Clear. In various places, leading characters claim that "I will trust you for a lifetime [and] I will fulfill my promise." The association between their friendship/trust and the product is further buttressed by the regular presence of the Clear ads featuring Little S with the slogan, "Clear, Unbeatable, and Do What Is Promised." The values embodied by these leading characters are highly valued in China in the last two decades when individual entrepreneurship is highly promoted and consumer-citizens are expected to take care of themselves and be self-reliant in the market economy.

Furthermore, the storylines of *Unbeatable* reflect Clear's advertising journey in China. The show focuses on Clear's anti-dandruff function because Unilever's internal research found that as many as 70 percent of Chinese claim to be concerned with dandruff (Madden, 2007, April 30). Their concern is due to the fact that dandruff appears more visible on black hair and on the dark clothing that modern professionals wear. While China has more than 2,000 shampoo brands, professional anti-dandruff products constitute about 18 percent of total shampoo sales in the Chinese market. Clear faced a huge challenge, however, when it launched its anti-dandruff shampoo in 2007. Its major competitor P&G literally created the product category with its Head & Shoulders (H & S), which dominated China's shampoo market for two decades. Clear sold three versions: one for men, one for women, and another unisex version. Targeting young consumers aged between eighteen and thirty-five, Clear promised to make consumers more confident, young, sexy, and more cosmopolitan through the use of stylish and global elements such as jazz, foreign technology, and Western imagery. Unilever publicized stylish ads using Little S, a Taiwanese talk-show host, to endorse Clear's formula, which combines vitamins and minerals to restore the scalp's natural balance. In various versions of the ads and commercials, Little S. states, "if someone lies to you repeatedly, what you should do is to dump him," "While not everyone is worthy of my trust, I trust Clear for my lifetime," "Clear is my anti-dandruff partner," and "Dandruff never comes back." These commercials urge consumers to dump H & S and choose Clear, since Clear is a more trustworthy partner. *Unbeatable* constantly refers to these commercial messages and reinforces the information that H & S has repeatedly lied to consumers. In Episode 14, for instance, a leading character states, "anti-dandruff shampoo has sold in China for decades, but it has not resolved the problem. Instead, more problems have emerged, which suggests that some brand's anti-dandruff function is not realized. What else can you do if you do not dump it?" Not only is the competitor repeatedly evoked as dishonest and old-fashioned, but Clear is also recurrently and explicitly associated with trust and newness. Just as the heroine achieves breakthroughs, Clear's Frenchness and new technologies are breakthroughs. Reinforcing Clear's cosmopolitan image, the show predominantly uses white and black for costuming, which connotes modernity and fashionable style as well as Clear's celebration of black hair. This is also connected to Clear's branding strategy in general. For example, in a commercial aired across Asia, South Korean celebrity Rain states, "I like black; I trust Clear; dandruff never comes back ... Clear means no dandruff; confidence means no dandruff." Through fusing commercial messages, the storylines and TV personas, *Unbeatable* fetishizes the products and persuades consumers in a subtle way.

Because both shows feature professionals in advertising and PR firms, advertising campaigns are a natural part of their daily work. They constantly discuss the core values, functions, and benefits of products in meetings and conversations. They share their experience after using the products in the show. Logos, props, posters, and products are naturally displayed in the background, thus making it impossible for viewers to escape the commercial messages. What is more, the revelation of the branding process also gives pleasure to consumers and turns them into co-conspirators. Instead of treating consumers as passive dupes, the shows treat them as intelligent co-producers on the same level as ad professionals. The second season of *Unbeatable* even includes the launch of a branded entertainment campaign for Clear as part of the storyline, with the good side and the dark side competing to produce the best campaign.

In branded entertainments in China, the main or supporting characters are often portrayed as not only being successful in China, but also enjoying global currency through their education, travel, and business connections in the West. In *Wudi*, Du Weidong has been living and working in the United States, Lei Jiong has studied abroad, and Li Anqian travels constantly to the United States and works with foreign agencies. The inclusion of foreign elements in the shows localize the global and globalize the local, thus creating glocalized style and contents. In the first season of *Unbeatable*, the location is a French PR agency and the professionals at the agency constantly deal with foreigners and travel to other countries. In the second season of *Unbeatable*, the leading hero studied in the United States, and many characters had international connections. Branded entertainments are thus cosmopolitan glocalizing vehicles for profits.

XIAOMI'S PARTICIPATORY MARKETING

While sponsors of branded entertainment often collaborate with traditional broadcasters, Xiaomi's phenomenal success relies almost exclusively on online marketing.[106] Founded in 2010, Xiaomi is China's top smartphone brand, valued at $45 billion USD in 2015, making it the world's most valuable technology startup (Cendrowski, 2015; FRPT Research, 2015). Incorporating users' input at all stages, the company creates a distinctive participatory culture.

XIAOMI'S USER AND FAN COMMUNITY

In 2010, Xiaomi began developing MIUI, a free operating system for android phones. The user-friendly software and its appealing interface attracted half a million users before the company released its first smartphone on August 16, 2011 (Li, 2014). These early users are foundational for the company's later success. Witnessing the enthusiastic participation of these free beta-testers, Xiaomi's founder Lei Jun developed a smartphone using the slogan "born for fans" as a positioning statement to differentiate the brand from the competitors. The phone had high configurations, but sold typically at 1,999 yuan (approximately $300), much lower than major Chinese and global brands in the Chinese market.

The company can sell at cheaper prices because it only spends 1 percent of its revenue on marketing in contrast with Samsung's 5.4

percent, for example (Einhorn & Larson, 2014, June 9) and its exclusive online marketing also saves 20 to 25 percent normally paid to retailers. Not surprisingly, Xiaomi's users are price-conscious consumers, including college students, migrant workers, and lower-middle-class consumers living in third- and fourth-tier cities.

The company's name Xiaomi (small rice) connotes its humble position. Its logo represents the pinyin of the company's name "Mi" and the Chinese character "heart," connoting its care and attention to consumers. Xiaomi uses terms such as *mifen* (Mi fans), *baomihua* (Pop Mi or Pop Rice), *mifen jie* (Mi fan festivals), and *mitu* (the mascot Mi bunny) to construct a special relationship with consumers, aiming to turn users into fans and Mi family members. The company has also founded twenty flagship stores for product displays and services. Called Xiaomi Zhijia (meaning "Xiaomi family"), these stores are also important networking sites.

Incorporating users into product development and marketing is key to Xiaomi's success. The co-founder and marketing director Li Wanqiang in his book *The Sense of Participation* (2014) provides details about how Xiaomi cultivates users' participation; he asserts that the company does not sell products but participation. The management even requires the engineers and developers to constantly interact with users online. With in-house teams handling marketing events, press releases, public relations, and creative communications, Xiaomi can respond quickly to market changes and users' concerns. It is reported that the company requires customer service people to respond to consumers' online complaints within fifteen minutes.

Xiaomi uses two major types of platforms to connect with consumers. First, it has four main websites: MIUI.com (focusing on the MIUI operating system), mi.com (the official website), xiaomi.cn (Xiaomi community), and miliao.com (a social networking software similar to WeChat). These interlinking websites do cross promotions. Second, Xiaomi has corporate social media accounts on Sina Weibo and

WeChat and collaborated with other social media networks such as Qzone and Baidu Zhihu. The company's online book site (Duokan.com) and a game site (game.xiaomi.com) also help develop the consumer base. Xiaomi now has a large number of online followers. As of July 10, 2015, its Sina Weibo account has more than 4 million followers, its WeChat account has more than 6 million followers, its bulletin board system (BBS) on mi.com has more than 10 million registered users, its MIUI has 60 million users, and its Qzone has 20 million visitors (He, Sep. 18; Li, 2014). In addition, the company has 15 million users on Miliao and 1 million daily users on its BBS community (He, 2014, Sep. 18). In November 2014, Xiaomi entered a strategic relationship with China's leading Internet video company Youku Toudou to develop online content.

Xiaomi hires more than 100 employees to manage its social media sites and the Xiaomi community. Different platforms are managed differently. The Xiaomi community management is hierarchical. Users are scored and badges are awarded based on online participation, purchases, and length of use. The users are classified as board masters, core users, consultants, cool players, the talented, VIPs, same-city fans, verified users, and regular users (Li, 2014). The hierarchy is linked to privileges for product purchases and access to discounts and free goods. Users' scores and levels are also publicized, thus creating an honor system and a competitive environment. Social media platforms, however, are managed in a less hierarchical way. For example, its Weibo team, consisting of customer service managers, chief editors, designers, and software engineers, supports user-generated content, sharing, and retweeting. The Qzone's management attempts to create more corporate content resonant with youth culture. Technicians manage Baidu Zhiwu since users access the site for technical issues. The mobile platform WeChat, with its audio and video capacity, is used accordingly. Xiaomi constantly monitors consumers and engages them through interesting topics and events, open interactions, and the effort to construct a sense of family (Shih, Lin, & Luarn, 2014).

The company provides F-codes (meaning "friend codes") to active participants and employees. F-codes are prequalifications for product purchases. F-codes are useful because Xiaomi often uses flash sales to promote new products. Many of their products reportedly sell out quickly. For example, at Xiaomi's second anniversary in 2012, 100,000 smartphones sold out in six minutes. The $370 Mi Note was reportedly sold out in three minutes in January 2015 (Cendrowski, 2015).

Xiaomi also organizes and sponsors offline activities. Each month, the company organizes approximately two Pop Rice events, allowing fans to have fun, including playing games and raffles, performing talent shows, and interacting with Xiaomi managers (He, 2014, Sep. 18). Since 2012, more than sixty such events have been held in China as well as Taiwan, Hong Kong, and Singapore, with 300 to 500 attendees in each gathering ("mipop.xiaomi.cn," n/a). Its annual Grand Pop Rice ceremony in December, launched in 2012, invites core fans to visit Xiaomi's headquarters in Beijing and tour the city. Xiaomi stars, voted by online users, walk the red carpet during the ceremony. These stars are also featured in an online magazine and the company's websites. In this way, Xiaomi produces its own celebrities who endorse their products with little or no cost.

Furthermore, Xiaomi has sponsored more than 500 fan-initiated *tongcheng hui* (same-city gatherings), each attracting dozens of participants. The company provides T-shirts with the corporate logo, and discounted or free products. Fans have complete control over the arrangement of these meetings and some *tongcheng hui* even have their own banners. About 130 *tongcheng hui* directors—recruited from among core fans—work for Xiaomi as volunteers (He, 2014, Sep. 18). The Xiaomi community also targets college students and organizes *tongcheng hui* for different universities. Through these meetings, fans establish connections with each other and the company. Guo Jun, the fan-turned-BBS manager, stated that "these fans came out of the virtual community and become friends in real life," and some even found marriage partners this way.

Sharing is essential for Xiaomi's success. The Xiaomi community and its Weibo accounts include fan pictures and user-generated content. Various corporate initiatives encourage fans to share selfies, photos, and life experience, and to trade impressions. Active participation provides material rewards and cultural capital. Xiaomi is skillful in producing media excitement through warm-up activities, discounts, and sweepstakes prior to major events, which are often prefaced by teasers. Targeting low-income ambitious members of younger generations, Xiaomi also incorporates youth and pop culture in promotional materials and online content. These efforts have paid off. A report by Aowei Consulting (AVC) finds that Xiaomi's BBS community participants were predominantly born after 1985 (about 74 percent), are career starters, male (about 92 percent), and price-conscious (Fu & Xiao, 2014). They like technology and games, and live in third- and fourth-tier cities or the industrial and service segments of first- and second-tier cities. The report also finds that opinion leaders play an important role in guiding the online community, since 71 percent of users only view others' comments, without posting their own. Xiaomi's strategy to privilege opinion leaders partially controls its branding and marketing communication.

XIAOMI'S RITUALISTIC COMMUNICATION

Xiaomi stresses ritualistic communication. First, the company has a fixed time for product sales, service updates, and promotions. It updates its MIUI system every Friday. Its sales start at noon every Tuesday, corresponding to the lunch break. It has annual promotions at the company's anniversary and during major Chinese holidays. Second, Xiaomi aims to associate its products with art and spirituality, despite their low prices. The company has released new products at the 789 Art District, a dynamic art community in suburban Beijing. Its slogan "born for fans" also implies that the company aims to achieve more than mere material satisfaction. Such a legendary mission is also reinforced by various online stories regarding how the founder, Lei Jun, and the company try everything to strive for product perfection. Xiaomi even publicized online videos disassembling its phones to show that the company uses the best parts in the world. Third, Lei Jun is a charismatic iconic figure in China's neoliberal economy. Before founding Xiaomi, he was already a successful entrepreneur and a venture capitalist. His entrepreneurship is much admired in China. Xiaomi is constantly compared to Apple and Lei to Steve Jobs. Lei has attracted more than 12 million followers on Sina Weibo and the co-founder and marketing director Li Wanqiang has 6 million followers.[107] As Xiaomi's natural spokesperson, Lei constantly interacts with consumers. He not only maintains a blog but has also put up posts on *Weibo* and Facebook, soon after the company was founded (Shih, Lin, & Luarn, 2014). As a hard-working and witty entrepreneur, Lei personifies the Xiaomi brand. He has appeared in numerous media interviews and his widely circulated remark, "a pig can fly if it stands in the path of a typhoon," pays tribute to China's exponential growth in the Internet industry and e-commerce. His Chinese background makes him a hero in the country's competition with global brands.

In the era when Chinese companies compete with global brands, Chinese media and consumers have a sincere desire to support quality Chinese brands. Xiaomi takes advantage of booming Chinese e-commerce and economy. By bringing the brand and customers closer through digital platforms, Xiaomi endears itself to consumers. Even though Xiaomi is generally viewed as a budget phone, the company's ritualistic communication transcends the product's utilitarian function and appeals to Chinese consumers' patriotic emotions. By inviting audiences to co-create the brand's future through brainstorming, crowdsourcing, voting, recommending, sharing, and sneak peaking, the company makes audience engagement a major driver for its business growth.

CONCLUSION

CCTV's media auction, Unilever's branded entertainment, and Xiaomi's participatory marketing reflect a general shift in China from mass marketing to more precise targeting and consumer engagement. Traditional top-down marketing practices are gradually being complemented by campaigns that focus on users' participation and integrate programming and advertising.

New communication technologies provide cheaper distribution, flatten hierarchies, and integrate fragmented audiences. While CCTV's mass-marketing model privileges content producers and broadcasters, branded entertainment and participatory marketing value audience engagement. The shift from centralized marketing to a more decentralized strategy means that advertisers have to empower consumers by allowing them to gain cultural, symbolic, and material benefits. While users may not be fully compensated, companies cannot take their free labor for granted. These shifts also suggest that media producers and marketers now have less control over commercial messages. Instead, content co-creation is essential for advertising and marketing success. Given the convergence of media forms and the blurring line of advertising and programming, as well as user-generated and corporate-generated contents, advertisers must always consider the holistic marketing environment in launching advertising campaigns.

Conclusion and Reflection

Many interdependent factors—culture, policies, markets, and technologies—have shaped Chinese advertising and consumer culture, both directly and through the intermediary dyads, including local-global, advertiser-consumer, and state-media relations. These factors influence not only Chinese advertising practices but also ideas about what are the best and normative practices.

China's search for modernity, together with globalization, functions as a grand narrative that defines the country's ambivalent attitude toward the West and toward the country itself. Generally speaking, Western brands still have more advantages and enjoy more prestige in comparison with Chinese brands. Western ad agencies have also enjoyed more prestige than their Chinese counterparts despite the fact that their attraction is in decline as Chinese ad professionals are now more knowledgeable about the West. Western modernity not only endows Western-style capitalism with authority and status but also simultaneously promotes China's desire to revive Chinese culture as a defensive mechanism. While Chineseness has increasingly become an appealing marketing strategy through which brands connect with consumers, it is also problematic, since Chineseness may be associated with labor exploitation, corruption, and patriarchy as well.

In response, Chinese ad practitioners use different voices to address varying constituents as an opportunistic tactic to achieve symbolic and material competitiveness. It is also a strategy to produce the Foucauldian "regime of truth." Foucault (1980) pointed out,

> Each society has its regime of truth, its "general politics" of truth; that is, the types of discourse which it accepts and makes function as true: the mechanisms and instances which enable one to distinguish true and false statements, the means by which each is sanctioned; the techniques and procedures accorded value in the acquisition of truth; the status of those who are charged with saying what counts as true. (p. 131)

Ultimately, Chinese advertisers and ad practitioners use these tactics to establish legitimacy in knowledge production and discursive power when they face increasing challenges from global capital and "universal" knowledge production and distribution. Chinese advertisers and ad practitioners have to constantly shift their ground to maintain a temporary advantage. Given that no Chinese corporations or ad agencies own Chineseness, foreign corporations and ad agencies can similarly use Chinese culture and tradition, thus further undermining the shaky ground of Chineseness. Further, pervasive developmentalism and neo-liberalism narrow the differences between Chinese and foreign ad practices, thus producing a hybrid form of marketing that combines Chineseness and cosmopolitanism. Indeed, Chinese corporations have long desired to globalize their businesses and personnel, and foreign corporations and ad agencies have already localized their practices and personnel and management. Foreign and Chinese advertising practices have been converging in China.

Advertising partially mirrors the society in which it operates. The changing social and cultural values in China influence advertising practices and ideologies. In particular, the 2007–8 global recession has caused substantial discussion about the desirability of the Western model of development. While the United States in specific and the West in general have been experiencing great difficulties, China has had rapid economic growth, which greatly enhances Chinese confidence in global affairs. China's growing wealth, together with a reconsideration of Western modernity and Chinese tradition, may produce a more sophisticated understanding about the West, Western advertising practices, capitalism, consumerism, and the country itself.

This does not necessarily mean that China will resist Western-style consumerism. On the contrary, I have noticed increasing conspicuous consumption and American-style consumerism. With the emergence of a large number of billionaires and millionaires and an expanding middle class, consumption is becoming an important way to define one's identity. Many media programs, books, and magazines instruct consumers on how to acquire a "highbrow" taste; now higher educational institutions also participate in producing a new wave of "cultured" consumerism. For example, in 2010, prestigious Chinese universities such as Qinghua University, Peking University, and Fudan University opened expensive classes and training programs for the children of the nouveau riche, teaching them business management skills as well as knowledge of "elite lifestyle" skills such as golf playing, horse-riding, dressing, wine, and tea-drinking (*China Daily*, 2010, April 8). What to consume and how to consume a product thus becomes a social marker distinguishing the cultured from the nouveau riche, which may in turn be converted into economic, cultural, and social capital.

Growing wealth also enables mainland Chinese consumers to travel globally and purchase goods in Europe, the United States, Japan, and Hong Kong. Chinese consumers are likely to diversify their consumption patterns and develop more sophisticated understanding of consumer culture. Although wealthy and middle-class Chinese consumers once preferred foreign products with visible logos, now sophisticated consumers have started paying more attention to goods sold to niche markets. Generally speaking, consumers are likely to support "safe cool" consumerism (Wang, 2008): that is, they use consumption to express individuality only within acceptable collective parameters.

An increasing need for glocalized advertising does not mean that it is easy for foreign companies to appropriate Chinese cultural symbols.

Foreign advertisers have to be cautious in what cultural symbols to appropriate and how to appropriate them. An inappropriate use of Chinese cultural symbols can backfire and damage a brand's image. Japanese brands, in particular, have to exert caution, because of the repeated invocations of Japanese invasions during World War II and beyond. Misused symbols can be linked to Japan's past aggression and contemporary neomilitarism.

Most recently, increasing media outlets and the development of new technologies have caused consumer and market fragmentation in China. In response, China has formed advertising and media groups and other strategic alliances. This trend also means that the mass marketing model represented by the CCTV media auction has been challenged. New practices such as branded entertainment and participatory marketing are being exploited. Using the Internet and social media as a hub to organize production, consumption, distribution, and audience participation, these new strategies attempt to integrate traditional and new media, advertising and media content, and advertisers and consumers. Digital technologies have also challenged Chinese marketers traditionally focusing on brick-and-mortar stores. With growing influence of e-commercial giants such as Alibaba and Jingdong, the market share of conventional advertisers has been shrinking dramatically. For example, footwear brands such as Li-Ning and Anta have recently closed a large number of stores and have been forced to find digital solutions.

A major challenge in the Chinese advertising industry is corruption. Similar to the pervasive corruption in Chinese society in general, Chinese media and advertising are afflicted with illegal activities, kickbacks, under-the-table transactions, and unethical practices. Advertisers, ad agencies, and media operators are likely to bend rules because of legal loopholes and loose implementation of laws. Private arrangements between media buyers, brokers, and operators that benefit individuals but harm corporate interests are common. Corruption is not limited to Chinese companies; foreign media buyers are also involved.

For example, the chief executive officer of Chongqing-based media buyer Huayu Advertising was arrested in 2010 for kickbacks, money laundering, and prostitution. The Huayu scandal led to the questioning of two senior managers of Vivaki Exchange, the Publicis Groupe's consolidated media buying agency for Starcom MediaVest Group, ZenithOptimedia, and Solutions Digitas. Indeed, foreign media buyers in China were estimated to earn more than half of their revenue from media operators rather than the clients' budget (Madden, 2010, Sep. 20), suggesting widespread questionable practices.

Media corruption is also associated with nontransparency in China's media market. Traditionally, Chinese advertisers relied on intuition for media planning and buying. Since the 1990s, there was an increasing demand for accountability and numerical data. As a result, firms focusing on monitoring media and consumer data appeared. Multinational corporations, P&G in particular, played an important role in pushing for the development of media metrics and quantitative data in China. Advertising groups were formed to increase their negotiating power against large media groups and rapidly growing advertisers. In contrast to the fervent discussion of creativity in the past, now economies of scale and efficiency are more celebrated in the advertising industry. Consequently, many ad agencies and media firms seek capital and management transformations through public listing and mergers and acquisitions, leading to cross-ownership and a blurred line between Chineseness and foreignness. Most recently, scholars and industry practitioners have expressed fervent interest in using big data in marketing, with particular attention to the "Internet plus" rhetoric that aims to lead business practices into becoming Internet-centered.

Advertising produces culture and values. Chinese consumer culture reflects global influence and local influence, as well as regional influence from Japan, Korea, Singapore, Hong Kong, and Taiwan. Chinese advertising is becoming increasingly complex and sophisticated as an industry, a profession, and a discourse.

Appendix: A Partial List of Ad Links

CHAPTER 2

P. 43. Yanwu Radio commercial. https://www.youtube.com/watch?v=kZITm9iRj94.

P. 43. Weili Washing Machine commercial: http://www.tudou.com/listplay/1pDHrHg3lko.html.

Pp. 43–4. Apollo Tonic commercial: https://www.youtube.com/watch?v=M3xS65ZzSTE.

CHAPTER 3

P. 85. Milu Jin Liufu commercial. http://v.youku.com/v_show/id_XMTc1MzgxNDA=.html?f=1305182.

CHAPTER 4

Pp. 109–11. Ads of Chinese.com. http://www.chinasmedia.net/2016/03/three-print-ads-of-chinesecom-yearbook.html.

Pp. 111–12. Chen Li Ji. http://www.chinasmedia.net/2016/03/chen-li-ji-commercial-yearbook-of.html.

P. 113. Ao Ni: http://v.youku.com/v_show/id_XMjI2MDQ5ODE2.html. (This commercial is not discussed in the book. Featuring Chou

Yun Fat and Elena Kong Mei-yee, the commercial sells Chineseness in a particular way.)

Pp. 115–16: Ads of Meng Niu Milk. http://www.chinasmedia.net/2016/03/mengniu-milk-ads.html.

Pp. 116–17: Xinhua Insurance Commercial. http://www.chinasmedia.net/2016/03/xinhua-insurance-commercial.html.

P. 117. Zhang Mingmin: My Chinese Heart. https://www.youtube.com/watch?v=y6qOTKWpA0E.

P. 118. Commercial of Confucius Mansion Wine. http://www.chinasmedia.net/2016/03/confucius-mansion-wine-commercial.html

P. 121. Oudian Floorboard. http://v.youku.com/v_show/id_XMzYyNDg1MjEy.html. Slogan: "Oudian Color Floorboard, Romanticism from Germany."

P. 121. Captaino ads: http://www.chinasmedia.net/2016/03/captaino-ads.html.

P. 122. Eenor Western Suit commercial. http://www.chinasmedia.net/2016/03/eenor-western-suit-commercial.html.

P. 123. Voit commercial. http://www.chinasmedia.net/2016/03/voit-commercial.html.

P. 126. China Mobile called "Holding Hands." https://www.youtube.com/watch?v=3IjZxMXONq8. Also available at: http://www.chinasmedia.net/2016/03/china-mobile-commercial.html.

P. 129. China Unicom commercial. http://www.chinasmedia.net/2016/03/china-unicom-commercial.html.

P. 131. Haier ads. http://www.chinasmedia.net/2016/03/haier-ads.html.

CHAPTER 5

Li-Ning website: http://www.lining.com.

P. 134. Li Ning lights cauldron of Beijing Olympic Games. https://www.youtube.com/watch?v=uYjgC6eY00I

p. 143. Li-Ning commercial featuring a French gymnast in Paris. https:// www.youtube.com/watch?v=32YDRWZFoCQ. Also available: http:// www.chinasmedia.net/2016/03/li-ning-ad-in-paris.html.

P. 145. Li-Ning commercial about the "sports spirit." https://www. youtube.com/watch?v=rp508nWaUQc. Also available: http://www .chinasmedia.net/2016/03/li-ning-one-team-commercial.html

P. 145. Li-Ning commercial "Awake the hero in our hearts." https://www. youtube.com/watch?v=BnUQTypHdY.c. Also available: http://www. chinasmedia.net/2016/03/li-ning-hero-commercial.html.

P. 148. Li-Ning's Shaquille O'Neal "Flying Armor" shoe commercial. http://www.chinasmedia.net/2016/03/li-ning-ad-featuring-oneal. html.

Pp. 148–9. Images of Lei Feng Shoes. http://www.chinasmedia. net/2016/03/lei-feng-shoes.html.

P. 149. Images of "The War of the Red Cliff" sneaker. http://www. chinasmedia.net/2016/03/the-war-of-red-cliff-shoe.html.

P. 150. Li-Ning's commercial after the Sichuan Earthquake. https://www. youtube.com/watch?v=dlQT_vBPw7A. Also available: http://www .chinasmedia.net/2016/03/li-ning-earthquake-ad.html.

P. 151. Li-Ning's "Inner Shine" commercial. http://www.chinasmedia. net/2016/03/li-ning-inner-shine.html

P. 152. Li-Ning post-'90s commercial. https://www.youtube.com/ watch?v=VsWg2PekdRU. Also available: http://www.chinasmedia. net/2016/03/li-ning-post-90s.html.

Pp. 154–5. Adidas Beijing Olympic commercial. http://www.china smedia.net/2016/03/adidas.html.

P. 155. Nike Beijing Olympic commercial featuring Liu Xiang. http:// www.chinasmedia.net/2016/03/nike-liu-xiang.html.

P. 159. Anta commercial "Keep Going." http://www.chinasmedia. net/2016/03/anta.html.

P. 159. Anta commercial "Pride" after the Sichuan Earthquake. http:// www.chinasmedia.net/2016/03/anta-pride.html.

CHAPTER 6

P. 167. Pond commercial featuring Tang Wei (in Cantonese). http://www.chinasmedia.net/2016/03/pond-tang-wei.html.

P. 175. Japanese Brand National's controversial window display in Beijing. http://www.chinasmedia.net/2016/03/nationals-window-display.html.

Pp. 181–2. Fuyanjie commercial featuring Fu Disheng and Fujing. http://v.youku.com/v_show/id_XODg5Ng==.html?from=s7.8-1.2.

P. 182. Jieerying commercial featuring Cecilia Cheung. http://v.youku.com/v_show/id_cl00XMTk1NDk2NzY=.html.

Pp. 182–3. Heng Yuan Xiang Beijing Olympic commercial. http://www.chinasmedia.net/2016/03/heng-yuan-xiang.html.

Pp. 183–5. Naobaijin commercials. http://www.chinasmedia.net/2016/03/naobaijin.html.

P. 188–9. Controversial Toyota ads. http://www.chinasmedia.net/2016/03/toyota-ads.html.

P. 189. Controversial Nippon paint ad. http://www.chinasmedia.net/2016/03/nippon-paint-ad.html.

P. 189. Controversial Nike commercial in China (2004). https://www.youtube.com/watch?v=pE4lR-5SgqI. Also available: http://www.chinasmedia.net/2016/03/nike-chamber-of-fear.html.

P. 193. Controversial KFC commercial about China's college exam. http://v.youku.com/v_show/id_XNjM5OTM1NDg=.html.

P. 194. Controversial KFC commercial about a Taoist master. http://www.chinasmedia.net/2016/03/kfc-taoism-commercial.html.

P. 196. Citroen's controversial ad featuring Mao Zedong. http://www.chinasmedia.net/2016/03/citroen-ad.html.

Notes

1 For example, the 1898 Reform Movement, led by Confucian scholars, attempted to rejuvenate traditional Confucian thoughts and institutions for modern China. This movement lasted only 100 days. Six Confucian scholars were executed as a result. Kang Youwei and Liang Qichao, the spiritual leaders of the movement and teachers of Emperor Guang Xu, fled abroad. In 1905, China abolished the 1,300-year-old scholar examination and selection system based on Confucianism.

2 Since their first appearance in South Korea in 2004, China has established hundreds of Confucius Institutes worldwide, aiming to disseminate Chinese language and culture. Within China, hundreds of patriotic education bases were also established to educate students about history, culture, and the Communist Party.

3 China's yearly ad revenue varies depending on the reporting agency. For example, the New York-based digital ad agency eMarketer estimated Chinese ad revenue in 2012 at $46.34 billion USD (eMarketer, 2012, Oct. 1); the Chinese Advertising Association claimed in 2013 that China had already surpassed Japan with an ad revenue of $76 billion USD ("zhongguo guanggao xiehui," 2013, April 15); and a McKinsey report (Yeh & Zhang, 2013) listed China as the third largest market after the United States and Japan, with expected ad revenue reaching $70 billion USD by 2016.

4 For example, Shanghai Media Group (SMG), with total assets now worth more than $70 billion USD, consists of thirteen radio channels, fifteen television channels, fifteen paid cable channels, eight newspapers and magazines, two influential websites, and a wide range of new media businesses. The agency also sells copyrighted materials, engages in cultural investment, and owns performing theatres and Shanghai's cultural landmarks such as the Oriental Pearl Television Tower, Shanghai International Conference Center, and Shanghai Oriental Green Boat. Another major media group, the Golden Eagle Broadcasting System in Hunan, now owns television and radio channels, newspapers, magazines, and Internet businesses, in addition to a publicly listed media company.

5 See the interview with Liu Yanming. *Twenty Years of Advertising in China* (in Chinese). Dir. Hui Lusheng, Wu Baowen and Wang Jun. CD-ROM. Disc 7. Episode 17, "Zhuangji yu Ronghe." Distributed by Shanghai Hairun Yingshi Gongsi. Beijing, China: Wujing Yinxiang Chubanshe, 1999.

6 Microblogging users experienced a decline recently. In 2013, there were 281 million microblogging users and 278 million social network site users, a drop of 9.2 percent and 3.8 percent respectively in comparison to 2012 (CNNIC, 2014, Jan.).

7 Beijing, Shanghai, and Guangzhou—sometimes Shenzhen—have been commonly referred to as the first-tier cities because of their economic growth, living standards, and infrastructure development. Second-tier cities refer to provincial capitals of economically developed regions, and third-tier cities refer to capitals of inland provinces as well as some coastal cities other than provincial capitals. In December 2013, *Chinese Business News Weekly* surveyed 400 Chinese cities and identified fifteen cities as the new first-tier cities, all of which are either capitals of economically developed provinces or coastal cities; Chengdu was at the top of the list (XinhuaNet, 2013, Dec. 16).

8 A few leading firms focusing on domestic businesses included Tangshan Fine Arts Advertising Firm (the first collectively owned advertising firm), the Beijing City Advertising Art Firm (formerly called the Beijing Fine Art Firm), the Guangzhou City Advertising Firm, Tianjin City Advertising Company, and the Shanghai Advertising Decorating Company (the former Shanghai City Fine Art Firm).

9 See the interview with Wang Zhicheng and Zou Fanyang. *Twenty Years of Advertising in China* (in Chinese). Dir. Hui Lusheng, Wu Baowen and Wang Jun. CD-ROM. Disc 1. Episode 3, "Jiannan Tansuo." Distributed by Shanghai Hairun Yingshi Gongsi. Beijing, China: Wujing Yinxiang Chubanshe, 1999.

10 A full-service agency provides services such as advertising creation, production, research, and media buying, as well as public relations. In contrast, a specialized agency only focuses on certain functions. In the last few decades, public relations and media buying have gradually separated from advertising firms.

11 Conditions for the joint venture were created by a director in O&M Hong Kong Office, who fabricated a series of letters and claimed the letters were authored by managers of joint ventures with foreign investment in Shanghai. These letters complained that joint ventures in Shanghai could not find corresponding advertising firms to provide adequate services and that the situation was symptomatic of China's problematic investment environment. These letters, together with a plan to establish a joint venture, were passed

through SAC to the Chinese authorities. Since China was sanctioned by the West after the June Fourth Movement in 1989, the Chinese authorities were concerned that they could not keep foreign businesses in the country. The plan for a joint venture was thus approved. See the interview with Xiong Jinhua. *Twenty Years of Advertising in China* (in Chinese). Dir. Hui Lusheng, Wu Baowen and Wang Jun. CD-ROM. Disc 6. Episode 16 "Kaifang Niandai." Distributed by Shanghai Hairun Yingshi Gongsi. Beijing, China: Wujing Yinxiang Chubanshe, 1999.

12 For example, a 1991 award-winning commercial for Black Sesame Porridge, created by SCAA, portrays a small boy eating black sesame porridge made by a kind-hearted woman and her daughter. With sentimental music and vintage images, the ad sells the idea of a simple life and nostalgia.

13 For example, although joint ventures with foreign investment took up only 0.69 percent of all ad agencies in China in 2001, they produced 20.33 percent of China's ad revenue (Fan, 2009). The trend is continuing. For example, surveys conducted by the Academic Committee of Chinese Advertising Association in 2004 found that ad firms in 2003 had an average yearly revenue of $80,000 USD, while the average for an agency with foreign investment was approximately $5 million USD, almost sixty times larger. The surveys collected information about Chinese advertising agencies, Chinese media, and Chinese advertisers in 2004 and published them in *Modern Advertising* in 2005. The project was directed by Chen Yong, director of *Modern Advertising*, and Ding Junjie and Huang Shenming, professors at Chinese Communication University. The agency survey was published in *Modern Advertising*, 2005 (3), pp. 14–37. The media survey was published in *Modern Advertising*, 2005 (2), pp. 14–41. The survey on advertisers was published in *Modern Advertising*, 2005 (1), pp. 16–41.

In 2007, the ad revenue of the 577 foreign-invested ad firms reached approximately $1.4 billion USD, worth 6 percent of China's total advertising revenue, with each agency averaging around $3 million USD. In contrast, 3,812 collectively-owned Chinese agencies earned only $200,000 USD on average; and more than 134,000 private firms each earned around $53,000 USD on average (Fan, 2009).

14 In 1993 only Saatchi & Saatchi (ranked sixth) was on the list of the top ten firms in China, and in 1994 two foreign advertising firms were on the top ten list, in addition to one Chinese firm with foreign investment (China Advertising Yearbook of 1995, 1996, p. 60). In 1995, Saatchi & Saatchi's advertising revenue rose to number one and two foreign firms—McCann Erickson, ranked fifth, and O&M, ranked eighth—and a Chinese firm with foreign investment were on the top ten list (China Advertising Yearbook of

1996, 1997). In 1998, six foreign firms and one Chinese firm with foreign investment were on the top ten list (China Advertising Yearbook of 1999, 2000, p. 52). In 2009, six foreign advertising agencies were on the list, including JWT, Leo Burnett, Saatchi & Saatchi, McCann, Dentsu, and DDB; the four Chinese firms on the list were much smaller, and all are firms with foreign investment (China Advertising Yearbook of 2010, 2011, p. 55).

15 For example, the survey on advertising agencies conducted by the Academic Committee of Chinese Advertising Association in 2004 found that 75.9 percent of the investigated ad agencies want to expand and increase their size through purchases, mergers, and branches. See note 13.

16 WPP now owns advertising, media, and public relations agencies such as Grey, J. Walter Thompson, Saatchi & Saatchi, O&M, Hill & Knowlton, Burson-Marsteller, Young & Rubicam, ZenithOptimedia, and GroupM. Sorrell estimated that WPP has a 15 percent market share in China, with an estimated revenue of $280 million USD. It is four to five times larger than the second advertising group (Mangan, 2012, Sep. 15).

17 In December 2012, Focus Media was unlisted and purchased by Giovanna, an entity that was equally controlled by Carlyle Group, private equity fund FountainVest, and CITIC.

18 For example, Focus Media had already obtained investments from Goldman Sachs, CDH FM, United Capital Investment, 3i Group, Draper Fisher Jurveston, Capital International Private Equity, and other international investors prior to its public listing. Focus Media established an offshore holding company in the British Virgin Islands in 2003 and moved its corporate headquarters to the Cayman Islands in 2005. The Beijing-based Charm Media (formerly Charm Advertising) moved its registration location to the Cayman Islands in January 2008 before it was publicly listed in the NASDAQ stock market in 2010.

19 "Above-the-line" advertising generally refers to the four traditional advertising forms: television, newspaper, magazine, and radio. Now, Internet advertising is also included as above-the-line. Outdoor advertising was considered "below-the-line," but now it is part of above-the-line forms. Below-the-line advertising now refers to all other advertising forms, such as promotion, store displays, direct marketing, and events. Above-the-line advertising has higher profit margins. Ad agencies that conduct above-the-line advertising were paid through commissions and annual fees, but now project-based fees are more common.

20 Seventeen agencies were selected based on two criteria: a minimum of 80-million-yuan Internet advertising expenditure in 2008–2009 and being competitive in terms of growth rate, volume, and market share (Web

Professional China, 2010, May 14). Among the top 10 agencies, five were fully or partially owned by multinational advertising groups, including neo@Ogilvy and GroupM Shanghai (owned by WPP), Optimum Media Direction and Nim advertising (owned by OmniCom Group), and a joint venture between Focus Media and Dentsu. Hylink Advertising was purchased by WPP in 2005 but became independent in 2008. Focus Media owned and partially owned three other digital agencies. Even the independent ad agency Tensyn had investments from foreign venture capitals.

21 WPP purchased social media research and consulting agency CIC through its fully owned agency Kantar Media. It also purchased mobile agency Wisereach through its consolidated investment operation GroupM and communication company Tenth Avenue. The purchased firms then formed a specialized mobile marketing presence MJoule. Publicis purchased Longtuo, a Beijing-based digital marketing and e-commerce company specialized in creative, customer acquisition, marketing solutions, and measurement, making Longtuo part of Publicis-owned Razorfish network. Omnicom Group purchased China's leading digital agency NIM advertising. Aegis Group bought Beijing-based Catch Stone, a digital agency specialized in automobile and financial services, as well as the Beijing-based interactive ad agency E-link (iResearch, 2013, Jan. 4).

22 For example, Yang Peiqing, President of Chinese Advertising Association, was SAIC's former party secretary and deputy director, who had also worked in the State Council and the Personnel Ministry.

23 On January 9, 1988, the Chinese government issued "Detailed Rules about Advertising Management" (*Guanggao Guanli Tiaoli Shixing Xize*), stipulating that domestic advertisers should pay 10 percent of their advertising money to their advertising agencies as commissions while foreign advertisers should pay 15 percent. SAIC modified the rules later and required all advertisers to pay 15 percent.

24 4A represents the Association of Accredited Advertising Agencies, but Chinese advertising professionals often mistakenly view this term as representing the Association of American Advertising Agencies. Thus, a 4A firm is often treated as one with foreign background.

25 Guangzhou 4A required its member organization to be a full-service agency, with an annual gross revenue of a minimum of $2.5 million USD, which had obtained three major clients, each having billings of at least $1.3 million USD (Jing Wang, 2003). The initial preparatory meeting involved seven transnational agencies and fourteen Chinese agencies (*International advertising*, 2001, no. 11, p. 46).

26 China cancelled the "Golden Week" for International Labor Day after 2007 and now there are only two golden-week holidays.

27 See the State Council's "Cultural Industry Revival Plan" (*wenhua chanye zhenxing guihua*) passed at the Seventeenth Congress meeting in 2009 (Xinhua, 2009, Sep. 26).

28 See "The 2011 Guiding Directory for Industrial Restructuring" (chanye jiegou tiaozheng zhidao mulu) issued by China's National Development and Reform Commission. April 26, 2011. Available: http://www.china.com.cn/policy/txt/2011-04/26/content_22444177.htm

29 For example, China's National Bureau of Statistics defined the "middle class" as the group with a yearly salary of 60,000 to 500,000 yuan. A group of researchers at Chinese Academy of Social Sciences (CASS) defined "middle class" based on career, middle-range income, consumption style and taste, social status, and sociopolitical attitudes. Lu Xueyi (2003), former director of the Sociology Institute of CASS, defined the middle class as salaried workers who earn wages mainly through mental labor, have ability to earn high income, and work in good environment and conditions, have the choice to enjoy quality leisure time, and have corresponding purchasing power and some degree of control over work (pp. 8–9).

30 For example, a research team from CASS surveyed people aged between 16 and 70 in twelve provinces and special municipalities, and seventy-three districts and countries between November and December 2001. The team defined the Chinese middle class using four criteria, including professional status, income, patterns of consumption and lifestyle, and subjective identification. Around 15.9 percent of those surveyed were classified as middle class by profession, 24.6 percent were viewed as middle class by income, 35 percent were middle class by standards of consumption and lifestyle, and 46.8 percent surveyed viewed themselves as middle class. When a comprehensive index for the middle class was created, the percentage dropped to 4.1–6.0 percent. The National Bureau of Statistics in 2005 set the yearly household income of a three-member middle-class family at a range between 60,000 yuan (approximately $7,300) and 500,000 yuan (approximately $80,000); according to this criterion, only 5.04 percent of families in urban China were middle class (cited in Wang 2008).

31 For example, a study by the Chinese Academy of Social Sciences (CASS) uses occupation as the primary criterion for the newly emerging middle class, which was estimated to be 80 million (cited in Wang, 2008 and Wang, 2013).

32 Other scholars have drawn similar conclusions. For example, Tsai's (2007) study finds that private entrepreneurs, belonging to the middle class, upper

middle class, and even the rich, support current political arrangements. Chen and his co-authors (Chen & Dickson, 2010; Chen & Lu, 2010) also argue that Chinese entrepreneurs, private business people, and middle-class consumers support the current social political order and are against radical changes.

33 For example, Ogilvy & Mather, arguably the most successful Western ad agency in China, has consistently claimed itself to be "the most localized multinational agency and the most globalized Chinese agency."

34 Considering China's gradual devaluation of its currency since the 1980s and a 60 percent devaluation of the exchange rate from renminbi to the US dollar between 1993–94, the degree of the loss for Chinese state-owned ad agencies was more severe. See the interview with Wen Weiping. *Twenty Years of Advertising in China* (in Chinese). Dir. Hui Lusheng, Wu Baowen and Wang Jun. CD-ROM. Disc 7. Episode 17, "Zhuangqi yu Ronghe." Distributed by Shanghai Hairun Yingshi Gongsi. Beijing, China: Wujing Yinxiang Chubanshe, 1999.

35 While the combination of its ad revenue and media fees—totaling 257 million yuan—was still ranked eighteenth, a large chunk of money was paid to media (China Advertising Yearbook of 2003, 2004).

36 All data came from China Advertising Yearbooks.

37 For example, SAC's general manager Guo Lijuan was a representative to Shanghai City's Thirteenth Congress. She held the titles of Vice President of the Chinese Advertising Association (CAA), Deputy Director of the Advertising Agency Commission under CAA, and Vice President of Shanghai City Advertising Association, among other titles. BAC's general manager Hu Jiping is Deputy Director of the Advertising Agency Commission under CAA. GAC's general manager was also Deputy Director of the Advertising Agency Commission. CAA, as a semi-official organization, provides an important platform for networking and business opportunities given its various component committees: media (TV, radio, newspaper), ad agencies, and advertisers.

38 I attended the conference and took notes on their talks.

39 For example, in 2005, on a mixed panel consisting of multinational and Chinese advertising agencies, Wang Yonghui, creative director of a foreign agency, stated, "a good local firm has things that 'international' firms can learn from." He further remarked that international and Chinese agencies should work together and that the latter probably have more advantages in serving Chinese clients. Zhang Dingjian, a panelist from a Chinese agency, responded, "Let's applaud for the tolerant attitude of Mr. Wang." The Chinese audience applauded (Wang, Chan & Zhang, 2005, Jan. 17).

40 Some of Ye's celebratory interviews might be paid ads, considering widespread media corruption in China.

41 The survey was conducted by the Academic Committee of the Chinese Advertising Association in 2004. It was titled "Guanggao Gongsi Shengtai Diaocha Baogao" (A Survey Report on Advertising Agencies). *Modern Advertising*, 2005 (3), pp. 14–37.

42 For example, Ye designed the ad campaign for Zhen-Ao Ribonucleic Acid, a generic nutrient that claimed to have the capacity to repair human cells and lengthen life. Ye used the theme "Thirty-eight Nobel Prize winners and Zhen-Ao Ribonucleic Acid," as if thirty-eight Nobel Prize winners endorsed the product. In March 2001, China's Ministry of Health issued a circular criticizing Zhen-Ao's misleading campaign. In April 2001, the Chinese Industry and Commercial Bureau investigated Zhen-Ao and other ribonucleic acid products and ordered the advertisers to provide accurate information. However, Ye's website and other media reports continued to list the campaign as a successful marketing case until 2006.

43 In spring 2005, a series of anti-Japanese demonstrations broke out in China to protest against Japan's effort to gain a permanent seat on the United Nations Security Council, as well as against a Japanese publisher's revisionist textbook that whitewashed the Japanese history of invasion. Carrefour was boycotted because of France's careless reception of the Beijing Olympic torch in Paris.

44 See Guangdong Advertising Agency, "Yanhuang zaixian pinpai gushi." Available: http://bbs.icxo.com/viewthread.php?tid=73&extra=page%3D1, accessed March 3, 2008.

45 See,"Jin nian zhen dong yumingjie de paimai: Chinese.com jiqi qianshi jinsheng." Available http://chinait.com.cn/blogs/chinait/archive/2007/11/18/1712.aspx, accessed March 25, 2008.

46 Su Wu (143 BC–60 BC), a diplomat in the Han Dynasty of China, was imprisoned during his official trip to Xiongnu. Despite the king of Xiongnu's promise for fame and fortune, Su Wu did not betray Han China. The king thus sent him into exile in an uninhabited area in North Sea (the current Lake Baikal area). He stayed there as a shepherd for over a decade without any human company. He was finally rescued by Chinese diplomats and returned to the Han court. The term Su Wu Mu Yang (Su Wu working as a shepherd) in Chinese suggests one's integrity and loyalty even when facing the enticement of power and wealth. Guan Tianpei (1781–1841) was a famous Chinese military commander who fought against the British army in the Opium War. He was killed on Feb. 26, 1841 by the British army when defending Humen, Guangdong province.

47 These two lines come from Chinese poet Su Shi's *ci* "Chibi Huaigu" (Recalling the Past at Chi Bi). Ci was a type of poetry originating in the Tang Dynasty (618–907) and was fully developed in the Song Dynasty (960–1279). It has fixed numbers of lines and words with strict rules about tonal patterns and rhyme schemes.

48 See the interview with Liu Yanming. *Twenty Years of Advertising in China* (in Chinese). Dir. Hui Lusheng, Wu Baowen and Wang Jun. CD-ROM. Disc 3, Episode 7, "*Pinpai Zhi Lu*." Distributed by Shanghai Hairun Yingshi Gongsi. Beijing, China: Wujing Yinxiang Chubanshe, 1999.

49 See A Pei Ke Si Advertising Agency, "Cheer for China." In Mu Hong and Li Wenlong (ed). *Advertising cases: Integrated cases* (in Chinese) (Beijing: Renmin Daxue Chubanshe, 2005), p. 416.

50 *Ru shi* can be literally translated as "entering the world." It is a shortened expression of "entering the WTO."

51 See, Captaino's website at http://www.captaino.online.sh.cn/, accessed June 12, 2005. Now the website is unavailable, suggesting the instability of Chinese companies.

52 Voit is a Chinese brand created in 1996 by Hua Feng Shoes, a Chinese company in Fujian Province founded in 1993.

53 The commercial is available at: https://www.youtube.com/watch?v=3IjZxMXONq8. Accessed May 21, 2015.

54 The commercial is available at: http://www.welovead.com/cn/works/details/31dzmlsE. Accessed May 21, 2015.

55 In 2003, Li-Ning lost its first position to Nike and a year later it lost its second position to Adidas.

56 In contrast, Anta's profit was 770 million yuan (approximately $121 million USD), followed by 361°'s 596 million yuan (approximately $94 million USD), and Peak's 240 million yuan (approximately $38 million USD) (Liu, 2012, Aug. 28). Nike's global sales reached $19.01 billion USD, with profits of $1.91 billion USD, in the fiscal year ending May 2010 and Adidas's global sales in fiscal year ending December 2010 reached $16.68 billion USD, with net income of $790 million USD (Marketline Industry Profile, 2013).

57 While other brands were later founded that bore other athletes' names such as Deng Yaping, Li Xiaoshuang, and Qiaobo, no other brand can match Li-Ning's influence.

58 At that time, the West was sanctioning China after the June Fourth movement in 1989 and the Chinese government desperately needed internal and external support to maintain the legitimacy of its control. Because of this, the government's support of the Li-Ning sponsorship was a political move as well.

59 While the brand celebrates its Chinese identity, its ownership is complicated. When it was founded, the brand was part of the state-owned enterprise Jianlibao. In 1994, it became independent from Jianlibao and was privatized. The company was publicly traded in the Hong Kong stock market in 2004. In 2012, investment firms TPG Capital and GIC announced a purchase of large amounts of Li-Ning shares.

60 However, because of the pervasive counterfeit culture and China's image as an imitator rather than innovator, Li-Ning's slogan was commonly viewed as a copycat of Adidas's "Impossible is Nothing," even though Adidas began using the slogan after Li-Ning.

61 China considered the Olympics as an opportunity to kick off its new global image as a rising economic power, a modern country, an open nation, and a harmonious society.

62 Though the official figure was never disclosed, Li-Ning reportedly offered 500 million yuan (approximately $60 million USD) initially to the Beijing Olympic Committee, and later doubled it. This offer was an "extravagant gamble," considering that Li-Ning's annual sales revenue in 2006 was merely 3.2 billion yuan (approximately $400 million USD) (Li-Ning, 2007, March).

63 Adidas was reported by Chinese media as having offered $160 million USD, but the amount reported by foreign media was between $800 million and $1 billion USD (*Chinese Economy Weekly*, 2008, Sept. 8).

64 Intending to become a major innovator, Li-Ning increased research and development investment prior to the Beijing Olympics. Its performance running shoe, "Li-Ning Arch," attracted much media attention.

65 See the commercial at: http://www.tudou.com/listplay/PNDkkz-X_Qg/xxwqwzXEF94.html. Accessed Jan. 5, 2016.

66 See the commercial at: http://v.youku.com/v_show/id_XNDU0Nzk0OTY=.html. Accessed Jan. 5, 2016.

67 For example, Yang Ge, a senior Chinese advertising professional, acknowledged the creativity of the campaign but warned that inner beauty would not resonate with consumers aged between fourteen and twenty-eight who value youthfulness and are driven by fashion and materialism (Yang, 2009).

68 Lin Zhiling was a model and was also criticized as a bad choice because she was a distraction from the brand's core value of athletics. Li-Ning's campaign also corresponded with Nike's online campaign in Asia called "Nike women, be transformed" that celebrates how women can transform theselves through exercise, with animations depicting women using punching bags, jump ropes, and bikes. Nike has long targeted women consumers through their empowerment rhetoric, such as its 2005 campaigns that celebrate women's

bodies ("My butt," "My hips," "My shoulders"). In this sense, Li-Ning's campaign is not unique, despite its interesting message.

69 Another meaning of its "post-90s" campaign refers to the fact that Li-Ning was established in 1990, but this meaning was lost in the campaign.

70 Li-Ning's one-hundred-strong distributors were very scattered, with none contributing more than 10 percent to its gross revenue. In contrast, Nike and Adidas each possess two accounts that own more than 50 percent of the turnover. Its Chinese competitor Anta also controls its franchise distributors, with most working merely with Anta (Knowledge @ Wharton, 2010 Aug. 18).

71 To resolve the problem of excessive inventory and leave room for new products, Li-Ning spent about 300 million yuan (approximately $50 million USD) buying back dated products from retailers in 2011 alone, expecting to spend hundreds of millions of yuan more in the following years (Lu, 2012, Feb. 20).

72 Images of the campaign can be found here at: http://brandchannel. com/2012/08/13/london-2012-success-as-li-ning-makes-a-change-in -olympics-strategy/

73 The commercial is available at: https://www.youtube.com/watch?v=8A0 xQSZJ7yg

74 For example, one Anta commercial features athletes who are competing. It includes taglines such as "You Do Not Have His Talents;" "Is the World Fair?" "But You Have the Right to Dream;" "Let the Heartbeat Be the Promise." The background music "We are the Champaign." This is a typical inspirational commercial for Anta. The commercial is available at: https:// www.youtube.com/watch?v=_FeJV-6uq8Y

75 For example, by June 2009, while Li-Ning had more than 1,300 retail stores in Beijing and Shanghai, Anta had already opened 353 stores, suggesting that Li-Ning experiences pressures from global and other expanding Chinese brands (Huang et al., 2011).

76 Global brands used a similar strategy as well. For example, Nike increased its retail stores by 500 yearly prior to and after the Beijing Olympics, and Adidas planned to double its store numbers from 2,500 to 5,000 in 2008–2010.

77 For example, after years of collaborations with NBA and individual NBA players, Peak opened an office and a flagship store in Los Angeles in 2011. Metersbonwe's recent campaign to build its MTEE brand as a "new Chinese product" uses classic Chinese cartoon characters and images to create a fashionable "throwback" style.

78 The ten government agencies include the Propaganda Ministry, Public Security Ministry, Ministry of Supervision, the State Council's Office of Readdressing Malpractices, the Ministry of Industry and Information Technology, the Ministry of Nation Health, SARFT, the News and Publications Administration, the State Food and Drug Administration, and the State Administration of Traditional Chinese Medicine.

79 See, "Commemorating the twenty-fifth anniversary of the Chinese Consumer Association," Available at: http://video.sina.com.cn/v/b/52549792-2034 950872.html

80 For example, on September 15, 2003, SARFT published a rule called "Provisional Rules for Radio and TV Advertising" (often called the No. 17 Decree), effective since January 1, 2004. This decree, for the first time, grants SARFT executive power to administer advertising content. It prohibits any station or program from allocating more than 20 percent of its airtime each day or allocating more than nine minutes for advertising each hour during prime time (11:00–13:00 for radio and 19:00–21:00 for TV). Further, the decree bans advertisements for offensive products during breakfast (6:30–7:30), lunch (11:30–12:30), and dinner (18:30–20:00). However, broadcasters regularly violate this rule, prompting the SARFT to introduce a decree called No. 61, effective since January 1, 2010, which repeats many previous requirements. SARFT issued another decree, effective since January 2012, banning satellite TV stations from inserting ads in the middle of a TV drama during prime time (17:00–22:00). In response to these rules, broadcasters raised advertising rates to compensate for the loss of revenue.

81 For example, since September 2011, SAIC worked with the Ministry of Commerce and a few other government agencies to clean up terms such as "tegong" and "zhuangong" (meaning "specially supplied") in advertising and promotional materials. Later, the Ministry of Finance, the Bureau of State Government Offices Administration, the Legal Affairs Office under the State Council, and the Information Office under the State Council also participated in cleaning up the Internet space (General Office of the Ministry of Commerce, 2012). In 2013, a campaign was launched to ban terms such as "specialized usage," "specially produced," and "internally used" ("Guojia Gongshang Zongju," 2013, March 29). Given the privileges enjoyed by Chinese bureaucrats, products with such labeling symbolize product quality and safety.

82 For example, in 2004, more than 1,400 newspapers and magazines were closed or merged with commercial media groups and thousands of television channels were required to commercialize and thus compete for advertising money (Tong, 2012).

83 Based on the scoring system of Corruption Perception Index, the higher a score, the cleaner a country is perceived to be. A score of 100 means that a country is perceived to be very clean. China's 2014 Corruption Perception Index scored 36 based on a 100-point scale and the country was ranked 100 out of 174 countries, falling from its rank of 80 in 2013.

84 For example, China's party-state put forward confusing concepts to reconcile the relationship between socialism and market economy. At the Chinese Communist Party's Twelfth Congress in 1982, China proposed the idea of "the primary role of a planned economy with the market as supplement." In 1984 at the Third Plenary Session of the Twelfth Central Committee of the Chinese Communist Party, it proposed the notion of a "planned commodity economy based on public ownership." In 1987 at the Chinese Communist Party's Thirteenth Congress, China proposed "a unified system of centralized planning and the market."

85 See the interview with Han Wenfeng. *Twenty Years of Advertising in China* (in Chinese). Dir. Lusheng Hui, Baowen Wu and Jun Wang. CD-ROM. Disc 1, Episode 3, "Jiannan Tansuo." Distributed by Shanghai Hairun Yingshi Gongsi. Beijing, China: Wujing Yinxiang Chubanshe, 1999.

86 See the interview with Hu Guiyi. *Twenty Years of Advertising in China* (in Chinese). Dir. Lusheng Hui, Baowen Wu and Jun Wang. CD-ROM. Disc 1, Episode 3, "*Jiannan Tansuo*." Distributed by Shanghai Hairun Yingshi Gongsi. Beijing, China: Wujing Yinxiang Chubanshe, 1999.

87 The Advertising Law, effective since 1995, has only one article that protects minors, which states, "An advertisement should not harm the physical and mental health of minors and the disabled" (Article 8). The Law of the People's Republic of China on the Protection of Minors, effective since January 1, 1992, and its revised version, effective since June 1, 2007, stipulates that media should be encouraged to make products "beneficial to the healthy growth of minors" (Article 24 in the 1992 version and Article 32 in the 2007 version). They also state, "no organizations or individuals can sell, rent or disseminate media products that contain pornography, violence, killing, terror or gambling information" (Article 25 in the 1992 version and Article 34 in the 2007 version; gambling is added to the 2007 version). The updated Advertising Law, effective since September 1, 2015 provides more protection for minors. For example, any form of tobacco advertising targeting minors is prohibited (Article 22). Children less than ten years old are not allowed to be spokespersons for any products or services (Article 38). The mass media targeting minors are not allowed to carry ads of medical services, medicines, medicinal foods, medical equipment, cosmetics, liquor, and online games that are considered unhealthy to minors (Article 40). What is

more, ads targeting minors less than fourteen years old should not contain such information that will "(1) allure the parents to buy the products or services; and (2) initiate the minors to emulate behaviors in an unsafe way" (Article 40).

88 The commercial is available at: https://www.youtube.com/watch?v=vbs-wK28VMw

89 A collection of Naobaijin commercials is available: https://www.youtube.com/watch?v=wJYn1ixN3Kg

90 The Nike commercial is available at: https://www.youtube.com/watch?v=pE4lR-5SgqI

91 Ai Cheng and Zhao Yihe, "The Power of Local Advertising," 9 Dec. 2004. Organized by Chinese Advertising Net (*Zhongguo Guanggao Wang*). July 3, 2006. <http://www.cnad.com/autonews/shichang/2004121510384947907.htm>

92 The commercial is available at: http://v.youku.com/v_show/id_XNjM5OTM1NDg=.html

93 The commercial is available at: http://v.youku.com/v_show/id_XMTQ0NzA3NzAw.html

94 For example, in November 2011, Chinese Internet celebrity Luo Yonghao, with several volunteers, smashed three Siemens refrigerators in front of Siemens's Beijing headquarters because Siemens refused to recall its faulty products or admit there was a problem. In 2011, a consumer in Jiangxi Province used a cow to drag a Volvo automobile—implying that a Volvo was slower than a cow—to protest the way Volvo handled his complaint. Finally, an upset buyer in Qingdao hired a group of people to smash a Lamborghini worth $500,000 USD and webcast the event on *Sina* because the car's customer service representatives had repeatedly failed to fix his car.

95 For example, in 2003, several real estate developers claimed Bill Clinton as their spokesman (Branigan, 2010). Obama was depicted in a commercial plugging the "Blockberry Whirlwind" smartphone, intending to cause customers to confuse it with the Blackberry Storm. A developer in Xi'an displayed images of Obama, Bill Gates, and Warren Buffett on the site to promote the Ivy Garden apartment building until the authorities intervened. In a commercial for USA Selikon, an anti-impotence drug made by Beijing-based private company, David Beckham, Sean Connery, and Keanu Reeves were illegally used as endorsers. In the commercial, Beckham claimed that the drug helped him "satisfy Victoria"; Connery stated that he had told his aged friends to try "USA Selikon capsules"; and Reeves asserted that his kidneys were cleaned by the pill (Brocklebank & Sheridan, 2009).

Entertainment stars such as Kelly Brooks and Mena Suvari were portrayed on Chinese condom packets without their knowledge (Branigan, 2010).

96 I translated the tagline into English from Chinese media reports.

97 CCTV's penetration rate was 95.9 percent in 2005 (CCTV.com, N/A). China's rapid media growth means that its penetration rate may be higher now.

98 See the interview with Tan Xisong. *Twenty Years of Advertising in China* (in Chinese). Dir. Hui Lusheng, Wu Baowen and Wang Jun. CD-ROM. Disc 4. Episode 11, "Jingzheng Shidai." Distributed by Shanghai Hairun Yingshi Gongsi. Beijing, China: Wujing Yinxiang Chubanshe, 1999.

99 The information is available at: http://tv.cntv.cn/videoset/C10437. Accessed June 30, 2015.

100 CCTV media auction generally sells airtime for the following year. The following year's bidding king is determined in the previous year. For example, the bidding king of 1995 was determined in November 1994.

101 Without capacity to produce enough wine to meet the market demand, Qinchi purchased wine in the market and branded it as its own. Even though this was a widespread practice in China's winery industry, media exposure put Qinchi at the center of the scandal. Two years later, the brand went to the brink of bankruptcy and gradually faded from the market.

102 For example, *Sina* set up a special forum for this issue (http://ent.sina.com. cn/f/v/shshzj/, accessed March 1, 2014); *Sohu* published many reports on fake media metrics (http://media.sohu.com/s2012/sslzj/, accessed March 1, 2014) and *People's Daily* published articles (http://media.people.com. cn/n/2012/0822/c120837-18798816.html, accessed March 1, 2014). TV and film producer Feng Xiaogang openly questioned CSM data and the reliability (People.cn, 2014, March 7).

103 For example, in September 2009, SARFT issued an order, requiring TV broadcasters to not exceed twelve minutes of advertising time each hour. Nor can a TV drama's commercial break exceed ninety seconds each time, effective since January 1, 2010.

104 Unilever promoted four brands for various reasons. The company began marketing Clear in China in 2007 as a challenger to Head & Shoulders. In the first season, the hero Fei Denan was a spokesperson for Clear and the show associates Fei's taste, sense of fashion, and socio-economic status with the brand. In later seasons, Clear was not included in the show. Instead, only Dove was prominently featured. Lipton Tea aimed to associate with white-collar professionals. China Toothpaste was included in the third and fourth seasons after Unilever purchased the brand in 2009.

105 *Unbeatable II* was a joint production between Omnijoi Media Corporation and Beijing Shiji Boying Media. It is situated in a foreign company selling deluxe products, including Clear. *Unbeatable III* was jointly produced by Zhejiang Satellite TV and Beijing Shiji Boying Media. It targets college graduates born after the 1980s, featuring their lifestyles and career in an advertising company. However, due to China's control over seasonal shows, these three seasons are unrelated and instead feature different actors and actresses, except that the Hong Kong actress Yumiko Cheng appears in all three seasons.

106 Even though Xiaomi placed commercials during CCTV's Spring Festival Gala in 2014, it treated CCTV as secondary to online marketing, in contrast with conventional advertising practices.

107 Xiaomi's Weibo account is at: http://www.weibo.com/xiaomikeji. While Guo Jun stated that Xiaom's BBS community has only 10 million users (He, 2014, Sep. 18), Li Wanqiang stated that it has 20 million (Li, 2014). Lei Jun's Weibo account is at http://www.weibo.com/leijun and Li Wanqiang's Weibo account is at http://www.weibo.com/wanqiangli

References

Aaker, D., & Bruzzone, D. E. (1985). Causes of irritation in advertising. *Journal of Marketing*, 49(2), 47–57.

Alden, D. L., Steenkamp, J.-B. E. M., & Batra, R. (1999). Brand positioning through advertising in Asia, North America, and Europe. *Journal of Marketing*, 63, 75–87.

Anderson, B. (1991). *Imagined communities*. London: Verso.

Andrew, D. L., Carrington, B., Jackson, S. J., & Mazur, Z. (1996). Jordanscapes: A preliminary analysis of the global popular. *Sociology of Sport Journal*, 13(4), 428–57.

Appadurai, A. (1996). *Modernity at large*. Minneapolis, MN: University of Minnesota Press.

Atsmon, Y., Dixit, V. & Wu. C. (2011, April). Topping China's luxury-goods market. McKinsey & Company Insights & Publications. Retrieved from http://www.mckinsey.com/insights/marketing_sales/tapping_chinas_luxury-goods_market.

Atsmon, Y. & Magni, M. (2012, March). Meet the 2020 Chinese consumer. *McKinsey & Company*. Retrieved from http://www.mckinsey.com/insights/asia-pacific/meet_the_chinese_consumer_of_2020.

Balfour, F. (2008, May 12). Acting globally, but selling locally. *Business Week*. 4083, 51–52. Database: Business Source Complete.

Barboza, D. (2008, July 20). Western Olympic ads cheerlead for China. *New York Times*. Retrieved from http://www.nytimes.com/2008/07/20/sports/olympics/20ads.html?_r=0.

———. (2012, April 3). In China press, best coverage cash can buy. *New York Times*, Business Section. Retrieved from http://www.nytimes.com/2012/04/04/business/media/flattering-news-coverage-has-a-price-in-china.html?pagewanted=all&_r=0.

Barnes, J. H. Jr., & Dotson, M. J. (1990). An exploratory investigation into the nature of offensive television advertising. *Journal of Advertising* 19(3), 61–69.

Batra, R., Ramaswamy, V., Alden, D. L., Steenkamp, J.-B. E. M., &Ramachander, S. (2000). Effects of brand local/nonlocal origin on consumer attitudes in developing countries. *Journal of Consumer Psychology*, 9(2), 83–95.

Baudelaire, C. (1972 [1863]). The painter of modern life. *Selected writings on art and literature*. Trans. P. E. Charvet. New York: Viking.

Bauman, Z. (1995). Searching for a center that holds. In M. Featherstone, S. Lash and R. Robertson (eds.), *Global modernities*, London: Sage Publications.

Berman, M. (1982). *All that is solid melts into air*. New York: Simon and Schuster.

Bhabha, H. (1994). *The location of culture*. New York: Routledge.

Bourdieu, P. (1984). *Distinction*. Trans. Richard Nice. Cambridge, Mass.: Harvard University Press.

Branigan, T. (2010, Sep. 5). China and the cult of "celebrity" advertising. *The Guardian*. http://www.guardian.co.uk/theguardian/2010/sep/05/china-cult -celebrity-advertising.

Bremmer, I. (2011). *The end of the free market*. Location: Portfolio Trade. Cambridge, Mass.: Harvard University Press.

Brocklebank, J. & Sheridan, E. (2009, February 25). "It's the secret weapon with which I can satisfy Victoria." *Mail Online*. http://www.dailymail.co.uk/ tvshowbiz/article-1154223/Its-secret-weapon-I-satisfy-Victoria-David-Beckham-used-sell-anti-impotence-drugs-China—knowing.html.

Canclini, N. G. (1992). Cultural reconversion. In G. Yudice, J. Franco, and J. Flores (eds.), *On edge: The crisis of Latin American culture* (29–44). Minneapolis: The University of Minnesota Press.

———. (2006). Hybrid cultures, oblique powers. In M. G. Durham & D. Kellner (eds.), *Media and culture studies: Keyworks* (422–44). Malden, Mass.: Blackwell Publishing.

Castells, M. (1996a). *The rise of the network society*. Oxford, UK & Malden, Mass.: Blackwell Publishers.

———. (1996b). *The power of identity*. Oxford, UK & Malden, Mass.: Blackwell Publishers.

CCTV.com (N/A). CCTV Jian Jie. Retrieved from http://www.cctv.com/ profile/intro.html.

Ce.cn (2011, March 24). Naobaiin shenhua jixu yanyi, xiaoliang chixu shinian diyi. Retrieved from http://www.ce.cn/cysc/newmain/yc/jsxw/201103/24/ t20110324_20955759.shtml.

Cendrowski, S. (2015). Enter the dragon. *Fortune*, 171(3), 108–14.

Chan, T. S, Cui, G. & Zhou, N. (2009). Competition between foreign and domestic brands: A study of consumer purchases in China. *Journal of Global Marketing*, 22(3), 181–97.

Chen, G. (2010). *Dangdai zhongguo guanggao shi* (*History of contemporary Chinese advertising*). Beijing, China: Peking University Press.

Chen, Jiu & Dickson, B. (2010). *Allies of the state: Private entrepreneurs and democratic change in China*. Cambridge, MA: Harvard University Press.

Chen, Jie & Lu, C. (2010). Democratization and the middle class in China. *Political Research Quarterly, 64*, 705–19.

Chen, Junsong & Price, L. J. (2005). Naobaijin. Reference No. 505-107-1. Abstract available: www.ceibs.edu/faculty/research/case/images/20060626/3653.pdf.

Chen, T. (2005). Waiqi zai zhonngguo de toufang celue yinggai you zhongguo de tedian. In Z. Guo (ed.), *Pinpai shixiao chuanbo* (69–74). Beijing: Communication University of China Press.

Chen, X. (1995). *Occidentalism: A theory of counter-discourse in post-Mao China*. New York: Oxford University Press.

Cheng, H. & Chan, K. (2009). Preface. In H. Cheng and K. Chan (eds.), *Advertising and Chinese society*. Copenhagen, Demark: Copenhagen Business School Press, 13–21.

Cheng, Q., Hao, C., & Yang, C. (2008, March 13). Naobaijin shinian fengguang xia de mitian dahuang. *Chinese Private Economy Weekly*. Retrieved from http://health.sohu.com/20080313/n255695191.shtml.

Chew, M. M. (2010). Delineating the emergent global cultural dynamic of "globalization": The case of pass-off menswear in China. *Continuum: Journal of Media & Cultural Studies, 24*(4), 559–71.

China Advertising Yearbook of 1994. (1995). *Zhongguo guanggao nianjian*. Beijing, China: Xinhua Chubanshe.

China Advertising Yearbook of 1995. (1996). *Zhongguo guanggao nianjian*. Beijing, China: Xinhua Chubanshe.

China Advertising Yearbook of 1996. (1997). *Zhongguo guanggao nianjian*. Beijing, China: Xinhua Chubanshe.

China Advertising Yearbook of 1999. (2000). *Zhongguo guanggao nianjian*. Beijing, China: Xinhua Chubanshe.

China Advertising Yearbook of 2000. (2001). *Zhongguo guanggao nianjian*. Beijing, China: Xinhua Chubanshe.

China Advertising Yearbook of 2002. (2003). *Zhongguo guanggao nianjian*. Beijing, China: Xinhua Chubanshe.

China Advertising Yearbook of 2003. (2004). *Zhongguo guanggao nianjian*. Beijing, China: Xinhua Chubanshe.

China Advertising Yearbook of 2007. (2008). *Zhongguo guanggao nianjian*. Beijing, China: Xinhua Chubanshe.

China Advertising Yearbook of 2008. (2009). *Zhongguo guanggao nianjian*. Beijing, China: Xinhua Chubanshe.

China Advertising Yearbook of 2009. (2010). *Zhongguo guanggao nianjian.* Beijing, China: Xinhua Chubanshe.

China Advertising Yearbook of 2010. (2011). *Zhongguo guanggao nianjian.* Beijing, China: Xinhua Chubanshe.

China Advertising Yearbook of 2011. (2012). *Zhongguo guanggao nianjian.* Beijing, China: Xinhua Chubanshe.

China Daily (2010, April 8). Wuxi "fu er dai" peixunban 3 geyue 66.8 wan yuan. Retrieved from http://www.chinadaily.com.cn/dfpd/2010-04/08/content _9700898.htm.

"China has world's second largest advertising market" (2014, May 10). Reprint from Xinhua News. Retrieved from http://www.chinadaily.com.cn/ business/2014-05/10/content_17498099.htm.

Chinanews.com (2011, Aug. 12). Shoushi lv bu zai shi wei yi, yangshi gaige feichu lanmu mowei taotai zhi. Retrieved from http://www.chinanews.com/ yl/2011/08-12/3253041.shtml.

Chinese Economy Weekly (2008, Sept. 8). Adidas: Zhongguo dian niannei jiang da 5000 jia. Retrieved from http://intl.ce.cn/zgysj/200809/08/ t20080908_16733698.shtml.

Chong, W. L. (2002). *China's Great Proletarian Cultural Revolution.* Rowman & Littlefield.

Chow, J. (2011, May 17). China's new rich. *The Wall Street Journal.* Retrieved from http://blogs.wsj.com/scene/2011/05/17/chinas-rich-status-is-out-travel -is-in/.

Chow, R. (1998). On Chineseness as a theoretical problem. *Boundary 2,* 25(3), 1–24.

———. (2007). Afterword. *Thamyris/Intersecting,* 16, 291–94.

Chow, Y. (2009). Me and the dragon. *Inter-Asia Cultural Studies,* 10(4), 544.

Clifford, J. (1992). Traveling cultures. In L. Grossberg, C. Nelson, and P. Treichler (eds.), *Cultural studies.* London: Routledge.

CNNIC (2014, Jan.). Zhongguo hulianwang fazhan tongji baogao. Retrieved from http://www.cnnic.net/hlwfzyj/hlwxzbg/hlwtjbg/201401/P020140221 599048456830.pdf.

———. (2015, Jan.). The 35th survey report on the Internet development in China. Retrieved from http://www.cnnic.net/hlwfzyj/hlwxzbg/201502/ P020150203551802054676.pdf.

Cohen, L. (2003). *A consumers' republic.* New York: Knopf.

Croll, E. (1995). *Changing identities of Chinese women.* Hong Kong: Hong Kong University Press.

Croteau, D. and Hoynes, W. (1997). *Media/Society.* Thousand Oaks, Ca.: Pine Forge Press.

Cui, G. and Yang, X. (2009). Responses of Chinese consumers to sex appeals in international advertising. *Journal of Global Marketing*, 22, 229–45.

Da, J. (2005, Oct.). Zhuanye daohang, Li Ning chaoyue. *Shichang yu Xiaoshou*, 29, 60–66.

Damn Digital (2011, Dec. 19). Hudong Zhongguo: "2011 nian zuishou huanying shuzi meijie dailishang" piao xuan huodong. Retrieved from http://www.damndigital.com/archives/18998.

Davis, D. (2000). Introduction. In D. Davis (ed.), *The consumer revolution in China* (1–22). Berkeley: University of California Press.

———. (2005). Urban consumer culture. *The Chinese Quarterly*, 183, 692–709.

De Certeau, M. (1984). *The practice of everyday life*. Berkeley: University of California Press.

de Kloet, J. (2007). Cosmopatriot contaminations. *Thamyris/Intersecting*, 16, 133–54.

de Kloet, J. & Jurriens, E. (2007). Introduction: Cosmopatriots. *Thamyris/Intersecting*, 16, 9–18.

Dikotter, F. (1996). Culture, "race" and nation: The formation of national identity in twentieth century China. *Journal of International Affairs [online]*, 49(2), 590–605.

Ding, J. (2005). Yangshi zhaobiao beihou you shenme (What is behind CCTV media auction). In Z. Guo (ed.), *Pinpai shixiao chuanbo (Brand effectiveness communication)* (218–20). Beijing: Communication University of China Press.

———. (2015). Yangshi zhaobiao bianhua yu chuanmei guanggaoye qushi sikao. *Shenping Shijie. Guangao Ren (Admen Culture)*, January, 39–40.

Dirlik, A. (1996). The global in the local. In R. Wilson and W. Dissanayake (eds.), *Global/Local* (21–45). Durham, N.C.: Duke University Press.

———. (2002). Modernity as history: Post-revolutionary China, globalization and the question of modernity. *Social History*, 27 (1), 16–39.

Doctoroff, T. (2012). *What Chinese want: Culture, communism, and China's modern consumer*. New York: Palgrave Macmillan.

Dongnan Satellite TV (2013, Nov. 27). Host: Yuan Min. Aipin Dajiangtang (*Biz Talk*). Retrieved from http://www.yemaozhong.com/meitizhuanfang/2013_1127/589.html.

Dorfman, A. & Mattelart, A. (1984). *How to read Donald Duck: Imperialist ideology in the Disney comic* (2nd ed.). International General.

Dou, H. (2012, Oct. 13). Baiwei zhongguo fuhao zong zichan suoshui 7%. *news.youth.cn*. Retrieved from http://news.youth.cn/gn/201210/t20121013_2506978.htm.

Duara, P. (1993). De-constructing the Chinese nation. *The Australian Journal of Chinese Affairs*, July 30, 1–26.

———. (1997). Transnationalism and the predicament of sovereignty: China, 1900–1945. *The American Historical Review*, 102(4), 1030–51.

Eckhardt, G. M. (2005). Local branding in a foreign product category in an emerging market. *Journal of International Marketing*, 13(4), 57–79.

Einhorn, B. & Larson, C. (2014, June 9). *Bloomberg Businessweek*, 4382, 54–60.

eMarketer (2012, Oct. 1). Asia-Pacific poised to dominate North America as world's top ad market. Retrieved from http://www.emarketer.com/newsroom/index.php/asiapacific-poised-dominate-north-america-worlds-top-ad-market-comprehensive-edition-emarketer-global-media-intelligence-report/.

Fam, K.-S., Waller, D. & Yang, Z. (2009). Addressing the advertising of controversial products in China. *Journal of Business Ethics* 88, 43–58.

Fan, L. (2009). *Zhongguo guanggao 30 nian quan shuju (Complete data of Chinese advertising for 30 Years)*. Beijing, China: Zhongguo Shichang Chubanshe.

Featherstone, M. (1991). *Consumer culture and postmodernism*. London: Sage Publications.

Fejes, F. (1981). Media imperialism. *Media, Culture and Society*, 3, 281–9.

Fiddes, K. (1994, Dec. 8). Distribution, the ultimate market testing ground. *South China Morning Post* (Hong Kong), Chinese Business Review section, 6.

Finance.qq.com (2010, April 1). Guojia tongjiju gongbu quanguo baojian shipin xiaoshou paihangbang. Retrieved from http://finance.qq.com/a/20100401/005493.htm.

Fitzsimmons, E. (2008, May 16). Ban exposes China's ad censorship anomalies *Campaign* (UK), 19, 17.

"Focus Media to merge with Target Media" (2006, Jan. 6). Press Release. Retrieved from http://www.carlyle.com/news-room/news-release-archive/focus-media-merge-target-media-strengthening-its-position-out-home-audiovi.

Forney, M., Fonda, D. & Gough, N. (2004, Oct. 24). Marketing: How Nike figured out China, *Time Magazine*. Retrieved from http://www.time.com/time/magazine/article/0,9171,995462,00.html.

Foucault, M. (1978). *The history of sexuality*. Trans. Robert Hurley. New York: Random House.

———. (1980). *Knowledge/power: Selected interviews and other writings, 1972–1977*. Ed. and trans. Colin Gordin. New York: Pantheon.

Fowler, G. A. (2008, Dec. 29). Unilever to launch "Ugly Betty" remake in China. *The Wall Street Journal*, Business News.

Fox, R. W. & Lears, T. J. J. (eds.). (1983). *The culture of consumption: Critical essays in American History, 1880–1980*. New York: Pantheon Books.

Frisby, D. (1985). *Fragments of modernity*. Cambridge: Polity Press.

Frith, K. & Yang, F. (2009). Transnational cultural flows: An analysis of women's magazines in China. *Chinese Journal of Communication*, 2(2), 158–73.

FRPT Research (2015, Jan. 4). Xiaomi raises US$1.1-billion. *Software Industry Snapshot*, 1–2.

Fu, D. & Xiao, J. (2014). Xiaomi luntan fensi yunying shendu fenxi zhiyi. AVC Consulting. Available: http://wenku.baidu.com/view/358f3ca9fab069dc512 20131.html?re=view.

Gallup Organization (2001, June). Shichang xianzhuang yu xiaofei zhe fenceng yanjiu. Retrieved from http://doc.mbalib.com/view/e2277a6f67bc613eb0a29 267aa6d6cbb.html.

Gao, Z. (2007). An in-depth examination of China's advertising regulation system. *Asian Pacific Journal of Marketing and Logistics*, 19(2), 307–23.

———. (2008). Controlling deceptive advertising in China: An overview. *Journal of Public Policy & Marketing*, 27(2), 165–77.

Gellner, E. (1983). *Nations and nationalism*. Ithaca: Cornell University Press.

General Office of the Ministry of Commerce (2012, Oct. 12). Shangwubu ban gong ting guanyu jizhong qingli zhengdun liyong hulianwang xiaoshou lanyong "tegong", "zhuangong" deng biaoshi jiulei shuangpin de tongzhi. *Shanban Yunhan*, No. 1047.

Ger, G. & Belk, R. W. (1996). I'd like to buy the world a coke: Consumption-scapes of the "less affluent" world. *Journal of Consumer Policy*, 19, 271–304.

Gerth, K. (2003). *China made: Consumer culture and the creation of the nation*. Cambridge and London: Harvard University Press.

Giddens, A. (1990). *The consequences of modernity*. Cambridge: Polity Press.

———. (1991). *Modernity and self-identity*. Palo Alto, Ca.: Stanford University Press.

———. (1999, April 11). Comment: the 1999 Reith lecture. New world without end, *Observer*.

Gillette, M. B. (2000). *Between Mecca and Beijing: Modernization and consumption among Urban Chinese Muslims*. Palo Alto, Ca.: Stanford University Press.

Gilroy, P. (1993). *The black Atlantic: Modernity and double consciousness*. Cambridge, Mass.: Harvard University Press.

Goman, C. (2015). Cosmopolitanism born of trauma: Case studies of the South African Truth and Reconciliation Commission and the Rwandan Gacaca. Unpublished manuscript.

Gries, P. H. (2004). *China's new nationalism: Pride, politics, and diplomacy*. Berkeley: University of California Press.

Guangergaozhi (2004). 2004 nian quanguo shoushi xingwei ji shoushi shichang jingzheng geju fenxi (Analysis of reception behaviors and rating market in China in 200). Retrieved from http: www.cctv.com/download/04fenxi.doc.

Guillain, R. (1957). *The blue ants: 600 million Chinese under the red flag.* London: Secker & Warburg.

Guo, Z. (2005) (ed). *Pinpai shixiao chuanbo.* Beijing: Communication University of China Press.

Guo, Z. & Ding, J. (2005) (eds.). *Yingxiangli yingxiao (Influence marketing).* Beijing: Communication University of China Press.

Guojia Gongshang Zongju Guanggao Jiandu Guanlisi (2013, March 29). Guanyu yanjin zhongyang he guojia jiguan shiyong "tegong" "zhuangong" deng biaoshi de tongzhi. Retrieved from http://www.saic.gov.cn/zwgk/zyfb/lhfw/lhfw/ggjdgls/201303/t20130329_134274.html.

Guppy, D. (2008, Aug. 12) Can Li-Ning keep its Olympic glow? *CNBC.* Retrieved from http://www.cnbc.com/id/26147505/Can_Li_Ning_Keep_Its_Olympic_Glow.

"Half of China's urbanites to become middle class by 2023: report" (2011, Aug. 5). Consulate General of the People's Republic of China in Chicago. Retrieved from http://www.chinaconsulatechicago.org/eng/xw/t846014.htm.

Harvey, D. (1989). *The condition of postmodernity.* Oxford: Basil Blackwell.

———. (2005). *A brief history of neoliberalism.* New York: Oxford University Press.

He, B. & Guo, Y. (2000). *Nationalism, national identity and democratization in China.* Aldershot, Brooksfield: Ashgate.

He, Jia & Lu, Taibong (2004). *Zhongguo yingxiao 25 nian 1979–2003.* Beijing, China: Huaxia chubanshe.

He, Jun (2012, Jan. 19). Guojia tongjiju yinggai fangqi "tuoniao zhengce." *China in Perspective.* Retrieved from http://www.chinainperspective.com/ArtShow.aspx?AID=13771.

He, Yu (2014, Sep. 18). Xiaomi de fensi yingxiao xue. *Shangye Gushi,* 22–3.

Held, D. & McGrew, A. (2000) (ed.). *The global transformations reader: An introduction to the Globalization debate.* Cambridge: Polity Press.

Held, D., McGrew, A. G., Goldblatt, D., & Perraton, J. (1999). *Global transformations: Politics, economics and culture.* Cambridge: Polity Press.

Holt, D. B. (2004). *How brands become icons: The principles of cultural branding.* Cambridge, Mass.: Harvard Business Press.

Hong, Ji. (2005). *Advertising appeals and gender images in "Shishang," "Cosmopolitan," "Shishang," and "Esquire."* Ph.D dissertation, Ohio University.

Hong, Junhao, Lu, Y. & Zou, W. (2009). CCTV in the reform years. In Y. Zhu and C. Berry (eds), *TV China* (40–55). Indiana University Press.

Hu, A. (2004). *Zhongguo Zhanlue Gouxiang (Thoughts on Chinese strategy).* Foreword. Jiangsu: Zhengjia Renmin Chubanshe.

Hu, J. (2006, July 13). Kendeji Guanggao egao qijian gushi (KFC ad parodied the Seven Sword). http://news.xinhuanet.com/society/2006-07/13/content _4824661.htm.

Hu, Shen (2012, Dec. 10). China's Gini Index at 0.61, University Report Says. *Caixin Magazine*. Retrieved from http://english.caixin.com/2012-12-10/ 100470648.html.

Hu, Shuli (2013, Jan. 1). Zhongguo meiti zuida de beiai shi youchang xinwen yu chenmo. *Sohu Finance and Economics*. Retrieved from http://business.sohu. com/20130106/n362555439.shtml.

Huang, S. (2005). Qiye toubiao jinru gequ suoxu shidai. In Z. Guo (ed.), *Pinpai shixiao chuanbo* (214–217). Beijing: Communication University of China Press.

Huang, S., Zhou, Y., Qi, T. & Wang, Y. (2003, Aug.). *Zhongguo chuanmei shichang da bianju*. Beijing, China: Zhongxin Chubanshe.

Huang, S. et al. (2011). *Zhongguo guanggao zhu yingxiao chuanbo qushi baogao (Report on the promotion trend of China's advertisers)*, V.6. Beijing China: Social Sciences Academy Press.

Huang, W. & Wilkes, A. (2011). Analysis of China's overseas investment policies. Working Paper 79. *Center for International Forestry Research*. Retrieved from www.cifor.org.

Huang, Y., Lowry, T. D. (2012, April). An analysis of nudity in Chinese magazine advertising. *Sex Roles*, 66(7/8), 440–52.

Hughes, C. R. (2006). *Chinese nationalism in the global era*. London & New York: Routledge.

Huhmann, B. A. and Mott-Stenerson, B. (2008, Sep.). Controversial advertisement executions and involvement on elaborative processing and comprehension. *Journal of Marketing Communications*, 14(4), 293–313.

Hui, L., Wu, B., & Wang, J. (1999). Zhongguo Guangao Ershi Nian (*Twenty Years of Advertising in China*) [CD-ROM]. Disc 1. Episode 2, "Dapo Jianbing." Distributed by Shanghai Hairun Yingshi Gongsi. Beijing, China: Wujing Yinxiang Chubanshe.

Humphreys, P. (1996) *Mass media and media policy in Western Europe*. Manchester: Manchester University Press.

Hunan Weishi Zihui Pinpai (2008). *Guangao Daguan*, Zonghe ban. 11, 95–6.

iResearch (2012, Jan. 13). 2011 nian zhongguo wangluo guanggao shichang guimo da 511.9 yi yuan. Retrieved from http://www.iresearch.com.cn/View/ 161457.html.

———. (2013, Jan. 4). 2012 nian zhongguo wangluo guanggao hangye wu da pandian. Retrieved from http://a.iresearch.cn/new/20130104/190461.shtml.

———. (2015). Zhongguo wangluo guanggao hangye niandu jiance baogao jianban. Retrieved from http://doc.mbalib.com/view/c01c914269d2211b

539a80230514ec29.html. Also available at http://www.iyunying.org/seo/sjfx/12636.html.

————. (2015, March 2). 2014 niandu zhongguo hulianwang jingji shuju fabu. Retrieved from http://www.iresearch.com.cn/view/247017.html.

Jameson, F. (1993). Interviewed by Sara Danius and Stefan Jonsson. *Res Publica* 24, Dec.

Jhally, S. (1987). *The codes of advertising: Fetishism and the political economy of meaning in the consumer society*. New York: St. Martin's.

Ji, Y. (2013, March 12). Baidu guanggao shouru youwang chaoguo yangshi. Reprint: *Zhongguo Qiye Jia*. Retrieved from http://finance.sina.com.cn/chanjing/gsnews/20130312/135714804028.shtml.

Johansson, P. (1997). *Chinese women and consumer culture*. Institute of Oriental Languages, Stockholm University.

Jung, S. & Li, H. (2014). Global production, circulation, and consumption of Gangnam Style. *International Journal of Communication* [Online], 8, 2790–810.

Kant, I. (1795; 1996). Toward perpetual peace. *Practical philosophy*, 8, 836.

Katsanis, L. P. (1994). Do unmentionable products still exist? An empirical investigation, *Journal of Product & Brand Management*, 3(4), 5–14.

Kaviraj, S. (1992). The imaginary institution of India. In P. Chatterjee and G. Pandley (eds.), *Subaltern studies VII: Writings on South Asian history and society*. New York: Oxford University Press.

Kelsky, K. (1996). Flirting with the Foreign: Interracial Sex in Japan's "International" Age. In R. Wilson and W. Dissanayake (eds.), *Global/local: Cultural production and the transnational imaginary* (173–92). Durham and London: Duke University Press.

Klein, J. G., Ettenson, R., & Morris, M. D. (1998), The animosity model of foreign product purchase: an empirical test in the People's Republic of China, *Journal of Marketing*, 62, 89–100.

Kleingeld, P. & Brown, E. (2011, Spring). Cosmopolitanism. In Edward N. Zalta (ed.), *The Stanford Encyclopedia of Philosophy*. Retrieved from http://plato.stanford.edu/archives/spr2011/entries/cosmopolitanism/.

Knowledge @ Wharton (2010, Aug. 18). A run for their money: Li-Ning's new branding takes on Nike and Adidas in China. The Wharton Business School, University of Pennsylvania. Retrieved from http://www.knowledgeatwharton.com.cn/index.cfm?fa=viewArticle&Articleid=2278&languageid=1.

Kraidy, M. (2002). Hybridity in cultural globalization. *Communication Theory*, 12(3), 316–39.

Landis, D. (1985, Nov. 4). The China syndrome: Lyric Hughes learns how to sell. *Ad Week*. Accessed through LexisNexis.

Leach, W. (1993). *Land of desire*. New York: Pantheon.

Lears, J. (1994). *Fables of abundance: A cultural history of advertising in America*. New York: Basic Books.

Leibenluft, J. (2007, July 25). Female weightlifters, Spanish basketball stars, and Kim Jong-il: The strange world of Chinese sneaker endorsements. *Slate*. Retrieved from http://www.slate.com/articles/sports/sports_nut/2007/07/female_weightlifters_spanish_basketball_stars_and_kim_jongil.html.

Leng, X. & Zhang, M. (2011). Shanzhai as a weak brand in contemporary China marketing. *International Journal Of China Marketing*, 1(2), 81–94.

Leung, H. H.-S. (2007). Let's love Hong Kong: A queer look at cosmopatriotism. *Thamyris/Intersecting*, 16, 21–40.

Levenson, J. (1969). *Modern China and its Confucian fate*. Berkeley: University of California Press.

Li, H. (2008). Branding Chinese products: Between nationalism and transnationalism. *International Journal of Communication*, 2, 1125–163.

———. (2009). Marketing Japanese products in the context of Chinese nationalism. *Critical Studies in Media Communication*, 26(5), 435–56.

———. (2011). The gendered performance at the Beijing Olympics: The construction of Olympic misses and cheerleaders. *Communication Theory*, 2011 (21), 368–91.

Li, L. (2008, March 16). Zhang Baizhi daiyan "jieeryin" guanggao re fei yi (Controversy caused by Zhang Baizhi as a Spokesperson for Jieeryin). *Fazhi Daily*. Retrieved from http://news.xinhuanet.com/legal/2008-03/16/content_7800027.htm.

Li, Wanqiang (2014). *Can yu gan: Xiaomi koubei yingxiao neibu shouce*. Beijing: Zhongxin Chuban She.

Li, Y. (2016, Jan. 6). 2016 yinshi jianguan jiang chu naxie xin zhao. Zhongguo Xinwen Chuban Guangdian Wang. Published in *Zhongguo Xinwen Chuban Guangdian Bao*. Retrieved from http://data.chinaxwcb.com/epaper2016/epaper/d6177/d7b/201601/63695.html.

Liao, B. (2011). Oumei meijie goumai gongsi de fazhan, yingxiang ji duice fenxi. *Xinwen Yu Chuanbo Yanjiu*, 3, 85–89.

Liao, J. (2008, July 29). Zhongguo yundongyuan fushi linggan lizi bin ma yong. *Dayang Wang*. Retrieved from http://2008.163.com/08/0729/10/4I0V5IU500742437.html.

Liao, Y. (2013, Feb 25). Li Ning tan tianjia zanzhu CBA: bushi haodu, shi gei zhongguo lanqiu gongxian. *Guangzhou Daily*. Retrieved from http://www.chinanews.com/ty/2013/02-25/4591066.shtml.

Lin, M. & Galikowski, M. (1999). *The search for modernity: Chinese intellectuals and cultural discourse in the post-Mao era*. New York: St. Martin's Press.

Lin, X. (2012, April 27). Jiedu Jinjiang mima zhi san. *Diyi Caijing Ribao*. Retrieved from http://www.yicai.com/news/2012/04/1671750.html.

Li-Ning (2004, June 11). Corporate presentation. Retrieved from http://www. lining.com/eng/ir/presentations.php?year=2008.

————. (2007, March). Branding China, reaching global: 2006 annual results corporation presentation. Retrieved from http://www.lining.com/eng/ir/presentations.php.

————. (2012, March 30). 2011 Annual results corporate presentation. Retrieved from http://www.lining.com/eng/ir/presentations/pre120330.pdf.

"Li-Ning: Pinpai Jiema" (2011, Dec. 5). Retrieved from http://www.cntv.cn/pinpai/20111205/120879.shtml.

Liu, C. (2003, June 13). ADWATCH: Being regular on TV boosts constipation remedy's score. *Media: Asia's Media & Marketing Newspaper*, 18.

Liu, D. (2006, July 16). Jinjiangxie: fangmao pinpai zhi shang. *Financial Timely*. Retrieved from http://finance.sina.com.cn/chanjing/b/20060716/17502735 826.shtml.

Liu, J. (2007). Chen Tianlong tan shengguang "guanggao binfa." *Advertiser: Market Observation*. 2, 72–73. Available: http://www.mie168.com/manage/2007-02/257896.htm.

Liu, W. (2012, Aug. 28). Li Ning Anta liuda tiyu pinpai zhongbao chulu, wujia shouru fu zengzhang. *Quanzhou Evening*. Retrieved from http://news.xin-huanet.com/fortune/2012-08/28/c_123639777.htm.

Liu, Y. (2010, April 7). Shoushi lv diaoyan de zhongguo jingguan: jishu, shichang he yishi xingtai. *Aisixiang.com*. Retrieved from http://www.aisixiang.com/data/related-32865.html.

"Liu Xiang turan tuisai" (2008, Aug. 19). *Sina.com* http://news.sina.com/sports/phoenixtv/406-105-105-124/2008-08-19/19143222731.html.

Low, M. (1994, Oct. 21). Winning the consumer war in China. *Business Times* (Singapore), Advertising & Marketing section, 11.

Lu, Tonglin (2002). *Confronting modernity in the cinemas of Taiwan and mainland China*. Cambridge: Cambridge University Press.

Lu, T. & He, J. (2000). *Lanse zhihui*. Guangzhou, China: Yangchen Wanbao Chubansh.

Lu, X. (2003). Preface. In Xu, H (ed.), *Ni "zhongchan" le ma?* Beijing: Jingji Ribao chubanshe.

Lu, Z. (2012, Feb. 20). Li Ning shenxian gaoceng chuzou yu gao kucun mengyan. *Yangcheng Wanbao*. Retrieved from http://finance.people.com.cn/GB/70846/17165289.html.

Lyotard, J.-F. (1984). *The postmodern condition: A report on knowledge*. Minneapolis: University of Minnesota Press.

Ma, E. K.-W. (2000). Rethinking media studies: The case of China. In J. Curran & M.-J. Park (eds.), *De-Westernizing Media Studies*. London and New York: Routledge.

Madden, N. (2007, April 30). Unilever takes aim at dandruff, as well as P&G, in China. *Adage. Com*. Retrieved from http://adage.com/article/print-edition/unilever-takes-aim-dandruff-p-g-china/116365/.

———. (2010, Sep. 20). Ad probe spotlights murky media practices in China. *Advertising Age*, 81 (33).

Mangan, V. (2012, Sep. 15). Britain has to realise it's no longer the power it used to be, says WPP chief Martin Sorrell. *The Telegraph*. Retrieved from http://www.telegraph.co.uk/finance/newsbysector/mediatechnologyandtelecoms/media/9544721/Britain-has-to-realise-its-no-longer-the-power-it-used-to-be-says-WPP-chief-Martin-Sorrell.html#disqus_thread.

Marchand, R. (1985). *Advertising the American dream: Making way for modernity, 1920–1940*. Berkeley: University of California Press.

Marketline industry profile (2013). *Footwear industry profile: China*. 1–13.

Martin-Barbero, J. (1993). The methods: From media to mediations. *Modernization and mass mediation in Latin America*, 187–245.

McDonald, H. & London, T. (2002). *Expanding the playing field: Nike's world shoe project* (A). World Resource Institute. Sustainable Enterprise Center.

McGovern, C. F. (2006). *Sold American: Consumption and citizenship, 1890–1945*. Chapel Hill: University of North Carolina Press.

Miao, W., Yue, X., & Lu, S. (2012). 2011 nian zhongguo chuanmei hangye jingying zhuangkuang fenxi. In B. Cui. (ed.), *Zhongguo chuanmei chanye fazhan baogao* (30–38). Beijing, China: Social Sciences Academy Press.

Mittelman, J. H. (2006). Globalization and development: Learning from debates in China. *Globalizations*, 3(3): 377–91.

"Mipop.xiaomi.cn" (n/a). Shenme shi baomihua huodong. Retrieved from http://mipop.xiaomi.cn/default/about.

Modern Advertising (2012). Chinese advertising industry and audience development report. In B. Cui (ed.), *Report on the development of China's media industries*. Beijing, China: Social Sciences Academic Press.

Morley, D. & Robins, K. (1995). *Spaces of identity*. London: Routledge.

Netease (2004, April 23). Jinjiang xieye de zaopai yundong. Retrieved from http://biz.163.com/40423/4/0KLLJGSV00020RNK.html.

Niu, C. & Bai, M. (2013, Oct. 10). Yong xin zuo, zhiru jiu meiyou lei ren de. *Zhongguo Xinwen Chubanwang*. Retrieved from http://data.chinaxwcb.com/epaper2013/epaper/d5674/d7b/201312/39807.htm.

Nonini, D. M. & Ong, A. (1997). Chinese transnationalism as an alternative modernity. In A. Ong and D. Nonini (eds.), *Ungrounded empires* (3–33). New York: Routledge.

Norris, P. & Inglehart, R. (2009). *Cosmopolitan communications: Cultural diversity in a globalized world*. Cambridge: Cambridge University Press.

Notoji, M. (2000). Cultural transformation of John Philip Sousa and Disneyland in Japan. In R. Wagnleitner and E. T. May (eds.), *Here, there and everywhere: The foreign politics of American popular culture*. Hanover, N.H.: University Press of New England.

Nussbaum, M. (1997). *Cultivating humanity: A classical defense of reform in liberal education*. Cambridge Mass.: Harvard University Press.

Ong, A. (1997). Chinese modernities: Narratives of nation and capitalism. In A. Ong and D. Nonini (eds.), *Ungrounded empires* (171–202). New York: Routledge.

———. (1999) *Flexible citizenship: The cultural logics of transnationality*. Durham, N.C.: Duke University Press.

Oriental TV (2011, Sept. 20). *Bo Shi Tang*. Retrieved from http://www.yemao zhong.com/meitizhuanfang/2011_0920/83.html.

"Oudian diban shijian quancheng jiexiao" (2006, Sept. 26). *Xinhua Net*. Retrieved from http://news.xinhuanet.com/classad/2006-09/26/content_5140636.htm.

People.cn (2014, March 7). Feng Xiaogang lianghui kaiqiang: guonei shoushilv tongji zaojia. Retrieved from http://culture.people.com.cn/n/2014/0307/c87423-24553984.html.

———. (2014, June 17). Guo Zhenxi ceng 8 nian nei lao 20 yi. Retrieved from http://politics.people.com.cn/n/2014/0617/c1001-25161266.html.

Pollay, R. & Gallagher, K. (1990). Advertising and cultural values: Reflections in the distorted mirror. *International Journal of Advertising*, 9, 359–72.

Prendergast, G., Cheung, W. and West, D. (2008). How far is too far? The antecedents of offensive advertising in modern China. *Journal of Advertising Research*, 48 (4), 484–95.

Pusey, J. R. (1983). *China and Charles Darwin*. Cambridge, Mass.: Harvard University Press.

Qin, X. (2009). Dangdai Zhongguo Wenti Yanjiu. In X. Qin (ed.), *Dangdai zhongguo wenti: Xiandai hua haishi xiandai xing* (3–10). Beijing, China: Social Sciences Academic Press.

Quanzhou Footwear Association (2006, June 28). Quanzhou xie ye ershi nian huihuang lu. Retrieved from http://www.qzshoes.org/news/newshtml/sh-info/20060621110421.htm.

Raboy, M. (1997) (ed.). *Public broadcasting for the 21st century*. Luton: University of Luton Press.

Ramo, J. C. (2004, May). *The Beijing consensus*. The Foreign Policy Center, London, UK.

Reichert, T. & Carpenter, C. (2004). An update on sex in magazine advertising: 1983 to 2003. *Journalism & Mass Communication Quarterly*, 81, 823–37.

Reid, A. (2009). Chineseness unbound. *Asian Ethnicity*, 10 (3), 197. doi:10.1080/14631360903232045.

Robertson, R. (1992). *Globalization: Social theory and global culture*. London: Sage.

Robins, K, Cornford, J. & Aksoy, A. (1997). Overview: From cultural rights to cultural responsibilities. In K. Robins (ed.), *Programming for people*. Newcastle: Centre for Urban and Regional Development Studies, University of Newcastle and European Broadcasting Union.

Rofel, L. (2007). *Desiring China: Experiments in neoliberalism, sexuality, and public culture*. Durham, N.C.: Duke University Press.

Rosen, S. (2004). The victory of materialism: Aspirations to join China's urban moneyed classes and the commercialization of education. *The China Journal*, 51, 27–51.

SAIC Advertising Censorship Personnel Management Methods (1996). SAIC (1996), document No. 239. Retrieved from http://www.hzgs.gov.cn/fgzx/gsfg/gggl/42_079.html.

Said, E. (1978). *Orientalism*. New York: Vintage Books.

Sautman, B. (1997). Racial nationalism and China's external behavior. *World Affairs* (Washington, D.C),16, 78–95.

Schein, L. (2001). Chinese consumerism and the politics of envy: Cargo in the 1990s. In X. Zhang (ed.), *Whither China?* Durham, N.C.: Duke University Press.

Schiller, H. (1996). *Information inequality*. New York: Routledge.

Shi, Y. (2004, Oct. 27). Shiwu nian liang qi yi luo Shi Yuzhu Naobaijin. An Interview. *Zhongguo Jingji Shibao. Beifang Wang*. Retrieved from http://economy.enorth.com.cn/system/2004/10/27/000890398.shtml.

Shih, C., Lin, T. M., & Luarn, P. (2014). Fan-centric social media: The Xiaomi phenomenon in China. *Business Horizons*, 57 (3), 349–58. doi:10.1016/j.bushor.2013.12.006.

Shih, S.-M. (2001). *The lure of the modern: Writing modernism in semicolonial China, 1917–1937*. Berkeley: University of California Press.

Shimp, T.A. and Sharma, S. (1987). Consumer ethnocentrism: construction and validation of the CETSCALE, *Journal of Marketing Research*, 24, 280–9.

Shirk, S. (2007). *China: Fragile superpower*. Oxford: Oxford University Press.

———. (2010). *Changing media, changing China*. Oxford: Oxford University Press.

"Situ Leideng 'daiyan' Hangzhou fangdichan guanggao yin zhengyi." (2011, March 30). *House 365*. Retrieved from http://news.house365.com/gbk/njestate/system/2011/03/30/010280558.shtml.

Sklair, L. (1994). The culture-ideology of consumerism in urban China: Some findings from a survey in Shanghai. In C. J. Schultz II, R. W. Belk and G. Ger (eds.), *Research in consumer behavior, 7,* 259–92). Greenwich, Conn.: JAI.

Sohu (2003, Feb. 16). Li Tie daiyan guohuo jingpin. *The Beijing Youth Daily,* Retrieved from http://sports.sohu.com/85/97/news206399785.shtml.

———. (2007, May 19). Beijingshi gongshang yancha "xuanfu," guanggao jinyong fukua cihui. Retrieved from http://news.sohu.com/20070519/n250105470.shtml.

———. (2010, Oct. 15). Jieli sohu duowei juzheng: Wu Xie Ke Ji kaiqi yingshiju wangluo yingxiao 2.0 shidai. *Admen,* 221–2.

Sohu IT (2012, Jan.1). 2011 nian wangluo guanggao chaoyue baozhi. *Sohu.com.* Available from http://it.sohu.com/20120111/n331821067.shtml.

Sohu zhengquan (2007, Jan. 15). Li Ning: Beijing aoyun ling mingnian shichang tuiguang fei weisheng, yue zhan yingyee 16%. http://business.sohu.com/20070115/n247620449.shtml.

Song, G. & Lee, T. K. (2010). Consumption, class formation and sexuality: Reading men's lifestyle magazines in China. *China Journal,* 64, 159–77.

Song, Q., Zhang, C., Qiao, B., & Gu, Q. (1996). *China can say No.* Beijing, China: Zhongguo Gongshanglian Chubanshe.

Straubhaar, J. (1991). Beyond media imperialism: Asymmetrical interdependence and cultural proximity. *Critical Studies in Mass Communication,* 8, 29–38.

Sturken, M. & Cartwright, L. (2001). *Practices of looking.* Oxford: Oxford University Press.

Sun, L. (2003). *Duan lie (Fractured China).* Beijing, China: Sheke Wenxian Chubanshe.

Sun, Q. (2015, Jan. 30). Zhongjiwei jiang yacha yingshi ye "qian guize." *Jinghua Wang.* Retrieved from http://epaper.jinghua.cn/html/2015-01/30/content_168516.htm.

Sun, S. (2010, April 1). Trends in Chinese cinema, Part II. Shaoyi Sun's Film Review Blog. Retrieved from http://shaoyis.wordpress.com/2010/04/01/trends-in-chinese-cinema-part-ii/.

Sun, Z. (2013). Cultural values conveyed through celebrity endorsers. *International Journal of Communication,* 7, 2631–52.

Sweney, M. (2012, March 1). WPP breaks £1bn profit barrier. *The Guardian.* Retrieved from http://www.guardian.co.uk/media/2012/mar/01/wpp-breaks-10bn-revenue-barrier.

Tan, L. (2012, Aug. 24). Weile shoushi lv nuoben de xin dou you. Retrieved from http://www.zcom.com/article/81262/.

Tang, X. (2000) *Chinese modern: The heroic and the quotidian*. Durham, N.C.: Duke University Press.

Tang, Z. (2011, Feb. 28). Health supplements bring in the Business. *China Daily*. Retrieved from http://www.chinadaily.com.cn/bizchina/2011-02/28/content _12087266.htm.

Tech.163.com (2014, Sep. 29). 21 Shiji baoxi she xinwen qiaozha duoren bei cha. Retrieved from http://tech.163.com/14/0929/21/A7BFDNMD000915BD _all.html.

Tian, A., Fang, N. & Wang, H. (2012, Sept. 18). Lining "e meng." *The Southern Metropolitan. Changyejia.com.* Retrieved from http://www.chuangyejia.com/ index1.php?m=content&c=index&a=show&catid=17&id=8254.

Tian, T. (2008, November 28). Zhongguo jingdian guanggao zhuge shu: Ao Ni zaojiao xifa jingao. *Guanggao Men*, Retrieved from http://www.adquan.com/ post-1-1527.html.

Ting, T. (2008). Rang pinpai huo qilai: Lianhelihua pinpai zhiru Chounu Wudi hudong zhi mianmian guan. [Interviews with Unilever China Media Director Patrick Zhou, Mindshare CEO Andrew Meaden, Minshare ESP General Manager Mateo Eaton, Mindshare's Unilever Account Manager Alex Reynold, and Nesound Producer Zhou Heng]. *Chinese Advertising*, 7, 106–11.

Tomba, L (2004). Creating an urban middle class. *The China Journal*, Jan., 51, 1–26.

Tong, L. (2012). Decoding the regulatory system for advertising in contemporary China. *Global Conference on Business & Finance Proceedings*, 7(1), 200–212.

Transparency International (2014). *Corruption Perceptions Index 2014: Results*. Retrieved from http://www.transparency.org/cpi2014.

Tsai, K. S. (2007). *Capitalism without democracy*. Ithaca, N.Y.: Cornell University Press.

Turow, J. (2011). *The daily you: How the new advertising industry is defining your identity and your worth*. New Haven & London: Yale University Press.

Van der Veer, P. (2002). Empathy or empire. *Biblio: A Review of Books*, 1, 10–13.

Voice of America (2011, March 21). Beijing jinzhi xuanchuan xiangle zhuyi de huwai guanggao. *VOAChinese.com.* Retrieved from http://m.voachinese. com/a/article-20110321-beijing-targets-luxury-ads-amid-wealth-gap-11835 3014/779561.html

Waller, D. S. (1999). Attitudes towards offensive advertising: An Australian study, *Journal of Consumer Marketing*, 16 (3), 288–94.

———. (2005). A proposed response model for controversial advertising. *Journal of Promotion Management*, 11(2/3), 3–15.

Wang, F. (2008, Jan. 14). Xibanya xuetielong guanggao qingman Mao Zedong (Spanish Citroen ad insulted Mao Zedong. *The Global Times*. Retrieved from http://news.163.com/08/0114/10/425NCIH70001121M.html.)

Wang, F. (2012, July 27). Anta da aoyun jihua. *Jingji Guanchao Bao*. Retrieved from http://news.hexun.com/2012-07-27/144076492.html.

Wang, G. (1991). *The Chineseness of China*. Hong Kong: Oxford University Press.

Wang, H. (2003). *China's new order*. Ed. Theodore Huters. Cambridge, Mass.: Harvard University Press.

Wang, Jian (2000). *Foreign advertising in China*. Iowa City: Iowa State University Press.

———. (2005). Consumer nationalism and corporate reputation management in the global era. *Corporate Communications*, 10(3), 223–39.

———. (2006). The politics of goods: A case study of consumer nationalism and media discourse in contemporary China. *Asian Journal of Communication*, 16(2), June, 187–206.

Wang, Jian, and Wang, Z. (2007). The political symbolism of Business. *Journal of Communication Management*, 11(2), 134–49.

Wang, Jing (2003). Framing Chinese advertising: Some industry perspectives on the production of culture. *Continuum: Journal of Media & Cultural Studies*, 17(2), 247–60.

———. (2008). *Brand new China*. Cambridge, Mass.: Harvard University Press.

Wang, Xiaoyu (2011, Jan. 12). Qingyang, shifou zhende wuxie keji. Originally published in *Sales and Marketing*. Retrieved from http://mag.cnyes.com/Content/20110112/0D083B8715844B0B9C64985BC4771145.shtml.

Wang, Xin (2013). Desperately seeking status: Political, social and cultural attributes of China's rising middle class. *Modern China Studies*, 20 (1), 1–44.

Wang, Y. Chan, V. & Zhang, D. (2005, Jan. 17). A panel on "client relationship management." *Guanggao Sanren Xing*. cnad.com, http://www.a.com.cn/News/Infos/200601/17453921416.shtml.

Wang, Z. & Chen, F. (2007). *History of Chinese and foreign advertising*. Changsha, China: Hunan University Press.

Web Professional China (2010, May 14). China released a list of best Internet advertising agencies. Retrieved from http://www.webprochina.com/2010/05/china-released-a-list-of-best-internet-advertising-agencies/.

Weir, T. (1993, Oct. 7). Goodbye to the game, Michael Jordan, one of a kind, retires. *USA Today*. News, 1A. Accessed through LexisNexis.

Whyte, M. K. & Parish, W. (1984). *Urban life in contemporary China*. Chicago: University of Chicago Press.

Wilson, A. and West, C. (1981, January-February). The marketing of "unmentionables." *Harvard Business Review*, 91–102.

Wilson, Y. & Dissanayake, W. (1996). Introduction: Tracking the global/local. In R. Wilson and W. Dissanayake (eds.), *Global/local: cultural production and the transnational imaginary* (1–18). Durham, N.C.: Duke University Press.

Wind, J., Sthanunathan, S., & Malcom, R. (2013, March 29). Great advertising is both local and global. *Harvard Business Review*. Retrieved from http://blogs.hbr.org/2013/03/great-advertising-is-both-loca/.

Wu, L. (2008, Feb. 15). Bi Naobaijin geng "lingren bengkui," Hengyuanxiang aoyun guanggao shou pengji (Being more offensive than Naobaijin advertising, Henyuanxiang Olympic ad was attacked). *Shanghai Diyi Caijing*. Retrieved from http://money.163.com/08/0215/04/44ND9HR6002524 SC.html.

Xia, X. (2001). *Zhuanxing zhong de zhongguoren* (Chinese in Transition). Tianjin, China: Tianjin Renmin Press.

Xiao, D. (2013, March 17). Yangshi 3.15 wanhui zong daoyan fouren baohu guanggao kehu. Reprint from *Beijing Morning Post*. Retrieved from http://finance.sina.com.cn/china/20130317/015914856178.shtml.

Xie, S. (2014). Similarities and differences or similarities in differences? China's TV programming in global trend of neo-liberal imperialism. *China Media Research*, 10(1), 91–102.

Xinhua (2008, Aug. 1). China tightens control on TV ads. Retrieved from http://www.chinadaily.com.cn/bizchina/2008-08/01/content_6897431.htm.

———. (2009, Sep. 26). Wenhua chanye zhenxing guihua. Retrieved from http://www.gov.cn/jrzg/2009-09/26/content_1427394.htm.

XinhuaNet (2012, Nov. 20). Xishuo lijie yangshi guanggao biaowang de mingyun. Retrieved from http://news.xinhuanet.com/fortune/2012-11/20/c_12397 6051.htm.

———. (2013, Feb. 21). Xinlang Weibo yonghu shu chao 5 yi, ri huoyue yonghu dadao 4620 wan. Retrieved from http://news.xinhuanet.com/info/2013-02/21/c_132181760.htm.

———. (2013, Nov. 12). China's mobile phone users hit 1.22 bln. Retrieved from http://news.xinhuanet.com/english/china/2013-11/21/c_132907784.htm.

———. (2013, Dec. 16). Zhongguo xin chengshi zuixin fenji chulu. Reprint from: *Sichuan Online*. Retrieved from http://news.xinhuanet.com/fortune/ 2013-12/16/c_125868485.htm.

Xinmin Wanbao (2006, March 2). Guochan fuzhuang weihe jie yangming 'yangming'? Retrieved from http://www.texindex.com.cn/Articles/2006-3-2/ 55534.html.

Xiong, Z. (2005). *Zhongguo shengji weishi fazhan zhanlue*. Shanghai, China: Shanghai Renmin Chubanshe.

Yan, S. (2004). *Traditional Chinese clothing*. San Francisco: Long River Press.

Yan, T. (2008, Dec. 24). Chounu Wudi de hudong yingxiao. *Chuanmei Jingji Xue*. Retrieved from http://211.71.215.185/ChuanMeiJingJi/content/2008-12/24/content_2589.htm.

Yang, Ge (2009). Li Ning Inner Shine, bie ta kong. *Shichang Guancha*, Issue 4. Retrieved from *Zhongguo Zhiwang*.

Yang, Guobin (2009). *The power of the Internet in China*. New York: Columbia University Press.

Yang, T. (2008, March 13). 2007 nian yangshi guanggao shouru tupo baiyi yuan. Retrieved from http://finance.sina.com.cn/china/hgjj/20080313/00274614443.shtml.

Yang, Y. (2010, June 12). Changrong Chuanbo de "zhongguo shi WPP" zhi lu. *21 Shiji Jingji Baodao*. Retrieved from http://it.sohu.com/20100612/n272737383.shtml.

"Yangshi guanggao zhaobiao zong e chao qu nian, xinwen lianbo 10 miao xijin 35 yi yuan" (2013, November 19). *Guan Cha Zhe*. Retrieved from http://www.guancha.cn/economy/2013_11_19_186652.shtml.

Ye, M. (2014, Nov. 7). Yingxiao guandian: 16 ge xingxiao guanjian ci 13: Jie shi. Retrieved from http: www.yemaochong.com/yemaozhongzhisideblog/2014_1107/733.html.

Yearbook of Chinese Advertisements (2000). Compiled by Journal of International Advertising, Beijing Broadcasting University and IAI International Advertising Research Institute. Beijing, China: Zhongguo Sheying Chubanshe.

———. (2001). Compiled by Journal of International Advertising, Beijing Broadcasting University and IAI International Advertising Research Institute. Beijing, China: Zhongguo Sheying Chubanshe.

Yeh, J. & Zhang, M. (2013). Taking the pulse of China's ad spending. Insights & Publications, *McKinsey Quarterly*. June. Retrieved from http://www.mckinsey.com/insights/media_entertainment/taking_the_pulse_of_chinas_ad_spending.

Yu, L. (2008). *Li Ning: A champion's heart*. Beijing, China: Zhongxin chubanshe. Also available: http://vip.book.sina.com.cn/book/index_65089.html.

———. (2009, Feb.). Li Ning de guojihua. CEIBS Business Review. Retrieved from http://www.ceibsreview.com/show/index/classid/28/id/469.

Yule.sohu.com (2014, October 17). Xinwen Lianbo shoushi lv baoguang. Retrieved from http://yule.sohu.com/20141017/n405190685.shtml.

Zhang, G. (2009). Gaige kaifang yilai woguo guangbo dianshi guanggao guizhi de fazhan he wenti. *Zhongguo Guangbo Dianshi Xuekan*, 1, 43–44. Retrieved from Zhongguo Zhiwang.

Zhang, J., Wang, F., Li, Y., & Liu, Y. (2008, Jan. 15). Xuetielong tingkan qingman Mao Zedong Guanggao. *The Global Times.* Retrieved from http://news .xinhuanet.com/world/2008-01/15/content_7422869.htm.

Zhang, Peng & Li, Wangyan (2008, Aug. 15). Huangjin dadang haineng "songli" ma? *Southern Metropolis Weekly.* Retrieved from http://past.nbweekly.com/ Print/Article/5574_0.shtml.

Zhang, S. (2009). What's wrong with Chinese journalists? *Journal of Mass Media Ethics*, 24(2/3), 73–188.

Zhang, W.-W. (2000). *Transforming China: Economic Reform and its Political Implications.* London: Macmillan.

Zhang, Xiwen (2006). Pleasingly plump or fashionably thin? *China Today*, 55(11), 22–25.

Zhang, Xudong (2001). The Making of the post-Tiananmen intellectual field: A critical overview. In X. Zhang (ed.), *Whither China? Intellectual politics in contemporary China*, 1–75. Durham, N.C.: Duke University Press.

Zhang, Xiaoxiao & Fung, Anthony (2011). Producing Chinese *Ugly Betty*: Decentered political and centered economical controls. Conference presentation. *International Communication Association.* Boston, Massachusetts, May 26–30, 2011.

Zhang, Y. & Harwood, J. (2004). Modernization and tradition in an age of globalization: Cultural values in Chinese TV commercials. *Journal of Communication*, 54(1), 156–72.

Zhao, S. (2000). Chinese nationalism and its international orientations. *Political Science Quarterly*, 115(1), 1–33.

Zhao, Y. (1998). *Media, market and democracy in China.* University of Illinois Press.

———. (2008). *Communication in China.* Lanham, Md.: Rowman & Littlefield.

Zhongguo chengshi fazhan baogao bianweihui (2012). (eds.). Zhongguo chengshi fazhan baogao, No. 5 (*Annual report on urban development of China*, No. 5). Beijing, China: Shehui Kexue Wenxian Chubanshe.

"Zhongguo chuanmeijituan fazhan baogao" (2004, May). *Zhongguo chuanmeijituan fazhan baogao.* Changsha, China: Hunan Jiaoyu Chubanshe.

Zhongguo guanggao xiehui (2013, April 15). Zhongguo yi cheng shijie dier da guanggao shichang. Retrieved from http://finance.sina.com.cn/chanjing/ cyxw/20130415/200915154425.shtml.

"Zhongguo pinpai weilie waizi jutou, jin si cheng ren renwei Li Ning shi Beijing Aoyunhui Zazhushang" (2008, Aug. 19). Reprinted from *Guoji Xianqu*

Daobao. Retrieved from http://finance.ifeng.com/news/industry/200808/08 19_2202_731763.shtml.

"Zhongyang dianshi tai 2015 nian huangjin guanggao ziyuan zhaobiao shu" (2014). Retrieved from download.cntv.cn/biaoshu/2015biaoshu_141102.pdf.

Zhou, L. & Hui, M. (2003). Symbolic value of non-local origin in the PRC. *Journal of International Marketing*. 11(2), 36–58.

Zhou, L., Yang, Z., & Hui, M. K. (2010) Non-local or local brands? *Journal of the Academy of Marketing Science*, 38(2), 202–18.

Zhou, N., & Belk, R. W. (2004). Chinese consumer readings of global and local advertising appeals. *Journal of Advertising*, 33(3), 63–76.

Zhu, Y. (2012). *Two billion eyes*. New York: The New Press.

Zhuang, G., Wang, X., Zhou, L. and Zhou, N. (2008). Asymmetric effects of brand origin confusion. *International Marketing Review*. 25(4), 441–57.

Index of Names

General Index